Sir John Northcote

Note book of Sir John Northcote

Containing memoranda of proceedings in the House of commons during the first

session of the Long parliament 1640

Sir John Northcote

Note book of Sir John Northcote
Containing memoranda of proceedings in the House of commons during the first session of the Long parliament 1640

ISBN/EAN: 9783337154554

Printed in Europe, USA, Canada, Australia, Japan

Cover: Foto ©ninafisch / pixelio.de

More available books at **www.hansebooks.com**

NOTE BOOK

OF

SIR JOHN NORTHCOTE.

NOTE BOOK

OF

SIR JOHN NORTHCOTE

SOMETIME M.P. FOR ASHBURTON,
AND AFTERWARDS FOR THE COUNTY OF DEVON.

CONTAINING

MEMORANDA OF PROCEEDINGS IN THE HOUSE
OF COMMONS DURING THE FIRST SESSION
OF THE LONG PARLIAMENT, 1640.

From the MS. Original in the Possession of the Right Hon.
Sir Stafford Northcote, Bart., M.P.

TRANSCRIBED AND EDITED, WITH A MEMOIR,

By A. H. A. HAMILTON.

LONDON:
JOHN MURRAY, ALBEMARLE STREET.
1877.
[*Right of Translation reserved.*]

LONDON:
BRADBURY, AGNEW, & CO., PRINTERS, WHITEFRIARS.

TO

THE RIGHT HON.

SIR STAFFORD HENRY NORTHCOTE,

BART., C.B., D.C.L., F.R.S.,

CHANCELLOR OF THE EXCHEQUER,

KNIGHT OF THE SHIRE FOR THE NORTHERN DIVISION OF DEVON,

AND LEADER OF THAT HOUSE OF PARLIAMENT

WHOSE MOST FAMOUS SESSION IN FORMER TIMES

IS HERE RECORDED BY HIS ANCESTOR,

This Volume is Dedicated.

Fairfield Lodge, Exeter,
1877.

CONTENTS.

	PAGE
MEMOIR OF SIR JOHN NORTHCOTE	ix
INTRODUCTION TO THE NOTE BOOK	xlvii
SIR JOHN NORTHCOTE'S NOTE BOOK	1
ABSTRACT OF AN ACT OF PARLIAMENT	123
NOTES OF THE SESSION OF 1661	127

MEMOIR

OF

SIR JOHN NORTHCOTE.

SIR JOHN NORTHCOTE of Hayne, in the parish of Newton St. Cyres, in the county of Devon, first Baronet of his family, and a lineal ancestor of Sir Stafford Henry Northcote, was one of those country gentlemen who, though their names do not appear in biographical dictionaries among those of the Vanes and Hampdens, played a not inconsiderable part in the great events of the seventeenth century. Had it been otherwise,— had he been one of those who trust in the length of their ancestry rather than in their own personal exertions, the race to which he belonged was by no means wanting in distinction of the former kind. A pedigree preserved at Pynes, which was examined and verified at the Heralds' Visitation of Devonshire in the reign of James the First, contains a complete and minute account of the family from the days of Galfridus de Northcote, knight, who held the lands of Northcote in the parish of East Down, near Barnstaple, in the year 1103, the third of the reign of Henry the First.

James Northcote, the eminent painter, who descended from Samuel Northcot, Mayor of Plymouth in 1658, and who delighted to trace his origin to an offshoot which branched away from the parent stem in the 15th century, collected various records of the family in two large manuscript volumes, which, illustrated by many sketches of his own, by several rare engravings, and much curious heraldry, are also preserved in the library at Pynes.

From these sources we learn that the Northcotes, as generations went by, allied themselves with many distinguished houses, such as those of Courtenay and Luttrell, which are still flourishing ; of Hillion, whose ancestor came over with the Conqueror ; of Meoles, whose name appears in Domesday Book ; and others well known to the antiquaries of the West of England. Through the Courtenays and Luttrells they acquired a strain of the blood of the Plantagenets. We also find that, by the marriage of heiresses, they absorbed into their own several of the ancient families of Devonshire. Many deeds and wills preserved in the Heralds' College attest their importance, and John de Northcote served the office of Sheriff in the 27th year of Edward III. (1354). As they acquired new estates, either by marriage or purchase, they repeatedly changed their residence. In the middle of the sixteenth century, Walter Northcote, great-grandfather of the first Baronet, was living at Uton, in the parish of Crediton.

Memoir of Sir John Northcote. xi

There exists in the State Paper Office an incidental notice of him, contained in a declaration of John Prediaux, the then owner of Pynes, which, some generations afterwards, was brought into the Northcote family by the heiress of the Staffords. John Prediaux's declaration relates mainly to the disturbances which might be expected if King Philip of Spain landed in Devonshire on his way to marry Queen Mary, but he mentions casually that at the time of Quarter Sessions he was partly busied with other affairs, "also with Norcot of "Kyrto (Crediton) for and consernyng his assur-"ances for land that he bought of Sir Hugh "Pollard, knight." The name is so frequently spelt *Norcot* by writers of the sixteenth and seventeenth centuries, including Lord Clarendon, that we may perhaps infer that it was so pronounced, as North-west is often pronounced Nor'-west, and as the county of Northfolk has become Norfolk. It will be seen afterwards that the Northcotes were connected in various ways with the once flourishing family of the Pollards.

Walter Northcote was succeeded by his son John, and John Northcote's eldest son, Walter, married the heiress of Edmund Drew, of Hayne, which place then became the principal seat of the family. He died young, and his widow married Sir Edward Giles. His only child, Elizabeth, married first George Yard of Churston Ferrers, an ancestor of Lord Churston, and secondly

Dr. Barnabas Potter, who was Vicar of Dean Prior (a living in the gift of Sir Edward Giles), and afterwards Bishop of Carlisle. The estate of Hayne, however, did not pass to her, but to her uncle John Northcote, father of the Baronet.

The name of this John Northcote appears in the list of Devonshire justices who attended Quarter Sessions during the latter part of the reign of Elizabeth. He lived till 1632. It seems from his epitaph that he was tried by the Star Chamber.

> " Regia pacificæ commisit chartula libram
> Justitiæ, lustris ætatis quinque peractis.
> Libravit rectum purâ cum mente, probatus
> Stellatâ Camerâ, spectatur ut ignibus aurum."

Which may be roughly translated, in case there yet remains any lady ignorant of Latin :

> To him the Queen's Commission in his youth
> Trusted the scales of Justice and of Truth.
> Fair was the balance held, and pure his fame,
> Though by Star-chamber tried, as gold by flame.

It is probable that his experience of the procedure of that Court, although he was not ruined by it, had a decisive effect in determining the side taken by his son in politics. We know how, in the case of Sir Simonds D'Ewes, the tyranny of the Star Chamber converted, at least for a time, a quiet antiquary into an active and zealous Roundhead. I think one may venture to guess

Memoir of Sir John Northcote. xiii

that Justice Northcote got into trouble for the very same cause as Sir Simonds, viz., a want of "forwardness" in collecting ship money for His Majesty. In the Diary of Walter Yonge, a Devonshire justice of the same period, we find that in April, 1627, there came letters to the justices of Devon, and the mayors of port towns, "for the setting forth of eight ships, viz., two for " Exon, two for Dartmouth and Totnes, two for " Plymouth, and two for Barnstaple." " The "towns are to provide the ships, and the country "men and victuals, and are to be ready against " the 20th May next." And in the next year there were sent letters into Devon, both by King Charles and his Council, "for the raising of " £17,400 out of this county, to set a fleet at sea, "which was appointed to be. at sea the 1st of " March, we having but six or seven days to raise "the money and to return it to London; *but our* "*county refused to meddle therein.*" It was exactly in this year, 1627-8, that John Northcote served the office of Sheriff of Devon, and must therefore have been required to levy the unpopular imposition.

His ill-luck in public affairs may perhaps have been compensated by his good fortune in private life. It is recorded of one of the three John Northcotes, and, I believe, may be safely attributed to this one, that he was one day playing piquet with his neighbour Master Dowrish, of Dowrish, near Crediton, who, having a particularly good hand, offered to stake the manor of Kennerleigh against the sum of six hundred pounds. But Master Northcote played his cards so well that he won the game, and the manor of Kennerleigh remains to this day in the possession of his descendant. The loser caused the two hands of cards to be inlaid in a marble table, to be preserved as an heir-loom,—an awful warning to his posterity to abstain from gambling. The family of Dowrish has long passed away, but the table is still preserved in their ancient manor-house.

John Northcote's first wife was Elizabeth, daughter of Sir Anthony Rous, Knight, of Halton in Cornwall, and sister of Francis Rous, afterwards Speaker of Barebone's Parliament, Provost of Eton, and one of Cromwell's Lords. His second wife was Susan, daughter of Sir Hugh Pollard of King's Nympton. By his first wife he had only one child, who died unmarried. By his second he had no less than twelve sons and six daughters.

Such a family suggested an obvious comparison with the patriarch Jacob, which was commemorated by his youngest son being called Benjamin, and also in his very curious monument in the Church of Newton St. Cyres. It is elaborate in design, though decidedly rude in execution. The deceased esquire is represented in complete armour, standing upon a pedestal, leaning upon his sword, and treading on a death's head with his left foot. His numerous progeny kneel beneath

Memoir of Sir John Northcote. xv

his statue, with the exception of three babies, who lie on the ground tightly wrapped in their swaddling clothes. On the right and left of the esquire are medallions in high relief of his two wives, each encircled by an oval frame bearing an inscription. The first wife is made to say, in a sad and apologetic manner :

> " My fruit was small,
> One son was all,
> That not at all ! "

Contrasted with this is the boastful statement of the second lady :

> " My Jacob had by me
> As many sons as he,
> Daughters twice three."

But even this lady did not rival her ancestress, the Lady Pollard, who had eleven sons and eleven daughters. Concerning this family, we are assured by the excellent Mr. Prince, in his *Worthies of Devon*, that four of the sons attained the honour of knighthood, one was Archdeacon of Barnstaple and Canon of Exeter, and all the rest were "well " advanced." " The daughters were married to " the most potent families," so that " almost all the " ancient gentry in the county became allied." The father of these twenty-two children, which Mr. Prince calls " a plentiful issue," was Sir Lewis Pollard, a justice of the Common Pleas in the reign of Henry the Eighth. He bought the estate and built the house of King's Nympton, near Chulmleigh, where his family flourished for several generations, and gave more than one representative to the county of Devon. Sir Hugh Pollard, father of Mistress Northcote, had the honour of being Sheriff of Devon in the year of the Armada, and was therefore the one immortalized, perhaps unconsciously, by Macaulay:

"With his white hair unbonneted, the stout old Sheriff comes,
Behind him march the halberdiers, before him sound the drums,
His yeomen round the market-cross make clear an ample space,
For there behoves him to set up the standard of Her Grace."

His son obtained a baronetcy soon after the institution of that order. In the reign of Charles the First another Sir Hugh Pollard distinguished himself on the King's side, especially by the defence of Dartmouth. At the Restoration he was elected Knight of the Shire for Devon, and was appointed Comptroller of the Household to Charles the Second. He was "a gentleman of a noble mind," and "magnificently hospitable," so that his mansion of King's Nympton became celebrated in a very bad rhyme, as

"Nympton Regis,
Where one drinks and t'other pledges."

It is not impossible that his hospitality may have

Memoir of Sir John Northcote. xvii

impaired his estate. At any rate he sold King's Nympton to Sir Arthur Northcote, and it continued for some time to be the principal seat of the latter family.

John Northcote, the eldest of the twelve sons before mentioned, was born in 1599. He married Grace, the heiress of Hugh Halswell, of Wells, in Somerset, and his eldest son, Arthur, was born in 1627. Of his early life no memorials have been preserved. I have tracked his public conduct through incidental mentions of him in many books and manuscript records. His career may perhaps serve as a type of the careers of other "Parlia-"ment-men" of that eventful period.

His name appears in the list of the Justices of the Peace for Devon in the year 1633, and also as an officer in John Bampfield's regiment of "trained soldiers," the second regiment of the southern division of the county. He took his seat in the Long Parliament as member for Ashburton in November, 1640, his colleague being Sir Edmund Fowel. In the Short Parliament of the preceding April, Ashburton did not return any members. That privilege, which had been suspended for many years, was restored to the borough in the first month of the Long Parliament. But the right seems to have been questioned. The first notes taken by Sir John were of the sitting of November 24. It is recorded by Rushworth, under the date Nov. 26, which pos

c

sibly ought to be Nov. 24, that the boroughs of Honiton and "Asperton" were restored to send burgesses to Parliament on a report by Mr. Maynard, Chairman of the Committee for Elections.

Sir Simonds D'Ewes, ever ready to instruct an ungrateful generation, tells us that he showed the House "the reason why they did forbear to send "was their poverty, being not able to maintain "their burgesses, but now, *gentlemen being gene-* "*rally chosen*, boroughs desire their ancient privi- "leges." The pay of a burgess had been usually four shillings a day. D'Ewes himself was a borough member.

John Northcote employed himself during the first few weeks in taking the notes which have been preserved in manuscript to the present day. In the earlier part of the same year, as we find by some rough memoranda on the fly-leaves of his Note Book, he had taken a journey to York, where the King's army was collected to oppose the invasion of the Scots. He took with him £21 "for Riding Charges," and he spent £9 6s. 1d. "from London to York and at York from the "last of March to the 9th of April." He seems to have held some appointment of the nature of secretary or aide-de-camp to a nobleman, probably the Earl of Northumberland, who was Lord General of the Northern Army. There are brief memoranda relating to North Shields, Scar-

Memoir of Sir John Northcote. xix

borough, and Newton upon Darwent. There is also one relating to the proclamation of martial law, and to the pay of the troops, a subject to which he seems to have paid special attention in his Parliamentary Notes. In July he paid Mr. Selden £20 "for drawing his Lordship's Com-" missions of General, by his Lordship's appoint-" ment." He also paid 4s. "for Maps for his " Lordship." And in January he paid the Clerk of the Parliament £1, "for copies of Scots " Articles against Lord of Cant. (Laud) and Lord " Lieutenant (Strafford) for his Lordship." There is at Pynes a very fine portrait by Vandyke of the Earl of Northumberland, wearing what appears to be a Chancellor's robe.

With the exception of a few more memoranda about the payment of money, the present Note Book throws no light on Sir John's personal history. But it seems certain that various MSS. of his were in existence about the middle of the last century, and we may hope that the present publication may have the effect of causing them to be discovered. We can hardly doubt that a man who took careful notes (and who took them exceedingly well) for a few weeks in 1640, and for a few days in 1661, and who lived till 1676, must have written much more of the same kind.

He was one of those who took the "Solemn "Protestation" on May 3, 1641, and he was created a Baronet on July 16, in the same year. I do not find that he ever took the Covenant, although he must have constantly acted with the Presbyterian party.

During the first year of his attendance in Parliament he seems to have kept silence and learnt his business, as became a new member. At the beginning of his second year he was the hero of a curious "scene" in the House, for the report of which we are indebted to Sir Simonds D'Ewes.

It was Friday, the fourteenth of January, 1641-2. Charles had made his spring at the Five Members, had missed his intended prey, and had slunk away from London in an agony of shame, "never to return till the day of a terrible and "memorable reckoning had arrived." The Five Members had been brought back in triumph. The four thousand freeholders of Bucks had ridden up to Westminster, and the Houses were in a state of unprecedented excitement.

"Sir H. Cholmely moved that he understood
" there were divers jealousies and fears put into
" the King's head, and the Queen's, as if we meant
" to diminish his authority, and impeach the Queen
" of high crimes, and therefore desired that we
" might think of some speedy way of removing
" these jealousies between the King and Parlia-
" ment. Others desired that we might first move
" the Lords to join with us to command the
" Marquis Hartford upon peril of his life to go

" to the Court (at Hampton) and to take the young
" prince into his custody, having been formerly
" appointed Governor of his Highness by the King
" himself.

" When some offered to speak against it, others
" interrupted them, although it was yet no order of
" the House, having not passed upon the question.
" Sir John Norcott said plainly that this would
" rather increase the jealousies between the King
" and us than any way diminish them, it being
" already reported by some *that there was an in-
" tention to crown the Prince and make him King.*
" But he was so interrupted as he was fain to give
" over before he had intended, and divers called to
" have the order read, which made me (D'Ewes),
" in respect of the weight of the business itself,
" and the orders of the House so extremely broken,
" to speak, &c."

Sir Simonds then gives us the substance of one of his instructive lectures in the "superior " person " style. As to the rest of the debate, he merely observes that " Divers spoke after me, "and, though all was not pursued which I had " moved, yet a good part of it was."

It was then resolved " that the Lords should " be moved to join with this House to command " Marquesse Hartford, being formerly appointed " by his Majesty to be governor of the Prince, " should take care of him and attend his person, " and take care that he might not be carried "beyond the seas; and that whosoever should give that advice or attend him on his passage shall be declared a public enemy to the kingdom." It was also resolved, on the motion of Sir Hugh Cholmley, to move the Lords to join in desiring his Majesty not to permit the Prince to be carried out of the Realm.

This was the memorable day on which Mr. Oliver Cromwell carried his motion "that a Committee might be named to consider of means to put the kingdom in a posture of defence."

Mr. Forster was misled by a very small error in his transcript of D'Ewes's notes into stating that Sir John Northcote said that *he* would rather increase the jealousies between the King and Parliament than diminish them. Having seen both the transcript and the original, I can confidently state that the word is *this*, *i.e.*, the proposal of Sir H. Cholmeley. The mistake is an example of the effect which a misreading of one syllable may sometimes produce in more important matters of history. The declaration which Mr. Forster attributes to Sir John Northcote would indeed have been a most audacious one at that time, when it was still the practice to mention the King personally in terms of most obsequious loyalty. Even in August, 1643, Henry Martin was sent by the House to the Tower for speaking against his Majesty. It is enough that Sir John was certainly the first to mention in the House the idea which had been suggested in conversation out of doors, that the habitual duplicity of the King left no hope of a satisfactory arrangement being made with him, and that the least dangerous course to adopt, in a choice of evils, was to depose him in favour of his son.

It is evident that Sir John did not give this as his own opinion, but he may have mentioned it as a means of testing the feeling of the House. That it was his real opinion is, I think, clear from the whole course of his life, and in this view his career during the next twenty years appears perfectly consistent. Nor would it be easy, even after the event, to suggest any scheme that would have been more likely to succeed. Lord Macaulay, writing with all the experience derived from two hundred additional years of English history, came to exactly the same conclusion as did Sir John Northcote.

"When a country is in the situation in which "England then was, when the kingly office is re- "garded with love and veneration, but the person "who fills that office is hated and distrusted, it "should seem that the course which ought to be "taken is obvious. The dignity of the office "should be preserved; the person should be dis- "carded."

Had it been possible to place Charles the Second on the throne in 1642, with Hampden for his governor, Bedford for Prime Minister, and Pym for Chancellor of the Exchequer and leader of the House of Commons, it seems probable that the Revolution of 1688 might have been anticipated, and that England might have been spared the miseries of the Civil War, the dominion of the Puritans of 1648, and the dominion of the Cavaliers of 1661.

In April, 1642, several members of the House of Commons subscribed money "towards the "speedy reducing of the rebels in Ireland," and we find that Sir J. Northcote put down his name for the sum of £450.

On June 15th he spoke in the House in favour of the appointment of Thomas Fuller as one of the Lecturers of the Savoy. It is pleasing to record that, even at that crisis, he was able to appreciate a good and wise man of the opposite party.

At this time both parties were preparing for war in England. The Houses of Parliament entrusted the work of raising the militia in Devonshire to the Earl of Bedford and other Commissioners, among whom Sir John Northcote was one of the most active. The King sent his Commission of Array to the Earl of Bath, and under him the principal leader seems to have been Sir John's Royalist relative, Sir Hugh Pollard, sometime member for Beeralston, who had been expelled the House and imprisoned

Memoir of Sir John Northcote. ⸺ xxv

for his share in the Army Plot, but had been released on bail at the instance of his cousin.

Among the De la Warr papers preserved at Knole are some letters written during that eventful summer and autumn.

On Sept. 25th, Sir Hugh Pollard wrote from King's Nympton to the Earl of Bath :

" The Earl of Bedford is now at Taunton, in "want of men and money ; he hath sent to his sure "friends Chudleigh, Bampfield, and Northcott, for "a supply of both, whose oratory cannot get one "trained man to move, nor above eight volun-"teers ; and their credits cannot procure him a "groat. I hear divers reports of an accommoda-"tion, but believe none ; and, my Lord, depend "upon it, his Majesty is in no ill condition."

This letter receives a curious comment from the succeeding ones. At that very time the Earl of Bedford was issuing orders for the arrest of Sir Hugh Pollard, and four days afterwards Sir George Chudleigh and Sir John Northcote wrote to Major Carey, expressing their approval of Captain Dewett's conduct in capturing the Earl of Bath.

" Northcote's oratory " resulted in placing him at the head of a regiment of 1200 men, which he appears to have commanded during the first two years of the civil war. He was slightly connected with several of the leaders in the West. His father's first wife, as has been already mentioned, was a sister of Francis Rous. His brother Robert married a daughter of Sir Richard Strode of Newnham, member for Plympton, and brother of the more famous William Strode, member for Beeralston. A sister of the Strodes was married to Sir George Chudleigh, perhaps the chief leader in Devonshire at the commencement of the war. At the beginning of the siege of Plymouth, we find Sir George " Governor of Plymouth, Mount " Wise, and other Castles thereabouts," having under his command about 2000 foot and 500 horse. Another sister was married to Sir Francis Drake, the first baronet, and their son had married a daughter of Pym.

In November, 1642, Sir George Chudleigh, Sir John Northcote, Sir Samuel Rolle, and Sir Nicholas Martyn, were proclaimed traitors by the King, and specially excepted from his offer of grace and pardon to all other offenders in Devonshire. The House of Commons sent up to the Lords a Declaration for their defence and protection. D'Ewes records the circumstances at some length, as he himself was named by Northcote and Hollis to be the messenger, "being the first " message I was ever sent up withal since my " being in this Parliament." Poor Sir Simonds was evidently proud of being selected, but the circumstances induce us to suspect that it was really a trap for him. His loyalty to the Parliament was considered very doubtful, and this

Memoir of Sir John Northcote. xxvii

was an opportunity to compel him to declare himself. He went up very complacently, and told the Earl of Manchester, who acted as Speaker of the House of Lords, that the Declaration was "for the vindication of some worthy "members of the House of Commons and others "*who have laboured to preserve the peace of the* "*kingdom in the county of Devon!*"

Four days afterwards, Sir Simonds appears to have seen reason to doubt the accuracy of his description of their conduct. In his journal for Dec. 24 we find that—

"Sir John Northcote brought in certain Articles "for an association to be made between the "county of Devon and one or two other counties, "which were read." As usual, D'Ewes proceeds to give his own speech, from which we have to gather what the proposal really was.

"After which I stood up and spake in effect "following :—

"That I conceived there were some particulars "in the said Articles which might be of dangerous "consequence. As first in forcing men to take a "Protestation, which perhaps many who would be "very willing to assist against Sir Ralph Hopton "may perhaps be unwilling to enter into any such "Protestation. The next particular is concerning "Martial Law, which is here permitted to some "private men in a county, whereas we would by "no means allow it to the general of our Royal xxviii *Memoir of Sir John Northcote.*

"Army when it was in the North the last year
"during the sitting of this Parliament. The third
"and last particular is to have power to seize
"horses for the service of the war, without excep-
"tion of so much as the very horses that must
"serve for ploughing the lands, by which in time
"a famine and dearth must be brought upon those
"parts."

Sir Simonds had as yet hardly realized what a civil war was.

"After I had spoken, Sir John Northcote stood
"up, and showed that the Protestation was only to
"assist against Sir Ralph Hopton and his forces,
"and that, for the other two particulars, how large
"soever the power that was given them was, *they*
"*would use it but moderately (!)*

"Whereupon the House passed the said
"Articles," and Sir Simonds shook the dust off his feet.

"After which I departed out of the House
"between 4 and 5 of the clock this afternoon, and
"returned no more thither again this day."

Sir John Northcote, having obtained the full powers he asked for, went off to take part in the defence of Plymouth, which began to be pressed by the Royal forces. A local annalist records that "Barronet Norcot," with his regiment, was quartered near Roborough Down, in order to hinder the passage from Cornwall by Saltash, where Sir Nicholas Slanning had 1000 men on the King's side. Robert Northcote commanded a troop of horse at the same time and place. In the "Siege Window," erected in the new Guildhall of Plymouth, "in memory of besiegers and besieged," the arms of the Northcotes have been introduced, in honour of the part which they bore in the defence of the town.

At the beginning of February the Houses received a letter from the Earl of Stamford, informing them that he was besieged in Plymouth. On the 27th they received news of a victory won at Modbury "by the forces under Lieut. Gen. "Ruthen, Sir J. Bampfield, and Sir John North-"cote, over the Lord Hopton's forces." About one hundred men were slain, and sixty taken prisoners. Nearly a thousand stand of arms were captured, and some artillery.

The Houses were much delighted at first, but were not so well satisfied afterwards. It appeared that the Cornish militia had run away, and that, if the Devonshire men had followed up their victory, the war in the West might have been at once terminated. The Parliament began to suspect that their soldiers were not anxious to bear too hard upon their enemies, and this suspicion was soon verified. Within a fortnight after the battle at Modbury, the Parliamentarian gentlemen of Devonshire, among whom was Sir John Northcote, and the Royalist gentlemen of Cornwall, had arranged preliminaries for an "associa-

"tion" or peace among themselves, which would have had the effect of neutralizing the two Western counties. It was arranged that the treaty should be ratified at Exeter, but the Houses received information of it, and hastily sent down Commissioners, who succeeded in preventing its completion.

We all know how the nation had "drifted into "war," without any definite resolution. What was at first a constitutional opposition became something more, and was met by the King with acts of violence. The military demonstration, with which the Parliament hoped to over-awe the Sovereign, was replied to by the Commissions of Array. The collision had become inevitable, but, as long as the conduct of the war was chiefly in the hands of country gentlemen, it was carried on only in a half-earnest sort of way, with constant attempts at accommodation, until at last the affair passed into the control of a fiercer spirit, possessed by a desire for very different objects, and utterly despising a rose-water revolution.

The fortune of war now changed in the West. The Royalists were victorious, and Exeter was besieged during a great part of the year 1643. On September 5 it capitulated to Prince Maurice on liberal articles, one of which provided that his Highness should procure "a free and general "pardon" for all persons in the city, among whom the Earl of Stamford, Sir J. Northcote,

Memoir of Sir John Northcote. xxxi

and other superior officers, were mentioned by name. This article was "much disgusted" in Parliament, and not unnaturally, as it seemed to admit that they were guilty of treason.

We next hear of Sir John at the siege of Sherborne. He is mentioned by Clarendon as having been sent by the Earl of Bedford, the Parliament's General of Horse, to negotiate a treaty with the Marquis of Hertford. His portrait appears in the magnificent illustrated copy of the History in the Bodleian Library.

Shortly after this he must have been taken prisoner, as we find by the Journals of the House of Commons for Oct. 16, 1644.

" Mr. Bond reports the case of the absence of " Sir John Northcott, a member of this House, a " prisoner to the King's Forces at Exon, and " come up upon his Parole, to solicit his exchange " for Colonel Gibson, a prisoner in the Tower.

" The humble Petition of Sir Jo. Northcote " was read, desiring that the Report concerning " him may be made, and his exchange expedited.

" *Resolved*, That this House doth allow that Sir " Jo. Northcote, a prisoner on his Parole to the " King's forces, shall be exchanged.

" That this House doth allow and approve of " the exchange of Sir Alexander Denton, a prisoner " to the Parliament, in the Tower, for Sir Jo. " Northcote, a Prisoner to the King's Forces.

" *Ordered*, That it be referred to the Committee

"of Prisoners, to take caution of Sir Alex. Den-
"ton; and to limit him a time to go to solicit
"his exchange, not exceeding the time limited and
"remaining to Sir Jo. Northcote."

This affair must have taken some time, as it is not until May 7, 1645, that we find it

"*Resolved*, That Sir Jo. Northcott be forthwith
"admitted to take his place, and to sit as a mem-
"ber in the House."

On June 3rd Sir John Northcott and Mr. Bond were appointed on the Committee for Plymouth, Lyme, and Poole.

On the same day Sir John's name appears in a long list of members who were to have "an allow-
"ance of Four Pounds per week, for their present
"maintenance," probably on account of their estates being in the power of the enemy.

On the 24th Nov., 1645, some suspicion appears to have been excited, and it was

Ordered, "That it be referred to the Committee
"of Examinations, to examine Sir John North-
"cote's servant, who was prisoner at Winchester,
"concerning any letter supposed to be carried by
"him to the Lord Digby. And likewise that the
"business concerning the Cypher, wherein Sir
"John Northcote was named, be by them likewise
"examined."

The result of this examination does not appear. On the 20th August, 1646, the order for the allowances of four pounds a week to certain

Memoir of Sir John Northcote. xxxiii

members was discharged, the whole country being now under the control of the Parliament.

It is pretty certain that Sir John never served in the field after the "self-denying ordinance." Having drawn his sword for the ancient liberties of England, he had no love for a military despotism, and he seems to have been constant in his opposition to the Cromwellian system. Even the author of the *Mystery of the Good Old Cause* does not accuse him of having made a profit of his political principles. He was one of the members "secluded" by the army in 1648, before the trial of the King, and in 1651 his name was omitted in the new Commission of the Peace for the County of Devon.

In 1654 the Protector called a Parliament, to be elected according to a scheme of Reform invented or adopted by himself. Devonshire had eleven members allotted to it, and of these Sir John Northcote was one. We may be sure that he went very heartily into opposition, which increased his popularity in his native county.

In the list of the Parliament of 1656 he appears as the first, or perhaps we may say the Captain, of the eleven. But this time Cromwell allowed no member to take his seat unless he had first obtained a certificate of having been "approved" by the Council." Some of the excluded members were bold enough to publish a Remonstrance, which may still be read, reflecting in unmeasured

d

xxxiv *Memoir of Sir John Northcote.*

language upon the tyranny of the Lord Protector, and among the signatures to that document we find the name of John Northcote.

Oliver died, and Richard Cromwell called a Parliament on the old system. Devonshire had again only two representatives, and the first of these was Sir John Northcote. His long experience of public affairs, as well as his opposition to Cromwell, had now evidently made him a man of considerable mark. He was placed upon many Committees, and at least once sent up with a message from the House to the Protector. We find by *Burton's Diary*, with which Goddard's Notes are incorporated, that he was at this time a frequent speaker in Parliament. Mr. Towill Rutt, the editor of that work, gives us a facsimile of his signature on the same page with those of Oliver and Richard Cromwell, Thurloe, Earle, Hesilrige and Vane.

His chief speeches which have been preserved were delivered in this Parliament, against the recognition of Cromwell's House of Lords. He appears as an enthusiast for representative government, and as entertaining a contempt for the pretended Peers which might have moved the admiration of an old Cavalier. On March 1, 1658,

SIR JOHN NORTHCOTE said: "It was minded "you by my learned countryman (Maynard) that "no law was rightly made but by King, Lords,

"and Commons. I am sure this law was not
"made so. If you admit this for a law, you give
"away all the rights and liberties of the people at
"once; such a thing as never was done. How
"that law was made, I shall not examine. The
"Triennial Bill had taken care for calling Par-
"liament, if the Petition and Advice had not; or
"the *lex naturæ* directs us how Parliaments should
"be called.
"In the Saxons' time, every May-day, the
"chief officer and the great council were chosen.
"All power, I do affirm, was derivative from the
"people. After the Conquest, in Henry the
"Third's time, the Lords were not hereditary.
"The first hereditary Lord was one Beaumont,
"in Henry the Sixth's time. If usage can make
"a right, they had it, but not for themselves, but
"for the good of the nation.
"I would have this examined, whether it be for
"the good or destruction of the nation that
"this House now in being should stand. They
"ventured their lives, but not their fortunes.
"The other Lords did venture both, and that
"they should be excluded and these advanced, is
"not just nor reasonable. I would have you first
"put the question, whether the Petition and
"Advice be a law."

Again, on March 5, Sir John Northcote said:
"We thought in the Long Parliament we
"might restrain the inordinate power of the Chief

"Magistrate. That was the ground of our quarrel "in the late war; but by this argument we cannot, "and it seems we cannot bound these Lords' "exorbitant powers. I am sorry to observe "the argument.

"It is said, we must take care we bring not "ourselves under Major Generals. I did not "expect that argument in this place. I did fight "against an exorbitant power in the King's hands, "*and I will fight against it again to the last drop* "*of blood*, if his Highness command me, whenever "such power shall be set up, if it be to-morrow, "and in whatever hands it be.

"It is objected that Lord Lieutenants heretofore "sat in the other House. That was introduced "but in Queen Elizabeth's days, and was then "complained of. Besides, they were great lovers "of the people. The Lieutenants were persons of "quality, and the captains men of estates. The "common soldiery were the yeomanry. None "had any pay. These are mean people, and "must be paid by you.

"You bring yourselves into the old condition "of slavery, if you go to establish those with this "external power. If you establish them not by a "law, if they be established in their power, you "establish slavery perpetually upon the people. "If the civil and military power be joined together "there by a law, some of them that offered force to "Parliaments, and disturbed us, are sitting there.

Memoir of Sir John Northcote. xxxvii

"What they have done they may do. Joab would "not take part with Absalom,¹ but he did with "Adonijah.

"I cannot be satisfied but that those persons, "in consequence, may join to set up themselves, "and pull down both the single person and this "House. I would have such an addition as may "so bound them, that they may not enslave the "people."

Richard Cromwell and his Parliament passed away, and the remnant of the Long Parliament returned to their House. Sir John does not appear at first to have taken any part in their proceedings. It is probable that few or none of the members secluded in 1648 took their seats on this occasion. It seems not unlikely that Sir John went down to his county to raise the militia for the defence of Parliament against the army, as he had once raised it for the defence of Parliament against the King. We next hear of him as a prisoner, and though, as on a former occasion, we are left to infer the fact of his imprisonment from the fact of his liberation, I think there can be little doubt that Lambert, when he again expelled the remnant of the House of Commons, took the precaution of arresting Sir John Northcote. After the second return of the members of that famous assembly, he is repeatedly mentioned in the

¹ 2 Sam. xiv. 29 ; 1 Kings, i. 7.

Journals. On Feb. 21st, 1659–60, it was ordered, That Sir John Norcott, Sir William Courtenay, Sir Richard Temple, and Sir Copleston Bampfield, *be discharged of their imprisonment.*[1] On Feb. 27, he was appointed one of a committee to consider "who are in Prison, and who are fit to be dis-"charged." On Feb. 29, he was placed on the Committee for Settling of Ministers and matters concerning Religion. He was also on the Committee for settling the Militia, and on some others, although the Parliament only lasted till the 16th of March.

The Convention Parliament met on the 25th April. The number of Knights of the Shire for Devon was again only two, and of these Sir John Northcote was one, his colleague being no less a personage than the Lord General Monk, destined soon to confer a crown, and himself to receive a ducal coronet. It must be considered a striking proof of Sir John's influence in his native county, that one so deeply compromised in the commencement of the rebellion should have been returned to Parliament in the first burst of reviving loyalty. Like Markham Everard in Sir Walter Scott's *Woodstock*, he cordially con-

---

[1] In the Clarendon Correspondence is a letter from Mr. Broderick, stating that "the gentlemen of "Devon take the imprisonment of "Sir Copleston Bampfield and the "rest so much to heart, that they are "sending to General Monk and the "City a declaration to live and die "with them in obtaining a free Par-"liament." See a paper on *Quarter Sessions under the Commonwealth*, in Fraser's Magazine, May, 1877.

curred in promoting the Restoration. Indeed, he showed his loyalty by moving a grant of £7000 to buy jewels for his Majesty at the Coronation, the former ones having been stolen, which was seconded by Lord Valentia, and carried, with the amendment that the sum should be £10,000. Such a motion, proceeding from a private member, would hardly be approved by a modern Chancellor of the Exchequer. It seems possible, judging from Sir John's constant appearance in debate and on almost every Committee at this time, and from his being the colleague of General Monk, that he may have held some office during the Convention Parliament. But, though he had become convinced, or perhaps always had been convinced, that the re-establishment of the Monarchy was necessary for the well-being of the country, he was not carried away by the violent re-action which tended to prostrate the ancient liberties of England at the feet of Charles the Second. He spoke repeatedly in favour of pardon and amnesty, and, when necessity arose, he seems to have confronted the triumphant Cavaliers in debate as boldly as he had met them, or their fathers, in the field.

A few fragments of his speeches have been preserved. In a debate on a Conference between the two Houses concerning the Indemnity Bill, Aug. 18, 1660, Colonel Jones exclaimed, "What "will the world think of those that speak for the "King's murderers?"

"Sir John Northcote got up and desired he "might be called to the Bar or explain himself. "Upon which the Colonel stood up again and "said he did not reflect upon any person." So early was the practice established of using words in a "Parliamentary" sense. In the same debate Sir Richard Brown the younger said he was for mercy, but it was for all the people in the land, and not for such horrid murderers as these were. "Sir John Northcote moved for a free conference, "and, if the Lords would not agree with them, "then to agree with the Lords as to their excep-"tions. Serjeant Hales said that the Proclamation "did not imply that those who came in should be "pardoned, though they did presume upon it," &c.

In a debate in the Commons on Religion, 16 July, 1660 (perhaps on the bill "for the confirming "and restoring of Ministers," 12 Charles II. Cap. XVII.), "Sir John Northcote began the debate "by speaking very highly against Deans and "Chapters, but spared the Bishops, saying the "former did nothing but eat and drink and rise "up to play, or something worse; upon which "Mr. —— stood up and reproved him, but he "was justified by Sir Walter Erle."

Sir John Northcote again moved in behalf of the ministry, and said "Many of those who were "ordained by Presbyters were active in bringing "in the King." Sir Anthony Ashley said our religion was too much mixed with interest, &c.

Memoir of Sir John Northcote. xli

On August 10 there was a debate in the Commons on the question whether the Money Bill should precede the Act of Grace. A motion was made by Mr. Annesley for carrying up the Money Bill, which had already been prepared, and only waited for the Royal assent. Sir John Northcote said, "That his duty to his King and "his love for his Country made a conflict within "him, and desired the Bill for Money might not "be carried before the Act of Indemnity was "passed." To which Mr. Pierpoint answered.

Sir John seems to have been sufficiently advanced to favour the Rights of Women. On Nov. 10 in the same year Mr. Ferrers brought in a bill for preventing the voluntary separation and living apart of Women from their Husbands, and that they should not be allowed Alimony, or have their debts paid, if they went away without consent. The bill was read a first time. In the course of the debate Sir John Northcote said, "It "was not improper for an old man to speak in "behalf of the women. That perhaps a young "man marrying a rich old woman, might also "take it into his head to part from her, and so "the woman might be ruined." He therefore moved to throw out the Bill, but was beaten on a division by 116 to 96.

We find his notions of finance expressed by a motion "to borrow money of the Hollanders at "6 per cent., and to give the excise for security."

On Nov. 13 the House resolved itself into a Grand Committee for consideration of the Public Debts. Mr. Knight moved to raise money by a Land Tax. Sir John Northcote was for not paying any of Cromwell's debts; *and to leave the raising money by a land tax to the last way of all.* On another occasion he even opposed a proposal to allow the cost of the funeral expenses of Cromwell and Bradshaw out of the forfeiture of their estates.

On Nov. 20, there was a debate on a seditious pamphlet "penned and published by William "Drake," arguing that the Long Parliament was still legally in being, and that the Convention Parliament was an unlawful assembly. Mr. Annesley said he did agree that the book was seditious, but the man repented of it, and had formerly merited; that it was hard to ruin a man for the first fault; and moved to forbear a while the severity of his punishment, but to burn the book. Sir John Northcote said it was not safe or honourable for them to spare him; and moved to agree in all with the Committee but the imprisonment. Mr. Howard said that he was writing a *Mene Tekel* upon the wall against them, &c.

Sir John was not returned to the Parliament of 1661, and it does not appear that he was a candidate. He was succeeded by his Cavalier cousin, Sir Hugh Pollard. It is probable that very few

Memoir of Sir John Northcote. xliii

who had ever borne arms against the King were returned in the midst of that loyal delirium. The old Parliamentarian must have felt a melancholy interest in haunting for a while the familiar scene, and observing the undoing of the great deeds of that House in which he had sat twenty years before. This interest is testified by a single sheet of foolscap which has been preserved, containing brief memoranda of the proceedings of the House of Commons in May and June, 1661.

His name was replaced on the Commission of the Peace for Devon, and he was for some years a regular attendant at Quarter Sessions. We may fancy him employing himself in his latter years by the erection of the monument of his father, and by the composition of the various mottos and epitaphs in English, French, and Latin, which are inscribed upon it. It may be that he felt rather weary and out of place in the England of Charles the Second, though not discontented, and not ashamed of the part which he had played among the men of a greater generation. So at least, we may interpret the inscription near the kneeling effigy of himself at the foot of his father's tomb :

"ITA VIXI UT NON PUDET VIVERE, NON PIGET MORI. JOHANNES NORTHCOTE, QUI HUNC TUMULUM IN MEMORIAM PARENTUM FIERI FECI."

He died in 1676, having attained the age of 77.

His wife had died in the preceding year, and they were both buried in the Church of Newton St. Cyres. No additional memorial of him marks the spot, nor is any required. There are two portraits of him at Pynes, one representing him in breastplate and gorget, as when he led his regiment to Plymouth, the other taken when he was an old man, with long white hair, and a stern expression of countenance, as when he sat in the Convention Parliament.

Sir John was succeeded by his son Sir Arthur, who seems to have been of a different shade in politics, if we may judge from the fact of his having been nominated one of the Knights of the projected Order of the Royal Oak, and from his concurrence with the majority of the Justices in signing the violent orders against Nonconformists issued at the Quarter Sessions of Devon about the time of the Rye House Plot. He married first the heiress of James Welsh of Alverdiscot, and secondly a daughter of Sir Francis Godolphin, and sister of that Sidney Godolphin who became Lord High Treasurer of England. From the latter lady is descended the present Chancellor of the Exchequer, who is also the representative of Tristram Risdon, a name dear to Western antiquaries as that of the author of the Survey of Devon in 1630. We need not repeat facts which are to be found in Baronetages and similar publications, but it may be worth recording that

Memoir of Sir John Northcote. xlv

certain members of the house seem to have sympathised with the exiled Stuarts. Several good portraits of that ill-fated race are preserved at Pynes, and it is recorded that a mass of correspondence with the Jacobites was destroyed in a season of danger.

The Northcotes have ever been a long-lived family. The present Baronet is only the eighth who has held the title in a space of 236 years. Not only his friends and followers, but most Englishmen, will join in the hope that he may long be spared for the service of his country in quieter times than those in which was cast the lot of his ancestor.

** The coat of arms on the cover is copied from Sir John Northcote's own seal.

INTRODUCTION TO THE NOTE BOOK.

Sir John Northcote's Note-book, which I have now the pleasure of introducing to the reader, is a small volume, about eight inches in length by four in breadth, of a convenient size and shape to be readily slipped into the pocket, stoutly bound in calf, and shewing the remains of two small brass clasps which once fastened it. It has been preserved continuously in the family of its writer, and there can be no doubt whatever of its authenticity. It is a genuine relic of that great epoch in English history which commenced in 1640.

Those who care for such matters may understand the pleasure of handling a manuscript book, which was frequently carried in and out of the House of Commons at the commencement of the Long Parliament, and of deciphering sentences traced by a hand perhaps warm from the pressure of the hand of Pym or Hampden, and guided by an eye which, when withdrawn for a moment from the paper, rested upon the face and figure of Falkland or Cromwell.

The leaves of the book are closely filled with writing on both sides, with the exception of two or three fly-leaves at each end, which contain miscellaneous memoranda. The report commences nearly in the middle of the volume, with the sitting of November 24th. The House had met three weeks before, and we may fancy that the writer intended to enter in the first part of the book the previous proceedings, as he might obtain them from some other source. But he omitted to do this, and, when he got to the end of his Note-book, he turned back to the beginning, and continued his report without a break. This seems to me an incidental confirmation, if any were needed, of the notes having been actually taken on the spot. No man copying out another person's notes, or even his own, would be likely to do it in such a way, unless compelled by a dearth of paper more severe than any that existed in the London of Charles the First.

The handwriting is small, hasty, and somewhat cramped, with many contractions, and rather trying to patience and eyesight, but sufficiently regular to offer no insuperable obstacle to one accustomed to decipher manuscripts of that period. Though some passages have cost me more trouble than would be imagined by those who have not tried a similar operation, and

Introduction. xlix

though one can hardly be quite sure of such contractions as *con*, or *com*, which might stand for common, commons, committee, convocation, concerning, canons, council, county, commission, and so on, I think I may say that there is scarcely a single word about which I feel any doubt, which is more than one would be disposed to say of the deliberate caligraphy of certain eminent living authors.

When we contemplate the fact of these Notes having been written amid the discomforts and distractions of the House of Commons of 1640, in the cold and gloom of a London winter, in a chapel destitute of stoves, and in an age undreaming of gas, we must form a high idea of the industry and determination of Sir John Northcote. And when we observe how well, without using short-hand, he took the chief points of a speech, and transferred them to his book in two or three pithy sentences, we must entertain an equally favourable opinion of his talent for Parliamentary life.

One or two of the speeches which he records, such as that of Falkland on Ship-money, and that of the Lord Keeper Finch in his own defence, have been preserved at some length by the historians of the Long Parliament, and so serve as a test of Sir John Northcote's powers of reporting. The celebrated Petition of the City of London against the Bishops, &c., has no doubt

Introduction.

been preserved *verbatim*. Sir John's notes of it shew just sufficient discrepancy to prove that they were taken when it was read *vivâ voce*, and therefore indicate the points which struck a very accurate observer as the most important at that moment.

I cannot pretend to claim for these Notes that they will alter the generally received views of English History. If they contained evidence proving that Pym was a Jesuit, that Laud was a Puritan, that Hampden was in the pay of the King, and Strafford a martyr for liberty, they would no doubt attain a wide popularity. All I can claim for them is that they furnish a few additional facts concerning matters that were in some measure previously known, that they indicate the line taken by various eminent men in particular debates, that they shew us a number of gentlemen generally supposed to have been mute inglorious members taking part in the discussions, and that they make us a little more familiar with the mode of transacting business in that famous assembly to which they refer.

I have met somewhere with the remark that the epoch was so great that no details concerning it can be small. Some readers may perhaps recognise, here and there, a touch that lets in a glimpse of light upon an obscure point. For instance, in presenting the Report upon Strafford on November 24, Pym observed that "altering "of Laws was to be avoided," which seems to prove that the Committee had already discussed the question whether to proceed by attainder or by impeachment.

We find in this little Note-book the record of the inception of great events, which afterwards shook the country from end to end. A few drops of water, trickling through a small crack in the embankment of the Mississippi, are the prelude to a deluge that sweeps away everything that stands in its way, and inundates many square miles of country. Even such were the proceedings of the first few weeks of the Long Parliament.

Those proceedings were very far removed from an age of shorthand writers, and telegraphs, and daily newspapers, and summaries of debates, and "Essences of Parliament," and "Sketches in "the House of Commons," and "Our London "Correspondents," and photographs, and caricatures, and all the apparatus which we are accustomed to see employed for turning the fiercest light of publicity upon our statesmen and politicians. There was no privilege of Parliament more jealously guarded at that time than the privilege of secrecy. The House of Commons discouraged in general any report of its proceedings, absolutely forbade the publication of its debates, and even visited with its displeasure the members who took notes for their own private satisfaction.

Sir Simonds D'Ewes, "the principal note-taker "in the House," records that he had to defend his conduct in that respect, and to protest that he should not communicate his journal to any man living. "If you will not permit us to write, we "must go to sleep, as some among us do, or go "to plays, as others have done,"—an awful scandal among Puritans. On that occasion Sir Walter Earle and Sir Henry Vane spoke against the practice, and Sir Edward Alford was required to give up to the Speaker some notes which he had taken.

Lord Digby's conduct in publishing a speech of his own was referred to a Committee, and he only escaped expulsion by being suddenly raised to the Peerage. His speech was burnt by the hangman. Sir Edward Dering for a similar reason was actually expelled the House and committed to the Tower. The member who moved that his speech should be burnt was Mr. Oliver Cromwell. He declared that Sir Edward was guilty of (1) discovering the secrets of the House; (2) disgracing the acts of the House; (3) naming members of the House to their disgrace.

On February 4, 1640-1, Mr. Francis Nevil, a member, was committed to the Tower for breach of privilege *in the preceding Parliament*, "by "discovering to the king and council what words "some members did let fall in their debate in "that House." It appears that any member who took notes was suspected of being a spy of the king, and was regarded with the same feelings with which a school-boy who "tells tales" is regarded by his companions.

On the occasion of the debate on the impeachment of Lord Strafford, with which Sir John Northcote's notes commence, an order was made "that no member should offer to go forth." The "outward rooms" were cleared, and the outward door kept locked, and so continued for four or five hours.

In this Note-book we may observe a remarkable entry on the 1st December. Sir John Hotham spoke "against Mr. Rushworth taking "notes by shorthand." A committee was appointed "to view the Clerk's book every Satur-"day, to allow of what they think fit to be "preserved, *and no copies of arguments*. And to "examine what copies have been given, and to "whom." Again, on Dec. 3rd, we find Pym obtaining an order for secrecy of those that were to be present at the examination of witnesses against Strafford, and " the Committee did "severally protest secrecy."

Sir John Northcote reports at some length the heads of a speech made by Mr. Holborne on Dec. 15 in defence of the new Canons, or rather of the Bishops. Of this speech Nalson, writing about the year 1680, only says, " Mr. Holborne "argued two hours in justification of them, but I "have not been able to gratify the reader with his "arguments, it being the constant method of that "age to discourage the printing of anything that "did oppose them, by which means very few "speeches or arguments of the loyal party have "been rescued from oblivion, or transmitted to "posterity." He goes on to say, with his usual unfairness, that the proceedings of the other party were "with great care and industry divulged and "spread abroad through the nation;" but this is certainly not generally true respecting their speeches in Parliament.

I have modernised the spelling of the "Notes," as it appears to me that the retention of the antique mode of spelling is wearisome both to the writer and reader, when continued through many pages, though it is often effective in an isolated quotation. I have made an exception with regard to proper names, as their original orthography is somewhat curious. Sir John Northcote's spelling is generally more regular and consistent than was usual in that age, but in the case of proper names he was, if possible, more careless than his contemporaries. The name of the great leader of the House of Commons, though it only consisted of three letters, is spelt in three, if not four, different ways. It is never Pym, the form which has been adopted in modern times. We find it spelt Pim, Pimm, Pimme, and

Introduction. lv

in one case I am inclined to think that it is represented by *Pem*. It is often represented simply by Mr. P.,—a tribute to Pym's importance, as there were plenty of other members whose names began with the same letter. Hampden's name is never spelt in the modern way. He is Hamden, or Hambden. The latter form seems to have been the correct one at that time, and is retained by Hume in his History. St. John is sometimes St. Johns, and Strode is always Stroud. Hyde is always spelt Hide, and Palmer is sometimes Paulmer. Sir John Strangways' name is spelt in various ways, which is very pardonable, and the difficulty is often avoided by simply calling him "Sir Jo. Strang." "Haselrig" and "Fiennes" also give considerable opportunities for variation. It is characteristic that, though the name may be contracted, the title of Mr., or Sir, is always prefixed. Cromwell does not appear at all in the debates of these weeks, and Hampden very seldom.

It would be absurd to affect ignorance of two works with which this Note-book may naturally be compared, Sir Ralph Verney's Notes, edited by Mr. Bruce for the Camden Society, and Sir Simonds D'Ewes's Reports of the Proceedings in the Long Parliament, which still remain in manuscript in the British Museum, but which have been made well known to the world by Mr. Carlyle and Mr. Forster.

Sir Ralph Verney's Notes cover a larger space of time than Sir John Northcote's, but in no other respect do they appear to me superior. A great part of them consists, like the Journals of the House, merely of resolutions without the debates, and those speeches which he reports are often set down without the names of the speakers. I may be prejudiced, and very likely am, but it appears to me that Sir Ralph was not so quick as Sir John in seizing the material points of a speech, and setting them down in a very few words. However, there is a great resemblance between the two, and it is curious that they do not in the least interfere with each other. Sir John Northcote's notes end on the 28th of December. Sir Ralph Verney's do not begin till the 10th of February, except as regards the Committee on Mr. Hobby's election, which Sir John dismisses in exactly three words.

The work of the other great note-taker of the Long Parliament, Sir Simonds D'Ewes, is of a very different character. It may almost rank with Pepys's Diary among the curiosities of literature. It is impossible for any careful student of the history of that period to feel otherwise than grateful to the writer of such a work, or to refuse a tribute of admiration to his extraordinary perseverance and industry. But Sir Simonds' manuscripts are not mere reports of the debates. It seems to me, having spent some time over them, that they were clearly intended to serve as

Introduction. lvii

materials for a complete History of the Long Parliament, and that, if their author's life had been prolonged, and his literary ability had been equal to his assiduity, he might have left us a book scarcely inferior to the History of Clarendon. But, like the History of Clarendon, it would have been a book written for a definite purpose. Clarendon wrote his History to exalt a party. Sir Simonds D'Ewes wrote his Journal, as he wrote his Autobiography, to exalt himself. He generally gives the speeches of other men in a brief, fragmentary style. His own speeches are given at length, often fairly copied out by a clerk, and, I suspect, written, or at least improved, after the predictions contained in them had been verified. There are passages in speeches delivered in 1642 which foretell the destruction, not only of the Monarchy, but of the Parliament, by the army that was being created, and which, if we believe their date, establish the speaker's claim to superhuman sagacity. His usual style is, "The " House fell into a most unnecessary debate," &c. ; " Whereupon, after three or four had spoken, I "stood up, and spake in effect following." Then comes a long speech, bristling with Latin, and adorned by copious quotations from the rolls of ancient Parliaments. " Then followed a great "*plaudite* or approbation in the House, many "speaking out loud, Well moved, Well moved!" " Divers expressed their approbation." "After "me, divers spake to small purpose!" "Mr. —— "spake long, and all of little moment!"

Once, after giving a long speech of his own, he honestly adds the memorandum, "This was not "spoken." Finding his success not equal to his merits, he became jealous of the leaders, "that "insolent proud fiery spirit Mr. Pym, whom I once "much esteemed for the piety I conceived had "been in him," and "his cunning companion Mr. "Hamden." It is curious to observe the small proportion of space allotted by Sir John Northcote and Sir Ralph Verney to the eloquent member for Sudbury, who, according to his own account, was the chief speaker in the House. It seems impossible to doubt that his careful, though unfinished, sketch of that great epoch, of the melancholy and dignified King, of the brilliant Strafford, of Pym, and Hampden, and Falkland, and Strode, and all the wise statesmen and dashing debaters of the House of Commons, was intended principally as a background for the principal figure, the great ME,—ME, Sir Simonds D'Ewes, Knight and Baronet, of Stowlangtoft, sometime High Sheriff of the County of Suffolk, heir of all the D'Eweses and of all the Simondses, husband of the heiress of all the Cloptons, the wise, the good, the eloquent, the learned, the depository of all the records of all the Parliaments of England, the elect of Sudbury in this world, but destined for a higher place in the world to come.

Introduction. lix

The commencement of the Long Parliament was one of those rare and brief periods when all honest men may be said to belong to one party. From every part of the kingdom the most prominent country gentlemen and lawyers had been sent up to Westminster, charged to put an end to the intolerable abuses of the preceding years. That fair brotherhood was afterwards dissolved in blood, but, for the time, Hyde, Falkland, and even Digby, were as eager as Pym and Hampden to pull down the minions who had almost ruined England. One of the most curious proceedings reported by Sir John Northcote is the appointment of a Committee to "interview" the Judges. Two members were to go to each judge separately, and get all the information they could out of him respecting the "solicitations" used by the Lord Keeper Finch to induce him to give an opinion favourable to the King on the question of ship-money. Of all this business it is evident that Falkland and Hyde were the prime movers.

The counties of Devon and Cornwall, and the boroughs with which they were then so thickly studded, sent up a strong Western Alliance. These men were indignant, not only at the general grievances of the country, but at the special wrongs of their own district,—the Stannary Courts and the pressing and billeting of soldiers and sailors in the neighbourhood of Plymouth.

Besides, they were closely bound together by the memory of the murdered Eliot. Their chief, the greatest Parliamentary leader that England had as yet seen, was John Pym, member for Tavistock. His colleague was a son of the House of Russell. William Strode sat for Beeralston, and his elder brother for Plympton. Totnes sent up Oliver St. John, soon to be Solicitor-General, and John Maynard, who was destined to play an important part in the revolutions of fifty years, and who, born in the reign of Elizabeth, lived to hold office under William the Third. Edward Hyde, afterwards Lord Clarendon, sat for Saltash. Robert Holborne, who had been counsel for Hampden, was chosen for St. Michael's, and George Peard, another rising lawyer, for Barnstaple. Hampden himself, now member for his native county, had been first returned to Parliament, twenty years before, for the borough of Grampound. Such was the party among whom John Northcote took his seat, a new member, but soon to be a very active one, though his energy at this period of his life developed itself rather in deeds than in words.

A close acquaintance with the proceedings of the Long Parliament cannot but increase our admiration of the courage with which, under the guidance of Pym, they entered upon their work. It must always be a subject of astonishment, how an assembly of squires and lawyers, drawn

Introduction. lxi

together from various quarters, many of them with no Parliamentary experience, none of them with recent Parliamentary experience, utterly unaccustomed to act together as an organised body, did, within a few days of their meeting, proceed to attack the fortress of tyranny which it had taken so many years to raise. Within a very few weeks they pulled down the principal promoters of despotism. They impeached the great Lord Lieutenant and the powerful Archbishop, the subtle Lord Keeper and the Popish Secretary of State, half the Bench of Bishops and the majority of the Judges. The worst offenders were safely lodged in the Tower. A judge of the King's Bench was arrested while sitting in his own Court. Finch and Windebank fled into exile. The less dangerous offenders were only bailed in enormous sums. And all these officials, whom the Commons were attacking, were men who, in case of failure, would certainly have had the lives and fortunes of their assailants at their disposal. The event shewed that, in such circumstances, the most extreme daring was the truest wisdom. When Strafford was struck down, no other instrument of tyranny could feel safe. Among all the able men of that age he was undoubtedly the ablest. Upon his life or death hung the destinies of England. Had he lived, the history of the next few years would probably have been entirely different. His talents appear to have been exactly of the kind most required in a civil war. Had Strafford been by the King's side in 1642, I believe that the Parliament would have been thoroughly beaten. On the other hand, had Strafford been a leader of the Parliament, I believe that Cromwell would never have risen above the rank of a Major-General. It is the highest proof of Pym's sagacity, that he clearly saw the key of the position, and succeeded in seizing it.

Lord Macaulay, in one of his early essays, after observing that "two men exercised a paramount influence over the legislature and the country, Pym and Hampden," ventures to assert that "by the universal consent of friends and enemies, the first place belonged to Hampden." It may be doubted whether he would have expressed this opinion after further research. It is true that Hampden was one of the best and wisest of men. It is true that his persecution by the Government, the dauntless courage with which he had met it, his sound judgment, his perfect honesty, his considerable abilities, his sweet temper, and his attractive manners, set off by the advantages of wealth and position, had made him most popular with the whole country as well as with his friends. The mode of his death, as in the case of Falkland, has added to the interest with which he has been regarded by succeeding generations. But in the

Introduction. lxiii

rare and peculiar talent which is required for leading the House of Commons, there seems no reason for supposing that he was equal to the statesman upon whom the Royalists, with a just appreciation of his power, fixed the nickname of "King Pym."

This opinion of the supremacy of Pym will be found fully confirmed in Sir John Northcote's Notes. Without official position, without rank, without wealth, without, so far as we know, any formal election, he was undoubtedly the leader of the House by the right of the ablest. Not only in the greatest affairs, such as the impeachments of Strafford and Laud, but in the every-day business of Parliament,—in conducting the frequent conferences with the Lords,—in questions as to the proper way of proceeding,—even in appointing the day for the Christmas recess,—we find the House voluntarily deferring to the advice of the member for Tavistock.

It may be convenient to refresh the reader's memory by a brief notice of the proceedings of the Long Parliament up to the commencement of this Note-book.

The Houses met on the 3rd November, a day already memorable as the anniversary of the meeting of that Parliament which pulled down Wolsey, and reformed the church. The King made a short speech, followed by a long one from the Lord Keeper. The House of Commons unani-

lxiv *Introduction.*

mously chose William Lenthall for their Speaker, on the nomination of Sir Henry Vane, senior.

On the 5th the Speaker was presented to the King, and made an elaborate oration, after the fashion of the period. The House then appointed its principal Committees, and at once proceeded to business. Petitions were poured in from all quarters, complaining of "grievances," the first being those of Bastwick, Burton, and Prynne. The House seems at once to have assumed administrative and judicial powers, ordering the liberation of prisoners, and the committal of officials and monopolists.

On the 7th speeches were made by numerous members, recounting the various grievances of the country. Of these the historians have preserved some record, especially of the speeches of Pym, Rudyard, Bagshaw, and Holland. By this time the petitions were so numerous that the House was divided into above forty Committees to examine them, "but the main were reducible into four heads:"

I. Committees concerning Religion, Innovations in the Church, and grievances by Ecclesiastical Courts.

II. Committees concerning public affairs in general, and particularly concerning Ireland and Scotland.

III. Committees relating to Ship-money, Judges, and Courts of Justice.

IV. Committees concerning Popery, the Popish Hierarchy, the Pope's Nuncio, Plots, Designs, &c.

These Committees went to work at once, and soon produced their reports.

A solemn Fast was decreed by both Houses on Nov. 9, and on that and the following days speeches on grievances were delivered by Lord Digby, Sir John Culpeper, Harbottle Grimston, Sir Edward Dering, Sir John Wray, and others.

On the 11th Pym declared that he had "some-"thing of importance to acquaint the House "with." Strangers were compelled to withdraw, and he then brought forward his accusation of Strafford, and obtained the appointment of a Committee of seven, whose report is the first matter noted by Sir John Northcote.

So the sittings went on, the principal business being the charges against Papists and Monopolists, and the consideration of the state and maintenance of the Scotch and English armies, which were still confronting each other in the Northern Counties.

On the 24th November, as I have already observed, Sir John Northcote began his Notes. They relate chiefly to the subjects already mentioned, and contain concise reports of debates, some of which were certainly conducted in strict secrecy. Brief as they are, they give us some idea of the preliminary proceedings against Strafford and Windebank, against Laud and the other

Bishops, against Finch and the other Judges. They also preserve the essence of certain discussions on the Canons, on Ship-money, on the Armies, on Priests and Recusants, on the London Petition, on the Revenue, and on some other matters. There is also a sort of Budget, presented five years after the money had been spent.

It may be observed that the speakers constantly refer to precedents, even of Roman Catholic times, and that their tone is exactly the reverse of that which prevailed during the great Revolution in France. So far from cutting themselves loose from former ties, they always professed, and probably believed, even when they were encroaching on the King's prerogative, that they were merely restoring the constitutional liberties of ancient times.

This short introduction, and also some of the notes which I have added to Sir John Northcote's concise memoranda, may probably be open to the charge of being too trite and simple. I am conscious of having inserted certain facts which "every school-boy knows,"—at least every school-boy who has the advantage of being within the circle of a critic's acquaintance. But I have endeavoured to make this little book readable by those who have no special knowledge of the period to which it refers. I can hardly hope, however, that Sir John Northcote's reports will be really appreciated by any but those who have small need of my annotations,—those whose minds are, so to speak, saturated with the history and literature of those eventful years,—who are able to clothe the dry bones with living flesh and blood,—who can call up before their mind's eye the actors in that great drama in their habits as they lived,—who can represent to themselves the tones in which their words were uttered, and the gestures with which they were accompanied;—even as the poet represents the same characters passing by in the vision of Cromwell:—

"There, as he gazed,—a wondrous band,—they came,
Pym's look of hate, and Strafford's glance of flame,
There Laud, with tott'ring steps and glittering eye,
In priestly garb, a frail old man, went by,
His drooping head bowed meekly on his breast,
His hands were folded, like a saint's at rest.
There Hampden bent him o'er his saddle-bow,
And Death's cold dews bedimmed his earnest brow,
Still turned to watch the battle,—still forgot
Himself—his fortunes, in his country's lot.
There Falkland eyed the strife that would not cease,
Flung back his tangled locks, and murmured, 'Peace.'"

SIR JOHN NORTHCOTE'S
NOTE BOOK.

[The notes commence without heading or date. The day, as we know from other sources, was Tuesday, Nov. 24, 1640. On that morning the "Outward Room" was cleared, the doors were locked, the keys laid on the table, and in secret session the great Parliamentary leader brought forward the charge against "the wicked Earl."]

[PROCEEDINGS AGAINST THE EARL OF STRAFFORD.]

MR. PIMM'S[1] REPORT. Long known the person charged by acts of friendship.

No use of Logic or Rhetoric.

Altering of Laws to be avoided.

1. It exceeds in extent—
    Divers great treasons.
    Murder, rapines, extortions.
2. In the Malignity against persons, justice, Nature, the public good.
3. The Mischievous effects.
    Bereaves Crown of its glory.
    Takes away Liberty of subject.

Seven Articles charging him with treason.

---

[1] John Pym was member for Tavistock, his colleague being Lord Russell, eldest son of the Earl of Bedford. The select Committee for preparing the accusation against Strafford, appointed on Nov. 11, consisted of Pym, Strode, St. John, Serjeant Grimston, Lord Digby, Sir John Clotworthy, Sir Walter Earle, and Hampden. Whitelocke and others were added afterwards.

Voted high treason (inserted afterwards).

1. He hath traitorously endeavoured to subvert the fundamental Laws and Government of England and Ireland, and to introduce tyrannical arbitrary government, against Law, giving his Majesty advice to enforce his subjects to submit to it. Information of Sir George Radclif's[2] words in Ireland, that with the Armies of Ireland and England the King need want no money.

One of his blood charged to say that England was sick of peace.

Lord S. himself to have said to a peer of Ireland, T[3] ... speaking of a case of his that he should have no other Law but what came out of his breast.

Five or six witnesses that he advised the King to make use of the Irish Army to reduce England, and to draw in the Nobility to assist with their fortunes and lives.

Musketeers sent to levy money in the North.

That he should say that those that refused to maintain these soldiers were little better than traitors. Warrants upon pain of death.

2. That he hath traitorously assumed regal power over the lives, lands, and goods of his Majesty's subjects, and exercised the same to the subversion of

---

[2] Sir George Radcliffe, an intimate friend and instrument of Strafford in his Irish policy. He was afterwards impeached by the Commons. Pym said, "In the crimes committed by the Earl there appears more haughtiness and fierceness, being acted by his own principles. In those of Sir George Radcliffe there seems to be more baseness and servility, having resigned and subjected himself to be acted by the corrupt will of another."

[3] This word is doubtful in the MS. It looks like *Teulcon*. There can be little doubt that it ought to be Dillon.

many. Judgement of death upon a peer, which was indicted in time of peace, when Courts of Law were open.

i. Lord Mountnorris's [4] cafe.

ii. Hath bereaved of lands, goods, offices, upon petition to himfelf alone and the board. Whole counties loft their eftates by Council orders.

iii. Difplaced Judges and officers, and placed others of his own.

Lord Chancellor [5] removed, and the Chief Baron in his room.

iv. Laid impofitions upon merchants (himfelf being farmer of Cuftoms). To be proved by Remon-(ftrance) of Ireland. Reftrained trade by monopolies for his own advantage.

3rd Article. Endeavoured to enrich himfelf. Hath detained his Majefty's revenue without giving Legal account to his own ufe, notwithftanding his Majefty's neceffities. Compofitions of papifts in North. Allow Revenue no perfect account. 40,000 taken out of the exchequer of Ireland for buying tobacco, himfelf being farmer of Cuftoms.

4th Article. Abufed the power of his Government to the encouraging of papifts, by their help to accomplifh his defigns. Erecting of Monafteries. Exercifing Jurifdiction from Rome. Raifed Army three parts papifts, and better paid than proteftants.

5th (Article). To ftir enmity between his Majefty's fubjects of England and Scotland. Acknowledged

[4] Lord Mountnorris was fentenced to death by a court martial for "fpeaking words" againft Strafford. The fentence was not carried out, but Lord M. was deprived of the manor of Tinmouth.

[5] Lord Chancellor Loftus.

before the Council that he advifed his Majefty's blocking up the fea. Counfelled it from Ireland.

6th (*Article*). Broken his Majefty's truft of Lieutenant-General by betraying the Army[6] at Newbor(n) and Newc(aftle). He had information that the King's Army was not able to encounter the Scots.

Writes to Lord Conway that he fhould fight, come what will. This without the King's knowledge, when he was near. Received counfel that Newc(aftle) could not be kept without works, and yet neglected.

My Lord Conway to produce his Letter.

7th (*Article*).—Laboured to fubvert rights of parliaments and incenfe his Majefty againft parliaments. In Ireland fummoned Liberties by *quo warr(anto)*, though they appeared the fame day, becaufe they would not choofe as *etc.*

Sir G. Radc(liffe) hath threatened fome for doing their duty in parliament.

For thefe they impeach him of high treafon.

Pray that he may be put to anfwer according to Law.

The Committee to prepare Interr(ogations) upon thefe Articles, to be fent up to the Lords.

[THE JUDGES, &c.]

SIR JO. STRANGWAYES.[7] The Judges not competent judges of fhip-money, which concerns the whole kingdom.

2. Againft the petition of right.

[6] A part of the King's army under Lord Conway was beaten by the Scots at Newburn, near Newcaftle, in Auguft, 1640.

[7] Sir John Strangways, of Melbury, Dorfet, member for Weymouth, maternal anceftor of Lord Ilchefter. He was difabled in 1642.

Old patents to Judges were *dum se bene gesserint*.
Proclamations questioned.
Fines upon them granted at a rent.
MR. WHISTLER.[8]

November 24th (25th ?).

[PETITIONS, &c.]
Divers imprisoned for refusing oath *ex officio*.
Petitioners.

MR. WHITE[9] charged Dr. Leyfield with divers words and acts of popery.

Ordered to be sent for as a delinquent, though he be of Convocation.

Sir H. Spiller refused to receive an indictment in Sessions against recusants. Referred to the Committee concerning him.

Idem. (Same day ?)

St. Gregor. Church. £1,500 bestowed four years since. My Lord Treasurer[1] and Lord Cottington

---

[8] Mr. Whistler, "of Gray's Inn," member for the City of Oxford. He was disabled in 1646.

[9] Mr. John White, member for Rye, afterwards a Royalist; "disabled," Feb. 5, 1643. He reported from the "Committee of Religion" that Dr. Layfield was charged with "setting the Communion Table altar-wise," causing rails and images to be set up, bowing to the images, setting up the letters I.H.S. in forty places, saying that the people saw Christ with their fleshly eyes, and telling them to confess their sins to him (Dr. L.), &c. A debate arose on the question whether members of Convocation did not enjoy the same privilege as members of Parliament. Dr. Layfield was imprisoned, but admitted to bail in January, himself in £1000, and a surety in £500. He was Vicar of All Hallows Barking, London.

[1] The Lord Treasurer was William Juxon, Bishop of London, and Archbishop of Canterbury after the Restoration. He died in 1663. The Church of St. Gregory, near St. Paul's, had been pulled down by order of the Lords

ordered the pulling it down, confirmed by order from board, againſt conſent of pariſhioners, who addreſſed ſeveral petitions to the board, and were forced to pull (it down) to ſave materials. After that part of Paul's was repaired, they petition again. Anſwered that either muſt build a new church, or diſtributed at appointment of Lord Treaſurer.

Committee deſire the Church may be re-edified. And that it be ſent up as a grievance.

[LORD STRAFFORD.]

LORD DIGBY[2] ſent with a meſſage to the Lords to deſire a conference of the Committee of both houſes concerning the Interrogations againſt Earl of Strafford, upon Sir John Hotham's motion.

[LOAN.]

ALDERMAN PENNINGTON.[3]—That the Lord Mayor hath ſent to thoſe that have underwritten to bring in their money, being about £28,000.

25th (November 26th?).

BOOK OF CANONS.[4]

of the Council, as mentioned in the text. Selden was Chairman of the Committee on this ſubject.

[2] Lord Digby, member for Dorſet, at this time a violent member of the Oppoſition. He ſeceded from the reforming party on Strafford's attainder, and became attached to the King. He was called up to the Houſe of Lords in 1641, in order to prevent his being expelled the Houſe of Commons. He is ſaid to have adviſed the King to ſeize the Five Members.

Sir John Hotham, Bart., member for Beverley, Governor of Hull at the beginning of the Civil War, was beheaded in 1643, together with his ſon, for treaſon againſt the Parliament.

[3] Alderman Iſaac Pennington, member for London, and afterwards Lord Mayor, an important perſonage in ſecuring the ſupport of the City for the Parliament. He was one of the regicides.

[4] The queſtion of the Book of Canons, which occupies a conſiderable ſpace in this Note Book,

Election for Tewkesbury⁵ recommitted.

The Convocation called as assistant to the houses by writ.

All oaths constituted by Parliament.

Opposes the King's supremacy that government of the Church shall be by Bishops, etc.

Mr. Glinn.⁶ What the Convocation did, not-

may be studied at great length in Nalson's Collection. After the Short Parliament was dissolved in May, 1640, Convocation continued to sit on, and, under the direction of Laud, passed seventeen Canons for the regulation of religion. It also imposed, under the name of a benevolence, a tax of four shillings in the pound on all benefices for a term of six years. These proceedings were confirmed by the King under the Great Seal of England, on the 30th of June, without giving Parliament any opportunity of expressing an opinion on them. They became the subject of long debates in the House of Commons, and formed the chief ground of the impeachment of Laud and the other Bishops. The Oath, which is so often mentioned, was imposed by the 6th Canon on all clergymen, graduates of the Universities, physicians, proctors, schoolmasters, and so forth. It was commonly called the *Etcætera* Oath, from the etcætera which appears in the middle of it. It was said to deny that the King was a Governor of the Church, unless he was included in the word *etc.*, "a scandalous place for his Majesty." It ran as follows:—"I A. B. do swear, That I do approve the Doctrine and Discipline or Government established in the Church of England, as containing all things necessary to Salvation ; and that I will not endeavour by myself or any other, directly or indirectly, to bring in any Popish Doctrine, contrary to that which is so Established ; nor will I ever give my consent to alter the Government of this Church by Archbishops, Bishops, Deans and Archdeacons, *&c.*, as it stands now Established ; and as by right it ought to stand, nor yet ever to subject it to the Usurpations and Superstitions of the See of Rome. And all these things I do plainly and sincerely acknowledge and swear, according to the plain and common sense and understanding of the same words, without any Equivocation, or mental Evasion or secret reservation whatsoever, and this I do heartily, willingly, and truly, upon the Faith of a Christian, So help me God in Jesus Christ."

⁵ Sir Edward Alford, being chosen for Tewkesbury and Arundel, made his election for the latter.

⁶ John Glyn, member for Westminster. He was a barrister, "a swearing, profane fellow," according to D'Ewes. At the Restoration he "ratted," was made one of the King's Serjeants, and joined with Maynard in prosecuting Vane. He was nearly killed by

withftanding his Majefty's Licence preceding and confirmation fubfequent, void.

1. What Law was before Sta. 25th H. 8 was, and what power the clergy had. No Canon can bind without Parliament.

Before Lateran Council every man might pay tithes where he would. That Canon which fettled it being received by continuance is good law.

No Canon can bind without common confent. By Stat. 24th H. 8, all convocations to be held by King's writ. All Canons to have confirmation from him. That all of them may be committed to 32 perfons, and being by them allowed then to be confirmed by Parliament, provided that no Canon be made contrary to laws, cuftoms, and ftatutes of this realm.

Henry the Eighth would not have prayed the aid of an act of Parliament if by law he could have done it of himfelf. Not a word to make the King to do more than what was before that law.

No Canons can be made with(out) King's confent, but no mention in provifion concerning King's confent.

No oath but by Parliament. And therein the Canon againft Common Law.

Mr. White. 1. The Author of thofe that made them.

2. The Convocation themfelves.

3. What penalty the makers have incurred.

1. That they have no power. Thofe matters that

his horfe falling on him at Charles the Second's Coronation, greatly to the delight of Mr. Pepys. The Statute 25 Henry VIII., which will be found frequently quoted in debate, was for "the fubmiffion of the clergy, and reftraint of appeals," &c., and placed the King to a great extent in the pofition of the Pope.

concern divine truth, if contrary to law of God, muſt be void.

Can make no Canon that trenches upon King's prerogative, or Common Law, or uſage of kingdom.

A dangerous plot[7] to blow up all religion. Not only at preſent, to blaſt future hopes. To overthrow our Liberties and Laws.

Supreme power given to Kings by God himſelf. No Miniſter ought to ſpeak againſt it.

In the firſt inſtitution of Kings,[8] God did ſet laws to limit them.

Againſt their making holyday for the King's inauguration, againſt the Statute what ſhall be kept and no other.

Againſt the oath. Binding all miniſters from exerciſing till taken in.

15 E. 3,[9] ſuch oath by act of Parliament yet revoked becauſe contrary to the laws and cuſtoms of kingdom.

Petition of Right, not to be put to any oath not warranted by laws of this kingdom.

25 *Ed.* 3,[1] the prelacy eſtabliſhed by the King and

---

[7] Alluſions to the Gunpowder Plot are common in the debates.

[8] "And Samuel ſaid unto Saul, Thou haſt done fooliſhly; thou haſt not kept the commandment of the Lord thy God, which he commanded thee, for now would the Lord have eſtabliſhed thy kingdom upon Iſrael for ever. But now thy kingdom ſhall not continue." 1 Sam. xiii. 13, 14.

[9] The ſecond Statute 15 Edward III. repealed the firſt ſtatute of the ſame year, reciting that "certain articles expreſſly contrary to the laws and cuſtoms of our realm of England, and to our prerogative and rights royal were pretended to be granted by us by the manner of a ſtatute."

[1] The Statute 25 Ed. III., called the Statute of Proviſors, recites that "the holy Church of England was founded in the eſtate of prelacy, within the realm of England, by the ſaid grandfather (of the King) and his progenitors, and the earls, barons, and other

his nobles. Therefore they (the Bishops) trench upon prerogative to bind it to themselves.

1 *Ma.* cap. 3, for restoring Bishop(ric) of Durham, which was taken by a former King.

The least punishment incurred is a *premunire*.

MR. PEARD.[2] The whole book of Canons is a bait and a hook. The whole book the bait. The oath the hook.

Brazen Serpent.

Keeper of a park.

28th November.

[ALDERMAN ABEL'S MONOPOLY.]

MR. GLIN. Report of Committee of grievances. Alderman Abell[3] threatening the vintners that petitioned the house in their Common hall, how they durst proffer petition without Licence of Company.

To be sent for as delinquent.

The petitioners to take copies of the writings brought in by Abell, Rowl. Wilson and Conradus, and the petitioners to be likewise sent for to charge them.

[MURDER OF MR. HAYWARD.[4]]

Report by SIR ARTHUR INGRAM and MR. GLINN concerning him that stabbed Justice Hayward.

---

nobles of his said realm, and their ancestors," &c. &c.

[2] Mr. George Peard, member for Barnstaple, "a lawyer of good repute in his profession." He afterwards moved the printing of the Grand Remonstrance, as an appeal to the nation. He died in 1646.

[3] Alderman Abel had a monopoly of soap, wine, &c. He appears to have exacted 40s. on every tun of wine imported. He was taken into custody, and bail for him refused in January, when Wilson and Conradus, who seem to have been his partners, were liberated on bail.

[4] Mr. Haywood, a Justice of

Motion that a bill be preferred to make it felony without clergy.

MR. PIM. Not to take away his life, but to lose his hand and his goods, and perpetual imprisonment.

SIR BENJAMIN REDYARD.[5] That his brother is in Court of Wards for lunatic, and that himself hath been often so, and therefore that he lose no more than what by the law.

One condemned to be boiled to death, judged in Parliament for poisoning a man before it was felony.

James his business recommitted, and to enquire of the lunacy.

CONCERNING SHIP-MONEY.

SIR THOMAS WIDDRINGTON.[6] Upon a doubt whether Acts of Parliament can take away ship-money, being an inherent right of the Crown.

MR. PIMME. That former judgments in Parliament against it. And therefore to rely upon them and not to argue it.

MR. ST. JOHNS.[7] The opinion of Judges and

---

the Peace who had distinguished himself by his activity in prosecuting "Popish recusants," was stabbed in the Palace of Whitehall by John James, son of Sir John James of Feversham.

Sir Arthur Ingram was member for Callington.

[5] Sir Benjamin Rudyard, member for Wilton, an old member of Parliament, and a very eloquent speaker. Sir Ed. Dering called him "that silver trumpet." He was a poet as well as an orator, and a friend of Ben Jonson, who praised him in some of his minor poems, as thus,—

"Writing thyself, or judging other's writ,
I know not which thou'st most, candor or wit;
But both thou'st so, as who affects the state
Of the best writer and judge should emulate."

He was secluded in 1648.

[6] Sir Thomas Widdrington, member for Berwick.

[7] Oliver St. John, member for Totnes, appointed Solicitor General in Jan. 1640-1. He had been counsel for Hampden, and prosecuted Strafford.

their reasons for it rather the grievance than the ship-money. No true ground. Wheresoever the kingdom is concerned the king may charge.

The power of Parliament questioned by it, in respect of many former judgments in Parliament.

Interpretation of laws belong to Judges, and not to Parliament. Added after the direction sent the Judges about ship-money.

[PETITION OF RIGHT.]

A clause desired to be added to the Petition of right.[8] Refused by the house. Destructive to the Petition upon the (words?) for the safety and protection of his people.

That a Committee be appointed to report former judgments, and to consider the proceedings in Parliament upon the Petition of Right.

[TONNAGE AND POUNDAGE.]

MR. SELDEN.[9] That Judgment in Chequer *primo Car.* for tonnage and poundage, and the decree there against replevins when the King's officers are possessed of a distress, be likewise referred to the Committee.

MR. PIMM. That another Committee be appointed to consider of tonnage and poundage, and to think of a recompense to his Majesty.

[DR. MANNERING, &C.]

Dr. Mannering's[1] book to be considered.

---

[8] The Petition of Right of the year 1628 is sufficiently known. It asserted the privileges of subjects, and recounted their grievances, especially in the four points of illegal exactions, arbitrary commitments, quartering of soldiers or sailors, and infliction of punishment by martial law.

[9] John Selden, the celebrated jurist and statesman, sat for the University of Oxford.

[1] Dr. Manwaring, Bishop of St. David's.

Dr. Beele's[2] doctrine delivered in a sermon in Cambridge.

[LORD STRAFFORD.]

A message for a conference concerning some of this house to be joined with the upper house about the examination of the E. of Strafford.

Mr. PIM. Difference twixt free conference where any of this house may speak as well as hear.

Answer returned that they are in great business, and will in convenient time send messengers of their own.

REPORT BY COMMITTEE OF RELIGION.

To consider of the special licence in the statute. A Committee.

MY LORD DIGBY for answer to the Lords for a conference. Divers arguments that some of the lower house ought to be present at the examinations of witnesses in the upper house.

Committee of six to consider of the opinions of the house, and upon their report a Committee of 60 to return answer to the Lords.

CONCERNING THE MONEY.

SIR J. HOTHAM.

The bond agreed upon.

[COMMUNION.]

Mr. Dowse[3] admitted to Communion.

---

[2] Dr. Beale, a member of the Lower House of Convocation, was accused of preaching sermons "tending to the disturbance of the state of this Realm."

[3] Edward Dowse was afterwards member for Portsmouth. The House received the Sacrament as a test of their Protestantism. The arrangements were made by a Committee, of which Sir Robert Harley was chairman, and no member who did not receive the Sacrament was to be allowed to sit. Mr. Dowse was admitted, although his return had not been received.

No Committees to fit this afternoon in regard of preparation.

Sir Th. Barrington[4] and Mr. Peard to receive the tickets of those that receive.

[MONEY FOR THE ARMY.]

Sir Wm. Udall[5] to receive the money and dispose of that for our Army. The rest to carry to Rippon to be delivered to the Committee of the North for contributions to be paid to Scots Army.

ALD. PENNINGTON. That the City money will be ready by night, and the most of them will require no security.

Ult. November.

[PETITIONS.]

Concerning bailing Mr. Hen. Darleye[6] upon petition of Ric. ———

Referred to the Committee of grievances.

Mr. Wilson's[7] petition to be read.

Petition of New Sarum against Sergeant Hide's[8] election, upon a schedule of divers misdemeanors. Referred to the hearing of a select Committee. And the petition of Mr. George[9] referred to the same Committee.

---

[4] Sir Thomas Barrington, Bart., member for Colchester, "an ancient parliament-man." He died in 1644.

[5] Sir W. Udall, or Uvedale, member for Petersfield, and "treasurer for wars." He was an officer of the army raised against the Scots at this time, and took the King's side in the Civil War.

[6] Richard Darley, member for Allerton, presented a petition from his brother Henry, a prisoner in York Castle. Henry Darley was elected for Malton.

[7] Mr. Wilson had been sequestered from his living for not reading the Book of Sports on the Lord's Day.

[8] Serjeant Robert Hyde was member for Salisbury. Edward Hyde, afterwards Lord Clarendon, sat for Saltash. They were both royalists in 1642.

[9] Mr. John George was member

One that is not in the houfe may not be named of a Committee, for that he hears not the direction of the houfe.

Wednefday morning appointed for hearing of all thofe that are under cuftody, meanwhile to go under fecurity.

SIR JO. CLOTWORTHY.¹ Concerning remonftrance prefented to Deputy of Ireland, upon report of a knight and a burgefs lately come thence.

Their petition read, and the petition to his Majefty, and anfwered that in convenient time they fhould be taken into confideration.

REPORT. MR. MAYNARD.²

Concerning prefence of fome Commons at examination of Lord Strafford. Agreeable to all proceedings in capital bufinefs at Common Law.

No Interr(ogation) to be prefented in writing to the Lords. Thofe that are from this houfe to attend the bufinefs may put in writing. Needs no precedent, becaufe conftant courfe of law warrants. But (precedents) muft be produced by Lords in denial of it.

[CONFERENCE WITH LORDS.]

A Committee of 60 fent to the conference with the Lords.

[MR. WALKER.]

Mr. Walker's³ petition read. Called in to avow his petition, and referred to felect Committee.

for Cirencefter. He followed the King to Oxford, and was of courfe difabled.

¹ Sir John Clotworthy, member for Malden.

² John Maynard, member for Totnes. He was Chairman of the Grand Committee for Privileges and Elections, which confifted of 47 members.

³ If we may believe Nalfon, Walker had publifhed a counter-

Moved by Mr. Controller[4] that no direction from the board, but only for commitment to examine from whom the order for the cruelty used did proceed. *Tuesd. in Cheqr. Chamber.*

Ordered that copies of all petitions against delinquents be granted.

Committee for Monopolies to sit this afternoon in Court of Requests.

[Burton and Prynne.]

Mr. Burton and Mr. Prynne[5] called in to avow their petitions.

Time given to Mr. Prin till Wednesday morning to add to his petition what he thinks fit, and to have a copy of that petition exhibited by his servants. Mr. Burton the like.

[Bishop of Rochester.]

Petition against Bishop of Rochester.[6] Parson of a church in London. For excommunicating the petitioner for refusing the ii*s.* ix*d.*

Referred to Committee of religion.

---

feit petition against Episcopacy, in the name of the County of Chester.

[4] Sir Thomas Jermyn, His Majesty's Comptroller, sat for Bury St. Edmund's. He was disabled in 1643. I may mention once for all that the members who were expelled for siding with the King were said to be "disabled." Those who were arrested or ejected by the Army in 1648 were said to be "secluded."

[5] The cases of Burton, Bastwick, and Prynne, are well known as examples of the brutality of the Star Chamber. They were all members of the learned professions, the first being a clergyman, the second a physician, and the third a lawyer. For having written against the Bishops and the Government, they were sentenced to pay a fine of £5000 each, to have their ears cut off, to stand in the pillory, and to be imprisoned for life in the distant castles of Lancaster, Launceston, and Carnarvon, whence they were afterwards transported to Jersey, Guernsey, and Scilly. One of the first deeds of the Long Parliament was to bring them up to London in triumph, and to impeach their judges.

[6] John Warner, Bishop of Rochester.

[DURHAM.]

Ordered that three pictures erected at Durham[7] be pulled down and brought by Dean and Chapter to the houfe, and to be enquired who fet them up.

[MONEY FOR THE ARMY.]

Report from the Lords' Committee for matter of monies. They left it to the houfe, but their advice (that the) whole (be) delivered to Sir Wm. Udall to go to Rippon. For the money to King's Army, to have his fees. For that for the Scots, he offers to give in a bill of charges. The like for the money from the City.

[SIR G. RADCLIFF.]

SIR WALTER EARLE.[8] That Sir Geo. Radcliff be reftrained from going to the Tower.

Mr. Speaker[9] hearing of it had granted warrant for his apprehenfion, and ordered that (*sic*) Lieutenant of Tower, that he may not himfelf, nor by interchange of letters, have accefs to Lord Lieutenant, being fent for upon information of high treafon.

[THE ARMY.]

SIR JO. HOTHAM. One with report that Lord General fhould mend.

Concerning popifh officers removing.

Ordered that meffage be fent him.

---

[7] See the curious Articles againft Dr. Cofins. "There were (in this church) the ruins of two Seraphims, with the picture of Chrift between them," erected in Queen Mary's time, and demolifhed in Queen Elizabeth's time, which Dr. Cofins, being Treafurer, "caufed to be repaired, and moft glorioufly painted."

[8] Sir Walter Earle, member for Weymouth, fecluded in 1648.

[9] The Speaker, of courfe, was William Lenthall, member for Woodftock, at this time a Bencher of Lincoln's Inn.

18   *Sir John Northcote's Note Book.*

Mr. Threr (*Treasurer*).[1]   Anfwer from Lord General.   Concerning fending officers of Army to their charge.

For hufbanding the money.

Lord Crawforth's troops unneceffary.   Their pay to hold till 8th of next month.   *Ordered.*

Reformadoes.   Moft of Lord Marq.[2] regiment. Stand £1,400 month.   To be removed.

Conveyance of Artillery. 3,638 per month. Conceived by Committee that £1,500 might be abated, but reporter's opinion 500 for extraordinary charges. 140 the pioneers per month. The laft refpited till Committee have debated till to-morrow morning. And payments upon fending payment to be made upon a new Mufter-roll, which my Lord General to be defired to make.   *Ordered.*

Proportioning the Money.

That £30,000 to the King's Army, and 20,000 to Northern Counties.

1ft December.

[Ecclesiastical Courts.]

A bill read for reformation of Ecclefiaftical Courts.

[County of Durham.]

A bill read for County of Durham to fend Knights and Burgeffes. County, Durham, Hartlepoole, and Barnycaftle.

---

[1] "Mr. Treasurer." Sir Henry Vane, fen., was Treafurer of the King's Household, as well as Secretary, and fat for Wilton. Sir H. Vane, jun., was Treafurer of the Navy, jointly with Sir William Ruffell, and fat for Hull.
  The Lord General was the Earl of Northumberland.
[2] "Lord Marq." perhaps Lord Marfhal, or the Marquefs of Hamilton.

Whether a fheriff that hath received his patent may be returned burgefs for another county.
Referred to a feleét Committee.

[PRIESTS AND JESUITS.]

MR. GLIN. Report.[3] Sixty-four priefts and Jefuits difcharged within four years, some by privy signet, others by warrant from Commiffion, most by Secr. Windebank.

Seventy-four letters of grace within fourteen years paft.

Committee find (from) two meffengers, Lane and Newton, that warrant was granted by Sec. Windebank to protect one[4] condemned, and the houfes that he fhould frequent.

Eleven houfes protected by being her Majefty's fervants.

Some under King's own hand at inftance of Ambaffadors or Queen mother, but with claufe that they be conveyed out of kingdom, save one Moffe, that was condemned, but upon mifinformation that he was (only) indicted, when in truth was condemned.

Another warrant under two Archbifhops' hands with Lords' commiffion.

Twenty-nine under Sec. Windebank('s hand) for difcharge of priefts and Jefuits.

One Cannon[5] difcharged by verbal warrant of Sec. Windebank to keeper of Clink, and the prieft faid he

---

[3] Report from the Committee to enquire about Priefts and Jefuits.
Sir Francis Windebank, Secretary of State, a concealed Roman Catholic, was member for Corfe Caftle. He fled to France to avoid impeachment.
[4] Mufkett, a condemned prieft.
[5] " Carrell, a fecular Prieft."

was employed about business of state and Lords' Council, which Sec. Windebank knew.

Petition of parish St. Giles against increase of popery. Instance three priests, and named twenty-one they had perverted.

Order given by board for prosecution.

Two of them after(wards) discharged by Sec. Windebank.

One Smith,[6] a priest, bailed by him, and had a note that none should molest him.

Mr. Reade's[7] letter for payment of fees. Close (of the letter), "it may be he means to keep you more free from trouble hereafter."

Upon petition of a priest in favour of himself and four others indicted of treason, Sec. Windebank orders suspending proceedings.

The letters of grace not entered in Signet office.

The frequenting Ambassadors' houses and Denmark house.

Printing books, making beads, etc., a trade.

Commission for compounding with recusants, from 3° Car. what revenue hath been answered by sheriffs. £4,083 in thirteen years. Nineteen peers and two countesses recusants; none of them convicted.

[TAKING NOTES.]

SIR JO. HOTHAM against Mr. RUSHWORTH[8] taking notes by short-hand.

---

[6] "One Smith, a Priest, called Gunpowder Smith."

[7] Robert Reade, Under Secretary to Windebank.

[8] John Rushworth, assistant clerk of the House of Commons, the principal Clerk being Henry Elsynge. He was Secretary to Fairfax in 1647. To the voluminous "Historical Collections" of Rushworth we are indebted for much of our knowledge of the Long Parliament. He died in 1690, aged about 83.

Sir John Northcote's Note Book. 21

A Committee to view Clerk's book every Saturday, to allow of what they think fit to be preserved, and no copies of Arguments. *Ordered.* And to examine what copies have been given out, and to whom.

[PRIESTS, RECUSANTS, &c.]

Letter to Sheriff (of) Sussex not to prosecute Commission of Recusants, signifying his Majesty's pleasure at instance of her Majesty. Sec. W. sent the like to divers other sheriffs.

Letter from his Majesty to Sir Jo. Bancks Attorney,[9] and his successors.

For Sir H. Beningfield[1] at instance of Queen Mother, dated 1634.

That petition be framed to his Majesty upon his protestation, 1º Car. (that), notwithstanding his then match, she should not intermeddle with matters of religion.

Concerning priests in Oxford.

Concerning Pope's Nuncio.

Ordered, That Committee make a charge against Sec. Windebank, to be sent (to) the Lords.

2. For a petition to his Majesty.

3. Preparation of Act against Recusants.

4. For Pope's Nuncio.

What powder and munition hath been sold to Papists.

Prayers in Lancas(hire) by order from Nuncio for prospering some great design.

Lo. Worster's[2] com(missi)on.

---

[9] Sir J. Banks, Attorney General, afterwards Chief Justice of the Common Pleas.

[1] " A Letter of Grace for exempting Sir Henry Beddinfield and his family from the danger of the laws against Recusants."

[2] Henry, 5th Earl of Worcester,

Horwood being under-sheriff Hamp. c. (county), upon letter from Sec. Windebank not to prosecute, imprisoned for doing somewhat against Recusancy, and entered bond not to prosecute any recusants, and to deliver up bonds by him taken. *Referred to this Committee.*

Secr. Windebank to answer to-morrow morning to such questions as shall be put to him by the House.

[CONFERENCE WITH LORDS CONCERNING STRAFFORD.]

Message from Lords to desire present conference by the same Committee, concerning the matter of the free conference.

The Committee give meeting presently.

Report. Lord Keeper,[3] that the Lords had reported to their house, and resolution that such of Committee as they shall choose be present at examination. And the Lords did desire a free conference. Lord Keeper, question whether they desired examination in house or at Committee.

MR. MAYNARD. Report of Conference. Lord Keeper, that for some they had resolved, some not, and herein desired free Conference.

1. To examine some of this house they were ready.

2. For members of Upper house, that all peers shall be examined upon oath when required.

3. That examination be speedy and private.

The Lords will have a speedy and strict examination of Lord Strafford.

---

held Ragland Castle for the King from 1642 to 1646.

[3] Lord Keeper Finch, the chief instrument of the King in enforcing the payment of ship-money. A great part of these notes relate to the proceedings against him.

For free conference, that some of lower house be present. Lord Keeper, that (he) spoke for himself, not the house, but Lords retired and gave no resolution.

That witnesses be examined concerning Lord Strafford to-morrow morning by Committee that frame the charge, and no examination to be public till the business be ripe.

That Message be sent to Lords that a Committee will be ready to examine witnesses to-morrow, and that all those present may be examined before they stir.

[SHIP-MONEY.]

Committee for ship-money to meet in Chequer Chamber, 3 o'clock.

[SIR G. RADCLIFFE.]

Sir G. Radcliff to appear on Thursday. To move the Lords on a proclamation to fetch him.

[LOAN.]

MR. HARRISON for time for raising the other £25,000.

2nd December.

[LOAN.]

ALDERMAN PENNINGTON. That out of the first money by the Act the Citizens be repaid, and that order of the house that it be secured by Act.

MR. HARRISON.[4] That the money first paid may be first repaid, but submits it to the house. *Ordered.*

---

[4] William Harrison, member for Queenborough. He was son of "Sir John Harrison of the Customs." He offered to advance £50,000 on the security of certain members who had volunteered to raise money for the Army. Nalson says he was a monopolist, who

[PETITIONS.]

Mr. Chambers,[5] petition avowed by him.

Mr. Vassall's[6] complaint of like.

Sixteen times committed. £5,000 damage. Loss of his trade, £10,000 more. His credit impaired. Total, £20,000.

Referred to Committee.

[LOAN.]

MR. PIM. That the house be bound by no order; for that there may be occasion to borrow more, and that it be no breach of promise if they make use of this money longer.

Message to Lords that they are ready with their witnesses to be examined concerning E. Strafford.

[THE ARMY.]

SIR WALTER EARLE. But 640 to be spared out of Artillery.

My Lord General's warrant to be discharge.

And for soldiers to be discharged, to receive no money unless they submit to their cashiering, and to time the money conveniently (?)

MR. THRES. Report of Lord General's[7] answer concerning popish commanders for reformed. Deferred till Lord General's answer.

---

hoped to mitigate his offence and obtain the favour of the House. He was disabled in 1643.

[5] Richard Chambers, an eminent merchant, whose goods had been seized in the Custom House, and who was ruined by the Star Chamber for comparing the Government of England to that of Turkey.

[6] Samuel Vassall, merchant, member for London. His complaint was of the same nature as that of Chambers. He was secluded in 1648.

[7] This should be the King's answer, "that he knew not of any popish commanders."

[SECRETARY WINDEBANK.]

Mr. Secr. Windebank to be first examined by Lords, and therefore his answer deferred to his accusation.

[BREACH OF PRIVILEGE.]

Petition from Leicestershire concerning affront done Sir Arthur Hesilrigg[8] (*sic*) at his election by Mr. Hallford.

Called in says that if he made no better speech than last he heard they would have little cause to joy in their choice.

LORD GRAY.[9] That he is no gent. That in memory of divers he kept hogs.

SIR ART. HASEL(RIG). That the petition moved not from him, nor expects reparation.

Offence to the house, because after election. To the County.

Ordered. To be sent to Tower, to make humble submission, to be drawn here, in house, and at Leicester assizes, and go to Tower.

[MESSAGE FROM LORDS.]

Report from Lords. They are now in serious debate, and will return answer in convenient time by their own (messenger).

[MR. WARNER.[1]]

Petition against Sheriff of Warwick, removing

---

[8] Sir Arthur Haslerig, the celebrated member for Leicestershire. Clarendon calls him "an absurd, bold man." The House of Commons was already becoming tyrannical. Mr. Richard Holford had said "They had chosen a man for the Knight of the Shire who had more will than wit, and it was to the disparagement of the county." His "humble submission" appears afterwards.

[9] Lord Grey of Groby, member for Leicester, eldest son of the Earl of Stamford, and one of the regicides.

[1] George Warner, Sheriff of the County of Warwick.

election from place to place, denied the poll, and granting poll, broke it up before 'twas done, and returned another. Ordered to the Tower, £100 fine, and to make submission in the house and at next assizes in county, as the house shall appoint.

Denying the poll to Mr. Speaker for Gloucester.[2] Referred to Committee of privileges, the first if his witnesses be ready.

December 3rd.

[SERGEANT HIDE.]

Report concerning complaints against Sergeant Hide. 1. Hinderer of the school. 2. Opposite to lectures. 3. Furtherer of ship-money. All fairly excused by the report. Much urged on both sides, but upon the question laid aside to further time.

[SIR G. RADCLIFFE.]

SIR WM. PENNYMAN.[3] That Sir G. Radcliff has attended.

[RECUSANTS.]

MR. PEARD. That order go from house to the Sessions at Newgate for quick proceeding against Recusants, that they may be convicted next Sessions. *Ordered.*

MR. MAYNARD. That a bill be passed that such as will not conform may stand convicted.

[PRISONERS TO BE BAILED.]

Upon Mr. Controller's motion for discharge of

---

[2] The Speaker had been nominated for Gloucester, but the poll was denied, and Thomas Pury and Henry Brett were returned.

[3] Sir William Pennyman, member for Richmond, a friend of Strafford's, commanded a regiment in the expedition against the Scots in 1640. He was disabled in 1642.

Sir John Northcote's Note Book. 27

the officer that brought up Mr. Prinn, to be upon bail.

The prisoners in Sergeant's hands to be bailed.

MR. SELDEN. That the names of the bailers and the sums be first presented to the house.

[LORD STRAFFORD.]

Message concerning examination of E. of Strafford. They have deputed some of theirs, and are ready to examine in presence of some deputed by this house.

[MR. BURTON.]

Mr. Burton's petition that he may have counsel assigned, and that he may take copies out of Star Chamber gratis. Called in, but was not here.

[SECRETARY WINDEBANK.]

An intimation to be sent to Secr. Windebank to come presently to the house, if it may stand with his Majesty's affairs. Answer that is gone sick to bed.

Appointed to-morrow morning.

[MR. PRYNNE.]

Mr. Prinn's petition read. To take consideration of his eight years sufferings.

Petition of some Chestermen,[4] Calvin Bruen, that were summoned to the High Commission at York for visiting Mr. Prinne.

[PETER LEE.]

Another petition. Peter Lee and Colborne gave Dr. Merrick £35, two butts of sack to Archbishop, 12 to one of his servants, to get access and favour from Archbishop, to their damage of £1000 in

---

[4] Calvin Bruen, Peter Leigh, and Richard Golburn, of Chester, were sentenced by the High Commission at York for visiting Prynne on his way to Carnarvon Castle.

trade, being forced to leave country for not making submission enjoined by High Commission. The form of submission read.

Dr. Snell's sermon (against them).

[MR. PRYNNE.]

Mr. Prinn's man's petition read.

Interr(ogation) against him about carrying the letter C. presenting one side Pope's head, other Army of men.

Archbishop vowed he should never be discharged unless he would confess or——.

MR. BAGSHAW.[5] For special committee for High Commission. *Ordered.* To sit to-morrow in Star Chamber.

[STAR CHAMBER.]

SIR T. WIDDR(INGTON). Report concerning Mr. Hunt's complaint against Star Chamber. To have power to send for records, and examine the exorbitancy of that Court, and the Military Charges for County of Leicester.

MR. SPEAKER. For reading general bills.

December 3rd (4th).

[ORDERS.]

That all take their places and keep silence upon pain xii*d.* to sergeant and poor.[6]

After xii o'clock no new motion be made without leave.

---

[5] Edward Bagshaw, member for Southwark. He distinguished himself by attacking the Ecclesiastical Courts as Reader at the Middle Temple, as well as in Parliament, but afterwards joined the King, and was disabled in 1643.

[6] "*Ordered,* That whosoever

[SECRETARY WINDEBANK.]

Motion concerning Secretary Windebanck's flight. Ordered to be sent for, both he and Mr. Reade, by the Sergeant's man, for 100 g. b. (good bail?)

SIR P. STAPYLTON.[7] Concerning warrant to Stockden Castle from officers of Army, to declare such as will not lend blankets and sheets enemies to the State, by Francis Trafford. Copy of the warrant avowed by Mr. H. Fowles.

[LORD STRAFFORD.]

MR. PIM. That order be made for secrecy of those that are to be present at the examinations. As the Lords have done.

The Committee did severally protest secrecy. Five of the Lords, and any four of the eight of Commons.

MR. PIM. Lord Digby, Sir W. Earle, Mr. Grimston, Mr. Stroude.

[FORESTS.]

MR. GRIMSTON.[8] Report concerning enlarging bounds of forests. That the judges have given opinion that King may make forest of any man's land.

Committee of all that will come to the business of forest. Chequer Court.

---

does not take his place when he comes into the House, or removes out of his place to the disturbance of the House, shall pay 12*d.* to be divided between the Sergeant and the Poor; and whosoever speaks so loud in the House when any Bill or other Matter is reading, as to disturb the House, shall pay the like Forfeiture."

[7] Sir Philip Stapylton, or Stapleton, member for Boroughbridge, He was a fellow-commissioner with Hampden and Nat. Fiennes in Scotland in 1641. He was disabled in 1647.

[8] Harbottle Grimstone, member for Colchester, Speaker in 1660, and afterwards Master of the Rolls.

SIR THO. BARRINGTON. That Lord Keeper said as before.

Mr. Burton called to avow his petition.

[THE ARMY.]

SIR JO. HOTHAM. The disorders of soldiers, that houses fired, and Minister's hand cut off by them.

SIR HU. CHOMLEY.[9] That their own trained bands committed the insolencies charged upon soldiers.

That E. of North(umberland) be moved to send for Col. Trafford.

MR. FINES.[1] That the house may do it.

MR. PIM. That the Lord General will give satisfaction, and that all due respects be held with him.

SIR H. ANDERSON.[2] That a Committee may present a draught to Lord Admiral.

Capt. Yeoward Sergeant Major to Sir Wm. Pennyman, with musketeers.

SIR WM. P. That he is not to answer for indiscretion of his officers.

SIR H. CHOMLEY produced Sir Wm. Pennyman's warrant for levying fortnight's pay upon — with the Musketeers; and that such as paid not should serve in person, and would fetch troop of horse to carry them away. Sent warrant Easter last for discharge of trained men, paying 15s. to officers. Upon that most of trained men changed.

Ordered that Committee consider of these illegal warrants.

---

[9] Sir Hugh Cholmondeley, member for Scarborough; disabled in 1643.

[1] Nathaniel Fiennes, member for Banbury, the eminent Parliamentary speaker, second son of Lord Saye. He was secluded in 1648.

[2] Sir H. Anderson, member for Newcastle; disabled in 1643.

Message by 2 Chief Justices.

The Lords desire present conference touching business of two kingdoms, about another month's cessation (of arms).

December 4th (5th), 1640.

Ordered. That no person (?)

[SHIP MONEY.]

Sheriff Hartford,³ rigorous levying shipmoney. Referred to Committee of any of the knights of shires that will come.

[RECUSANTS.]

MR. PIM. A bill of divers abuses in levying recusants' money in North.

[CUSTOMS.]

ALD. PENNINGTON. About wines stayed at Custom House for impost remitted 1636, the owner offering bond to answer all duties.

Sir Thomas Dawe⁴ sent for.

[THE ARMY.]

SIR WM. UDALL. For an order for Lord General's granting warrants for issuing the money, and the form of the acquittance from Northern Committees. Ordered for the money to King's Army. The latter referred to Committee to draw it.

[LORD COKE.]

Ransacking Lord Cook's⁵ study at his death.

---

³ Thomas Cunningsby, Esq., High Sheriff of Hertfordshire.
⁴ Sir Thomas Dawes seems to have claimed a monopoly of French wines. He was "sent for" by the House.
⁵ Sir Edward Coke's books, papers, and MSS. had been seized, also Mr. Noy's.

Taking away 19 manuscripts and other books, 3 ready for press, from his man.

Order. Committee gone to search.

Mr. Noye's books taken away by warrant of Secr. Windebank. *To be added to order.*

[ST. GREGORY'S.]

Business for St. Gregorye's referred to first Committee.

MR. WARNER and HARFORD.

Upon their petitions to make submission Monday next, and be released.

[LEAVE OF ABSENCE.]

One that sits in chair for privileges,[6] upon motion to be absent, to leave the petitions for the day to another. To be agreed by Committee.

[LORD STRAFFORD.]

Sir W. Pennyman. Leave to go to Lord Lieutenant concerning his own estate.

Like for Sir Ric. Buller, upon protestation to speak of nothing else.

[SECRETARY WINDEBANK.]

By SIR T. ROWE.[7] Desire of house that Sec. Windebank's study be searched for the books.

Monday appointed peremptorily for property (debate) of subjects' property. (*sic*).

ASSESSMENTS.

MR. SOLICITOR.[8] Report concerning £10,000

---

[6] "One that sits in Chair for privileges," *i.e.* Maynard.

[7] Sir T. Rowe, or Roe, member for Oxford University.

[8] The Solicitor was Sir Ed. Herbert, member for Old Sarum, Attorney General in Jan. 1640-1. He was impeached for framing articles of High Treason against the Five Members, and expelled the House.

Sir John Northcote's Note Book.

(100,000). To be affeffed in place of dwelling for his whole eftate, or where the land lies. *Laid afide after long debate.*

December 7th.

[PRIESTS AND RECUSANTS.]

Mr. Hanham's petition, that he would difcover priefts. Sir Tob. Mathew, Mr. Cotton, Mr. Sands, but they were all gone upon the proclamation.

Order for sending to all Juftices to proceed at next Seffions againft Recufants.

[PROPERTY OF SUBJECTS, AND SHIP MONEY.]

Report concerning property, and Clerk to take notes.

MR. ST. JOHN.[9] 1. Commiffion of Loan.

2. Commiffion of affize.

3. Addition to the Petition of Right defired by Lords.

Commiffion for Loans read. Being for neceffary defence of Kingdom, which would not permit calling Parliament.

Report that Committee find that both this and Upper houfe confider unlawful.

2. Commiffion for Affize. 2 Carol. For raifing money for defence of King and people in extremeft hazard. This Commiffion never enrolled. Sealed at Board. Copy of it read, taken when the commiffion was brought into the houfe, and then damned.

---

[9] Mr. St. John's Report on Ship Money, "which is very frequent, is not entered upon the Journal." (Nalfon.)

This by imposition or otherwise to raise money upon subjects.

Committee report that this in Parliament 3° Ca. adjudged by consent illegal, and desired to be cancelled. Lord Keeper presented it cancelled in King's presence.

3. Additions desired by Lords to Petition of Right. Copy of Journal in Lord's house read, viz., We present this petition to your Majesty not only to preserve own liberty, but to keep entire prerogative.

This taken into consideration.

Mr. Noye[1] presented exception against it to Lords,

---

[1] Shipmoney is said to have been invented, or rather re-introduced, by William Noy, whom Hallam calls a man "of venal diligence and prostituted learning." But he died in 1634, and the scheme was carried out and extended by Finch.

The question of Ship-money is generally understood, but it may make the following debate, and the proceedings against the Lord Keeper, clearer, if we quote the case submitted by the King to the Judges, and the "extra-judicial opinion" which they gave upon it.

"THE CASE.
 "CHARLES R.

"When the Good and Safety of the Kingdom in general is concerned, and the whole Kingdom in danger, whether may not the King by Writ under the Great Seal of England command all the subjects in his Kingdom at their charge to provide and furnish such number of Ships, with Men, Victuals, and Munition, and for such time as he shall think fit, for the Defence and Safeguard of the Kingdom from such Danger and Peril; and by Law compel the doing thereof in case of refusal or refractoriness? And whether in such case is not the King the sole Judge both of the Danger, and when and how the same is to be prevented and avoided?"

To which the Judges returned this answer:

"May it please your most Excellent Majesty, We have, according to your Majesty's Command, severally and every man by himself, and all of us together, taken into serious Consideration the case and questions signed by your Majesty, and inclosed in your letter. And we are of Opinion, That when the Good and Safety of the Kingdom in General is concerned, and the whole Kingdom in danger, Your Majesty may by Writ under your Great Seal of England Command all the Subjects of this Your Kingdom, at their Charge to provide and furnish such Number of Ships with Men, Victuals, and Munition, and for such time as Your Majesty shall think fit, for the Defence and Safeguard of the Kingdom from

who not accepting it, the second time sent, and then resolved not to be added. That this of itself, without relation to the petition, was lawful, but added to it, make it destructive of itself.

Report. The King though for safety, &c., cannot compel subjects to aid without consent in Parliament.

Violations stand on three legs.
1. Extrajudicial opinions of Judges.
2. The Ship-writs.
3. The judgment in Mr. Hamden's case.

The opinion of Judges read, upon his Majesty's letter to them and the case laid down, when the good and safety of Kingdom, &c. Their answer, that he may, and that he is sole judge. Judgment in Chequer accordingly.

2. *Ship-writs.* *Salus regni et populi periclitatur*, thereupon commanded that inhabitants of county should provide ships of war for 26 weeks, for which sheriff had power to (as)sess and levy, and to commit refractory persons. One of the writs read.

Judgment in Chequer and process upon it.

Message from Lords with a bill for the Queen's jointure.

Committee conceive that the Judges' opinion, and ship-writs, to be referred to consideration of house.

such Peril and Danger; and that by Law Your Majesty may compel the doing thereof in case of refusal or refractoriness. And we are also of Opinion, That in such case Your Majesty is the sole Judge both of the Danger, and when and how the same is to be prevented and avoided.

"JOHN BRAMSTON, WILLIAM JONES, ROBERT BERKLEY, JOHN FINCH, THOMAS TREVOR, FRANCIS CRAWLEY, HUMPHREY DAVENPORT, GEORGE VERNON, RICHARD WESTON, JOHN DENHAM.

"MR. JUSTICE HUTTON and MR. JUSTICE CROOK were against it, but afterwards they also subscribed it too."

MR. CRUE.[2] That if Committee have thought of any courſe to propoſe it.

MR. ST. JOHN. Upon reſolutions of this houſe, Judgment, and ſhip-writs. Committee conceived all to be againſt law and petition of right. Commiſſion of Loan and Commiſſion of Aſſize upon more urgent cauſes than *ſalus regni*.

That it be put to ſeveral votes. Opinion of Judges by ſelf, writs and Judgment by themſelves.

The charge impoſed upon ſubjects for providing ſhips and aſſeſſments for ſhip-money, againſt Law of Realm, ſubjects' property, reſolutions in Parliament, and petition of right.

MR. SOLICITOR. To provide otherwiſe for the Navy.

Voted illegal, and entered, *nullo contradicente*.

2. Extrajudicial opinions of Judges, publiſhed in Star Chamber, and enrolled in Courts at Weſtminſter. *Ut ſupra* in all particulars. *Voted, nullo contradicente.*

3. Queſtion. That the writ is againſt Law of Realm, &c., *Voted, nullo contradicente.*

4. Queſtion. The Judgment in Chequer in Mr. Hambden's caſe, againſt Law, *ut supra*. *Voted, nemine contradicente.*

MR. ST. JOHN. Select Committee to ſee the entries of reſolutions of houſe in this, and for Commiſſion of Loan, of aſſize, and petition of right. *Voted*, ſame Committee.

SIR TH. ROW. That Committee prepare the

---

[2] John Crew, member for Brackley; ſecluded in 1648.

resolutions of this house to be presented to Lords. *Voted.*

SERGEANT WILD.[3] That the Judgments be taken off the file.

MR. ST. JOHN. That to be respited till the resolution of the Lords.

LORD FAWKLAND.[4] Against Judges. They make *salus populi sola et suprema lex.* That could not stay 40 days for Parliament, and yet seven months for ship-money. Not so many to approve the judgment as those that judged it. All our sufferings from this, that a most excellent Prince hath been extremely abused. To take away judgment and judges together. Proceedings against S(trafford) for subverting laws. One excellent Solicitor[5] though abominable Judge. Joined his industry with his injustice. That 'tis not in power of Parliament to take it from King. Lord Keeper named. Dangerous to infuse into King's ear. The late declaration, undone us by wholesale, and now hath power put in his hands to undo us by retail.

MR. GOODWIN.[6] That the same committee prepare charge against Lord Keeper and rest of Judges.

SIR J. STRANGWAYS. That Lords first vote the cause.

[3] Serjeant Wylde, member for Worcestershire.
[4] Falkland, "that incomparable young man," as Clarendon calls him, was member for Newport, Hants. His speech is given by Rushworth, the only one in this debate. The chief point, the attack on the Lord Keeper, is sufficiently indicated in this summary.
[5] An "excellent Solicitor." He had *solicited* the Judges.
[6] There were three Goodwins in the Long Parliament; Arthur, Hampden's colleague for Bucks; Ralph, member for Ludlow, and Robert, who sat for East Grinstead.

MR. HIDE.[7] All our sufferings from the original of ship-money. That property of subjects not in their Judgment, but Parliament's. Of tampering and solicitation of the Judges. That some of the house be sent to the Judges to know what solicitations.

MR. PEARD. That Jones lying *in extremis* be sent to.

SIR JO. HOTHAM. That to have first concurrence of votes of Lords.

MR. RIGBY.[8] That it may require long discussion, and to prepare charge presently.

SIR FRANC. SEYMER.[9] That proof be first made.

MR. PELHAM.[1] That it will amount to high treason, and to prepare present charge.

SIR JO. WRAY.[2] The posy of his grandfather, Just and True. Sir Ed. Cook (said) whoever shall go about to overthrow Common Law, the Common Law will overthrow him. His motion, *Currat lex.*

SERGEANT EVERS.[3] To have first the votes of Lords.

SIR P. STAPYLTON. That Mr. Peard be sent to Judge Jones.

SIR JO. STRANGWAYES. That Justice Crook be sent to.

---

[7] Mr. Hyde. No one was keener in opposition at this time than the future Lord Clarendon. The curious suggestion to send members to "interview" the Judges proceeded from him.

[8] Alexander Rigby, member for Wigan.

[9] Sir Francis Seymour, member for Marlborough—created Baron Seymour in Feb. 1640-1.

[1] Henry Pelham was member for Grantham. He was secluded in 1648.

[2] Sir John Wray sat for Lincolnshire.

[3] Serjeant Sampson *Eure* was member for Leominster. He was disabled in 1643.

Lord Fawkland. That they be sent to all at once.

Sir Nevill Poole.[4] That Lord Keeper be forthcoming.

Mr. Controller. That respect be had to Judges. That none be urged to be accuser, but concluded that all be sent to.

Sir Jo. Culpeper.[5] Of twelve one was a Judas. To send to all the Judges that gave the Judgment, and to send immediately.

Mr. St. John. The Judges are assistants to Lords. Whether they may be examined without leave of the Lords.

Mr. Hollis.[6] That they have been sent to without leave, and desires that two members be sent to each.

Sir Jo. Strangways. That he was sent to Lord Brook without leave.

Sir Arth. Hesilrig. To go up presently and charge them before the Lords.

Mr. Treasurer. That no danger of Lord Keeper going away. That the same Committee may have time to consider of sending to Judges, and to prepare charge.

Mr. St. John. That it be instant and present.

Question. That some members go to several Judges to know what solicitations for their extra-judicial opinions. *Voted ut supra.*

---

[4] Sir Nevill Poole, member for Malmesbury. He was secluded in 1648.

[5] Sir John Colepeper, member for Kent, Chancellor of the Exchequer in 1641, disabled in 1643, and raised to the Peerage in 1644.

[6] Denzil Hollis, member for Dorchester, one of the Five Members.

SIR GUY PAULMES.[7] The like message sent heretofore, two to each Judge.

[SIR E. COKE.]

SIR THO. ROW. Report from his Majesty that the books (of) Sir E. Cook were by his order delivered Mr. Attorney, and returned to Sec. Windebank. Where now are his Majesty knows not, but within two or three days to cause them to be looked up.

December 8th.

Mayor of Norwich sent for for saying prerogative was triumphing.

To-morrow appointed for Canons.

[ELECTIONS.]

MR. HAMDEN's[8] motion that his double election may not be questioned, no complaint being brought within fourteen days.

A new election for Windsor.

MR. MAYNARD reports Sir Robt. Cran(e's)[9] election good.

Inhabitants of Windsor have voice in election.[1] SIR T. ROW.

And for want of notice given them Mr. Holland's election voted void.

REPORT FROM JUDGES.

LORD FAWKLAND. Bramston (said) that he had not been solicited in matter of ship money. Lord

---

[7] Sir Guy Palmes, member for Rutlandshire, disabled in 1643.

[8] The great patriot sat for Bucks, but he had also been returned for Wendover.

[9] Sir Robert Crane, member for Sudbury, Sir Simonds D'Ewes's colleague. He died in 1644.

[1] That is, not the Mayor and Corporation only.

Sir John Northcote's Note Book. 41

Chief Juftice Finch brought a cafe, Michaelmas term, before judgment. He had heard that order was given to fome Judges to conceal.

Mr. Hide. Lord Chief Baron denied any folicitation, nor knew of it till the cafe was delivered in Sergeant's Inn Hall.

Mr. Goodwin. Juftice Jones was fpoken to by Finch in fair way, but was not threatened. Dying men ufe to fpeak the truth, but reporter was perfuaded he meant not yet to die. For reafons of his opinion referred himfelf to his action.

Lord Waynman (Wenman).[2] Baron Trevor (faid) about 9^{ber} 1635, Lord Keeper came to his chamber with a writing, and defired him to fubfcribe it. Copy read. I am of opinion that where good of whole, etc. For my Brother Trevor. Subfcribed by him a day or two after. No threatenings ufed. For folicitations, Lord Keeper told him 'twas for King's fervice and good of Kingdom. Told him 'twas fubfcribed by moft other Judges. That Lord Keeper in this enjoined him fecrecy.

Sir Miles Fletwood.[3] Juftice Crook (faid) Lord Keeper had (been) feveral times with him. That by King's fpecial order cafe drawn, and that King enjoined upon allegiance to be fecret. That all Judges had fet their hands.[4] (On the) Wednefday

---

[2] Lord Wenman, member for Oxfordfhire. He was fecluded in 1648.

[3] Sir Miles Fletwood, member for Hindon.

[4] Of the twelve judges who gave judgment in the cafe of Hampden, feven, namely, Finch, Chief Juftice of the Common Pleas, Jones, Berkley, Vernon, Crawley, Trevor, and Wefton, decided for the Crown. Brampfton, Chief Juftice of the King's Bench, and Davenport, Chief Baron, pronounced for Hampden on technical grounds, but for the

before argument Lord Keeper preſſed him to do as four Judges had argued. If not, you do the King great diſſervice. For ſetting his hand, his opinion was involved in (that of) the greater number. That he meant the King was ſole judge of danger in Parliament, where has a negative voice.

SIR FR. SEYMER. Baron Weſton (ſaid) that (he) was never threatened nor ſolicited by writing under his hand. That records were brought him by a Judge, which he firſt ſaid was Lord Finch.

SIR JO. STRANGWAYS. Juſtice Barkley (ſaid) that a paper was ſhewn him by Keeper, that was, his Majeſty's pleaſure was that he ſhould give his opinion in the caſe brought him, which he ſubſcribed, that all kingdom (was) chargeable as well as maritime parts. After ſent paper, that debate between him and Judge Crook, that there was ſolicitation of them two.

SIR ARTH. HESILRIG. Juſtice Crawley (ſaid he was) never ſolicited nor threatened, nor any of the Judges to his knowledge. Lord Keeper gave him caſe, as to all other Judges, and enjoined ſecrecy.

LORD FAUKLAND. That members (of the) houſe (had heard) that Judge Hutton was weary of his life by ſolicitations of Lord Keeper.

MR. PEARD. That Sir Edw. Aſkew to hear him (ſay) that (he) was never weary being Judge till now, through his ſolicitations.

Averred by Sir. R. Aſkewe.

Crown on the principal queſtion. Denham, being very ill, ſent a ſhort written judgment in favour of Hampden. Croke and Hutton were decidedly in favour of Hampden, though they had ſigned the opinion for ſhipmoney on a previous occaſion, giving way to the majority of the Judges.

2. That letter to Judge Denham from Lord Keeper to folicit him.

Mr. Hamden. That has feen letter to him with fome relation to fhip-money.

Mr. Drake.[5] That had feen it, but was fo obfcure as he underftood it not. That Mr. Denham be spoken with in it.

3. That with evidence we have to give charge.

Mr. Grimston. Concerning Judge Crook, that fubfcribed cafe but againft his heart, Judge Jones urged him, You fee in Star Chamber, Council table, and other Courts, major part carries it, and that his vote was involved. But when he found it prefented *nullo contradicente,* was much troubled at it. That went to Lord Keeper Coventry[6] to acquaint the King that (it) was againft his opinion and judgment.

Mr. Palmer.[7] Common fame that Lord Keeper in his charge (faid) that fhip-money fo inherent in King, that Act of Parliament could not take it away.

Mr. St. John. That Baron Denham sent a paper that was for plaintiff. That Lord Keeper went to King (and told him) that Baron Denham (had) given his opinion for King, and told him of it, but he denied it.

Sir. Fr. Seymor. That had heard him fay that fhipmoney was binding till Act of Parliament took it away.

Mr. Nicholls.[8] The fame.

---

[5] William and Francis Drake both fat for Amerfham.

[6] Thomas Coventry, Lord Keeper, died in 1640.

[7] Geoffrey Palmer, member for Stamford, difabled in 1642.

[8] Edward Nicholas, member for Newton, Hants; was made Secretary of State, and knighted in 1641. Serjeant Robert Nichols fat

Mr. STROUD.⁹ That same Committee may draw up charge.

Mr. PERPOINTE.¹ That Sir W. Earle said last Parliament that a hundred Acts of Parliament could not take it away. He vouched Sir R. Hopton² for hearing the like in Chequer Chamber. That at Dorchester he gave his opinion that Parliament could not take it away.

SERGEANT WILD. That there was an offer of an argument in Chequer, whether it was so inherent or no.

Mr. JANE.³ That Keeper speaking of ship-money said that was so inherent in the Crown that Act (of) Parliament could not take it off.

Mr. LANE.⁴ That Baron Denham told him that Lord Keeper had said to him that if the King would make it annual he would be against it.

Mr. WHITLOCK.⁵ That the Lords might be sent to to have him sequestered.

Mr. PIM. That first a charge be presented to the house.

SIR JO. CULPEPER. That the Judges be likewise referred to Committee.

---

for Devizes, and Anthony Nicoll for Bodmin.

⁹ William Strode, the celebrated member for Beeralston, and probably the most violent politician in the House at this time. D'Ewes calls him a firebrand, "a notable profaner of the Scriptures," &c. He died in 1645.

¹ There were two Pierpoints, Francis, member for Nottingham, and William, for Great Wenlock.

² Sir Ralph Hopton, member for Wells, the gallant Royalist commander, "Hopton of the West." He was created Baron Hopton in 1642.

³ Joseph Jane, member for Liskeard; disabled in 1643.

⁴ Thomas Lane, member for Wycombe; secluded in 1648.

⁵ Bulstrode Whitelocke, member for Marlow, the well-known lawyer, statesman, and author. He died in 1676.

Mr. Stroude. That Sir Randall Crew[6] be sent to to know what was the caufe of his putting out.

That the gentlemen fent to the Judges be added to this Committee.

That they confider the denying *Habeas Corpora*, and Prohibitions. Meetings of Judges with ecclefiaſtical Judges. Concerning Jurifdictions of Courts and the Adm^{tie.} (Admiralty ?) Not allowable to divide the Inheritances of fubjects.

Mr. Str. That Lord Keeper's charge may not ſtay upon reſt of Judges.

Voted that all go to one Committee.

Sir R. Hopton. Lord Privy Seal gave his opinion to the Judges concerning legality of ſhip-money. That he be referred to Committee.

Mr. Pim. That the time not yet fit, coming upon Lord Keeper's words, being party culpable.

Committee to meet in Star Chamber to-morrow afternoon.

9th December.

[The Canons.]

[7] 25. H. 8. Statute requires for Canons (that) they had

1. The King's Writ.
2. The King's Royal Confirmation.
3. Provifo that they make no Canons contrary to the Law, etc.

No pofitive words in Statute that they ſhall have

---

[6] Sir Ranulph Crewe, Chief Juſtice of England, diſplaced in 1626, and ſucceeded by "Nick Hyde."

[7] According to D'Ewes, this ſpeech was delivered by Dr. Eden, member for Cambridge Univerſity.

power to make Canons. They had power before the Statute.

At Synod only Clergymen meet.

At Convocation others meet.

Why fhould Laymen be bound by Conftitutions of Clergy? he by that means may be excommunicated, and fo deprived of benefit of Law, and their eftate. Notwithftanding that reafon they may, for that they are parties to the ftatute by which 'tis done.

MR. BAGSHAW. Of legality of Canons, not of *præmunire*.

1. No Canons can be made to bind laity without our common confent.

2. Canons made by neither Synod nor Convocation void.

3. The whole Canons againft law.

Clergy divided in five ranks, firft 500 years till Conftantine's time. Canons made by Emperors and Kings, not by Clergy. From Conftantine to William Conqueror, Canons made by Civil Magiftrate. From thence to E. 3rd's time. Anfelm firft brought in Pope's Jurifdiction, though raifed of nothing to the Archbifhopric, and faid to King, *Tibi consilium, Papæ obedientia.*

In Henry 2nd's time a Council at Clarendon [8] undid what Anfelm had done.

In H. 3rd's time Common Law fet afoot, and no Common Law in force from E. 1st's time to 25 H. 8.

The Act 25 H. 8. no new law, but declaration of old Common Law.

Cowell's book, *Int.*[9] Parliament for advancing

---

[8] "The Conftitutions of Clarendon," A.D. 1164.

[9] Dr. Cowell's book, the *Interpreter*, was publifhed about 1607.

prerogative above law burnt, and by proclamation never to be printed, yet within seven years taken the boldness of printing it twice.

Three exceptions to oath. 1. No oath can be imposed but by Act of Parliament. Shall bring in no popish doctrine contrary to that established, which must relate to some popish doctrine. But upon confirmation have without warrant left out word popish, which alters oath. A Covenant against King's prerogative by Archbishops. Left out King, unless included in *etc.*,—an unworthy place for King. *Potestas ordinis, potestas jurisdictionis, jure divino.* Latter from the King. Difference 'twixt see of Rome and Church of Rome. One makes men traitors.

Benevolence granted by Clergy is against law.

Mr. Rigby. In preface to Archbishop's[1] speech in Star Chamber, says that not safe to govern by one way, the humours of men being various.

That the Canons in every part illegal.

25 E. 3rd, Oath do stand, *Jur(amentum) de parendo mandatis eccle(siæ)*. This oath taken by a Proctor *ex officio*. Give power to Archbishop every three years to make visitory articles, to which that oath will bind.

Conclude whole Canons illegal.

Mr. Bridgman.[2] That the Canons are illegal.

He attributed the most absolute power to the King, and was attacked by the House of Commons, who succeeded in getting the book suppressed by royal proclamation.

[1] Laud had published his speech on the censure of Bastwick, Burton, and Prynne, in 1637.

[2] Orlando Bridgeman, member for Wigan. He was a royalist lawyer, and was disabled in 1642.

1. Whether can make Canons.
2. Whether after Parliament.
3. Whether purfued it.

[SIR G. RADCLIFFE.]

Sir G. Radcliff prifoner to the gate-houfe, and none fpeak with him but in his keeper's prefence.

[IRISH PORTS.]

That the Irifh Ports are ftill ftopped. Mr. Treafurer to clear his Majefty's direction and intention.

December xth.

Mr. Marfh my Lord Marfhall's fervant. (Sent?) to Lord Marfhall.

[NEW WRIT.]

A new writ for election[3] in Secr. Windebank ('s place). And ordered that if he come not in tomorrow a charge to be preferred againft him.

[PETITION.]

A letter fent by Mayor of Salifbury found upon the downs, and directed unto the moft honourable affembly of the Houfe of Parliament, for benefit of his Majefty's Kingdom of England.

Debated whether to be opened without fending to the Lords.

A petition of all well-willers of the Realm of England.

That Juftice hath of late been neglected, vices cherifhed.

MR. THREA. That two or three may read it in

He was created a Baronet in 1660, and Lord Keeper in 1667.

[3] Mr. Burlace was elected for Corfe Caftle, on the flight of Secretary Windebank. He was difabled in 1643.

Committee Chamber, and if they find it scandalous to be laid aside, otherwise to report to the house, there being none to justify the petition.

(Written afterwards). Report that they think (it) fit to be burnt.

[ALGIERS.]

MR. PIM. Concerning Argier prisoners. That petition to be read.

SIR THO. ROW. That the Committee for trade have taken (it) into confideration, and shall prepare it without trouble to the house.

Referred to Select Committee.

[SUBSIDIES.]

MR. SOLICITOR. Concerning the raifing of the £160,000, whether at place of dwelling, or where the lands lie.

Put to question.

Subfidies given to particular ufes, and not to the King, thrice in Ric. 2. time.

That fum in every county may not exceed what was laft fubfidy.

---

xi*th* December.

[ELECTIONS.]

Malton and Allerton, Yorkfhire, towns reftored to fend Burgeffes.

Upon the queftion whether (at) Tewkefbury Bailiff, burgeffes, and commonalty, all the inhabitants are to give voices, and not the freemen only. After long debate referred to a Select Committee and all the Lawyers.

[THE LONDON PETITION AGAINST BISHOPS.]
(Presented by Alderman Pennington.)

Petition from Citizens of London, 15,000 names to it. *Read.*

Government of Archbishops, &c., dangerous to Commonwealth, and of human ordinance. Pray that the said government may be abolished.

Particulars of evils.

Subjecting ministers to their authority, which makes them faint-hearted to preach the truth.

The encouragement of ministers to despise magistracy.

The removing able zealous ministers.

5. Suppressing godly design for buying in impropriations.

6. Increase of idle and dissolute ministers.

8. Printing idle books to the increase of vices.

9. Hindering godly books against Arminianism and popery.

Publishing Arminian books, that no man has property.

Increase of priests. Making of crucifixes.

Impositions and customs.

Archbishops the same way of government as in Rome.

Others that have reversed popery have cast out prelates.

Also restrained ministers from praying for conversion of Queen.

The several habits of priests.[4]

---

[4] "The likeness to the Church of Rome in vestures * * * the Cope and Surplice, the Tippet, the Hood, and the Canonical Coat," &c.

Enumeration of ceremonies and invocations.
The Liturgy out of Romiſh Maſs-book.
Canons in Law. Sacred Synod.
Countenancing plurality of benefices.
Enjoining reading book of toleration of ſports upon Sundays.
Citing for working upon hólydays.
Abuſe of ordinance of excommunication.
Increaſe of whoredom by [5] commutations.
They claim their office *jure divino*, ſend proceſs in their own names.
Impoſing oaths and various articles upon church-wardens.
Oaths *ex officio*. Judges of late awed by them in granting prohibitions.
Many gone into (foreign) parts and tranſlating trade from hence.

Sir Mil(es) Fleet(wood). That many parts of it are worthy of conſideration.

Lord Fairfax.[6] That it follow Book of Canons.

Sir Ne(vill) Poole. That many parts of it ſcandalous.

Sir Sym. D'Eux [7] (D'Ewes). That in twenty years more we ſhould have loſt religion. Arch-biſhops have Pales (palliums?) from Pope. In

---

[5] The corrupt adminiſtration of Juſtice, taking money for the "commutation of Penance."

[6] Ferdinando Lord Fairfax, member for Yorkſhire. He died in 1647, and was ſucceeded by his more famous ſon.

[7] Sir Simonds D'Ewes, member for Sudbury, whoſe autobiography and Notes have made him, and the Houſe of Commons in which he ſat, so well-known to our generation. He was ſecluded in 1648, and died in 1650.

ancient times by preaching godly bishops they have got King's lands, and he wants them.

Mr. Treasurer. That the matter of petition not seasonable. Doth scandalize many things settled by Parliament. Many of petitioners Brownists. Scandalous against kneeling at Communion. Take care that own divisions bring not worse evils than papists.

Mr. Stroud. Not to give reproof to the multitude in their just complaints. To refer it to Committee of Religion.

Lord Digby. Of greatest consequence ever came to house. House not to enter into the business precipitately, but dismiss them and reserve it to hearing of whole house.

Ald. P(ennington). That 'tis not inconsiderately done, but that many should come to countenance.

Mr. Capell.[8] That roll of hands be sealed up, that no man's name be seen.

Mr. Craddock.[9] Against the disorders and oppressions of Bishops suppressing preaching.

Mr. Pim. That the names be sealed. That the Alderman dismiss them with fair answer, and that Thursday next be appointed for hearing it again.

Mr. Fines. In justification of petition. That nothing in it is scandalous. In Gloucester eleven

---

[8] Arthur Capel, member for Hertfordshire, was the first member who stood up to complain of the grievances of his country. He was created Lord Capel in 1641. He was a distinguished Royalist, and was beheaded in March, 1648-9.

[9] Matthew Craddock, member for London, died soon after this time.

Sir John Northcote's Note Book. 53

parifhes and but four fermons. Living under Bifhops, &c., and ferved by fhoemakers, &c., being finging-men. A free fchool, 400 fcholars. Lecture and fchool taken away. The trade of the city wholly decayed.

LORD FAWKLAND. That every member may have copy of petition to confider againft (the) day.

[COMMISSIONERS FOR SCOTLAND.] That their Army in great diftrefs and want of clothes, and therefore defire by Mr. Pim that the other 30,000 might be fpeedily fent, and debated to-morrow morning.

MR. PARGETER's[1] petition referred to Committee for Judges, that fits this afternoon.

Ellis, a conftable, inquiring in my Lord Marfhall's houfe for recufants, reproved by Mr. Marfh.

December xii*th*.

MR. HOBBIE's[2] ELECTION.

QUEEN's JOINTURE, read.

SIR B. RUDYER.[3] God bleft his Majefty with hopeful and fruitful progeny. To put in mind to

---

[1] Mr. Pargeter of Northamptonfhire had been committed for refufing to pay 5*s*. towards arming men againft the Scots, and Sir Robert Berkley had refufed to admit him to bail.

[2] Mr. Hobby's election is the only matter mentioned in the notes of Sir Ralph Verney, as well as in thofe of Sir John Northcote. Sir R. Verney's regular notes begin on February 10. Mr. Burlace difputed Mr. Hobby's return for Great Marlow, and the queftion was referred to a Committee, of which Sir R. Verney took notes. Mr. Hobby retained his feat, and Mr. Burlace found another at Corfe Caftle.

[3] Sir Benjamin Rudyard's fpeech is very characteriftic. He is defcribed by May as eager in expofing grievances, but always fparing the King, like a loyal gentleman.

provide for them. The first prince born amongst us this 100 years. Queen's good affection to Parliament. Concern her Majesty to uphold the glory and government of this Kingdom. The house to pass the bill with cheerfulness, and speedy reading it again.

SIR JO. STRANG(WAYS). That it may have certain day for reading.

MR. SOLICITOR. Concerning reading it Tuesday morning.

MR. PE(PEARD?). Against second reading for certain day. We servants of Commonwealth. No such bill twice read. And therefore to stay.

LORD FAWKLAND. For certain day.

REPORT.

MR. KING.[4] That ten Turkish Pirates upon Western Coasts. Committee advise that his Majesty be moved to send two ships from the Downs.

Mr. Treasurer and Capt. Rainsborow[5] sent about it presently.

[MONEY FOR ARMY.]

SIR J. HOTHAM for sending the rest of money

ALDER. PENYMAN (Pennington?). That the speeding the bill of subsidy will be first expected.

MR. SOLICITOR. That order be given to the Committee to attend this afternoon about it.

Lord General's answer delivered by Mr. Treasurer, and that part of the £50,000 may go to the payment of E. Crawforth's troops.

Referred to Committee to provide for garrisons,

---

[4] Richard King sat for Melcombe Regis. He was disabled in 1642.

[5] Captain Rainsborough was member for Aldborough. He died in 1641.

and to consider the state of them. And the words *justly suspected*[6] explained by them.

Sir Jo. Hotham. Upon Sir Wm. Udall's motion that Lord General's warrant may serve for issuing the money.

Sir T. Row. The speeding the money. Whether City mean not to part with more money till bill be past, that they might have security for other £25,000. The bill will hardly pass Royal assent under twenty days. That the money may be ready in a week.

Ald. Pennington. That upon the last they told City that bill would not pass under fourteen days. That to speak of twenty days more they will hardly pay their money without security.

Mr. Treasurer. That no time lost in preparing the bill. That citizens return answer that in four or five days the bill will be prepared.

Mr. Harrison. That he hath not taken bond of many noble gen(tlemen), and tenders them to the City. That he hath one-half of the rest ready.

[Petitions against Judges and Bishops.]

Petition of Browne, Juryman of Hertford, about removing Communion Table, for which Judge Barkley reproved and committed them, and next day caused all the Jury to retract what they had presented.

Sir Jo. Hotham. That (it) be referred to the Committee for drawing charge against Judges.

Sir Wm. Litton.[7] That the Judge required

---

[6] The words *justly suspected* occurred in the Order of the House concerning Recusants that held office in the Army. These words were to be explained by the Committee.

[7] Sir William Litton, knight, member for Hertfordshire; secluded in 1648.

him to tear the presentment and tread it under his foot.

Mr. STROUD. That the Judges are ready to comply with the Bishops. That at the Sessions, where he seldom comes, Sergeant Atkins had given the charge.

Mr. WINGATES.[8] A large relation of the manner of Justice Barkley's carriage. Sir Jo. Lamb and Dr. R. .... terrible to that country, yet not so much as this. Not to make new or more laws, but to have new or better Judges. His pressing the Jury to reveal secrets of their companions.

Petition of parishioners of Beckington[9] in Bath Diocese. About placing Communion Table altarwise. For refusing Bishop excommunicated Churchwardens. Upon appeal, Archbishop granted inhibition, and enjoined penance in three churches. Bishop said, What, dost prate of a Parliament? When the sky falls we shall catch larks. That the King referred all Church matters to Bishops. That divers ministers cut down rails about table, and placed it altarwise. Mr. Alex. Huish the principal parson there. Lord Keeper charged for countenancing the business at Assizes, and bound over Jury for finding indictment

---

[8] Edward Wingate, member for St. Alban's; secluded in 1648.

[9] A Petition of the inhabitants of Beckington against Mr. Alexander Huish their parson. Nalson says, "Upon every parish pique and unkindness (which seldom is wanting) between the Minister and any of his parishioners, Petitions were exhibited against them, and pressing of conformity was now become so criminal, that it certainly procured a petition and articles, those a summons, and vexatious attendance upon the Committee, with all the charges of the messengers' fees and others incident," &c. "That arbitrary power which was so much pretended to be feared from the Crown and Mitre, was really to be felt from the Cloak, and the then House of Commons."

Sir John Northcote's Note Book. 57

of riot. Fined petitioners 2500, and six months' imprisonment for advising parson not to remove table, and £100 charg(es) to parson. That the parson said he would willingly pay ship-money on condition there might never be parliament again.

Ordered, That the parsons be sent for as delinquents. The business referred to select Committee.

[CHRISTMAS RECESS.]

To resolve a time for recess.

MR. PIM. That two days before Christmas, and Tuesday following the house to be called.

[COMMITTEES.]

MR. CAGE.[1] That course be taken that none come to Committee but members of the house and parties.

[JUDGES.]

MR. MALLORY.[2] That the Judges require as a due presents from the sheriffs, which were formerly of courtesy.

[PETITION.]

Petition against one Ric. Greenburg for saying the petition[3] sent into the North was an insolent petition.

To be sent for as delinquent.

December 13th.

[SIR W. RUSSELL.]

Petition of Mr. Haselwood against Sir. Wm. Russell, deputy lieutenant there, said to be a recusant.

---

[1] William Cage, member for Ipswich, "an ancient parliament-man," died about 1644.

[2] William Mallory, member for Ripon, disabled in 1642.

[3] The petition presented to the King at York, requesting him to summon a Parliament.

Under pretence of levying 600 preffed men, preffed 3000, and taken rewards.

Mr. Goodwin. That he is no recufant, neither that he had not been at Church this twelvemonth.

Sergeant Wilde in his defence. *Cried down.*[4]

Sir Jo. Hotham. That a bill be prepared for a legal way for Deputy Lieutenants to walk, much of what hath been lately done being illegal.

Sir H. Herbert.[5] That Sir Wm. Ruffell faid none could be faved but in Church of Rome. Three other petitions againft him. Being High Sheriff there, he went not to Church, but ftayed in the ftreet to attend the Judges. That he hath had four or five removes in his religion, and not at Church this fix years.

[Lord and Deputy Lieutenants.]

Committee to enquire of the mifdemeanours of Lord and Deputy Lieutenants of Leicefter, and all officers whatfoever in the affeffment and levying all fums of money; and all other Lord Lieutenants and Deputies, and Clerks of Peace; and prepare Bill for regulating the actions of them, and rating Army. All petitions of that nature referred to fame Committee.

Mr. Kirton. That courfe be taken to regulate Lords of Council too, for they do nothing but by their bid (ding).

Sir Jo. Strangwayes. That foldiers changed for money like oxen. Coft the County Dorfet £2000.

---

[4] D'Ewes fays that he moved and carried a formal refolution that Serjeant Wilde "fhould hold his peace"!

[5] Sir Henry Herbert, knt., member for Bewdley, difabled in 1642.

Edward Kirton, member for Milborne Port, difabled in 1642.

[KING'S REVENUE.]

Mr. St. John. Resolved shipmoney against Law, and monopolies. These things not paid (palliated?) for Crown, when his Majesty sees the illegality of them. Crown Land taken away, and these taken away, Crown left poor. To provide a high subsistence for Majesty. That a Committee (be) appointed to consider of King's revenue.

Mr. Pim. That his expences be likewise looked to. To intimate the intention to his Majesty. That all officers may be sent to. Cromwell, Lord Treasurer, brought into the house particulars of King's expences in Henry VIII's time.

Sir Robert Pye.[6] That the King's officers may compute Revenue to his Majesty by Monopolies, and the disadvantage to subjects.

Mr. Hide. That consideration of issuing money of Exchequer last two years. Enough to conquer Germany.

Mr. Whistler. Concerning Escuage and Court of Wards.[7] To give his Majesty constant revenue above it, and be savers by it. That his Majesty be moved for liberty to treat. That a Committee may consider of last six years, and accordingly proportion. To examine what customs have been paid by subjects and not answered to King since last Parliament; and then need no impositions.

---

[6] Sir Robert Pye, member for Woodstock, secluded in 1648.

[7] Escuage and Court of Wards. The tenures by knight's service, and all the burdens connected with them, which pressed heavily on the landed gentry, and were therefore more hateful to the Cavaliers than to the Roundheads, were finally abolished immediately after the Restoration.

Mr. Selden. That Message and answer from his Majesty concerning leave to treat may precede.

Mr. Treasurer. That the way of proposing the particulars will be grateful to his Majesty. That subsidies in Queen Elizabeth's time came to greater sums than what hath since been raised by extraordinary ways.

Ordered, That the affections of house be presented to his Majesty, and desire of leave to treat of his revenue and expenses.

[The Judges.]

Mr. Stroud. For despatch of the Judges. Concerning ship-money, that Committee may have power to send some to examine witnesses and the judges. That the select Committee may have power to draw heads against Lord Keeper, and examine all things concerning him or them.

Sir Jo. Hotham. That Committee had two charges to prepare, voting against ship-money for the Lords, and charge against Judges. That the agreeing of Lords would conduce to the condemning the Judges in that Judgment.

Committee may make sub-committees. Select Committee is dividing of themselves for preparing businesses.

[The Canons.]

Mr. Whistler. Report that they have not yet looked upon former writs how they agree with last writ for Convocation.

That they have no power at all to make canons to bind Kingdom.

2. That their canons bind not themselves, *ad*

consentiendum juris quod ex communi consilio regni contigerint ordinari.

Stat. 21 Henr. VIII.[8] gives not King power in all things that the Pope had usurped.

Stat. 1 Eliz. concerning ceremonies (altered to *ornaments*) that shall continue till otherwise ordered.

SIR T. WIDDR(INGTON). Parliament summoned 13th of April. Writs to Bishops to appear day after. Another Commission to make Canons. Parliament ends 5th May. 2 Com. (second Commission) 12th May, in revocation of former. Doctors thus assembled make Canons. Three questions. 1. Whether (Canons) made by them and royal assent bind Commons without consent (of Parliament). 2. Admitting Convocation's order, where these bind? 3. Whether these thus made shall bind?

To 1st. That shall not bind. If so, either reviving former or introducing new. If affirming former, allowed, but as new, cannot bind, for that must be as altering former. Case 1607. Canon, Clerk to be chosen by parson. Resolved that, notwithstanding by custom, vestrymen shall choose, by judgment in several Courts. That no mention in books that any Canon before Stat. 25 Henry VIII. binds the Laity.

2. Parliament ended, their making those Canons illegal. *Ad consentiendum* Convocation men have relative power to Parliament. Like a man lying

---

[8] The Statute 21 Hen. VIII. c. 13, abridging spiritual persons from having pluralities of livings, &c.

Rushworth gives us two long speeches delivered in this debate by Sir Edward Dering and Nathaniel Fiennes, and a short one by Sir Benjamin Rudyard, but does not mention any other speakers.

speechless can make no will. Thirty two persons by that statute to consent to Canons.

3. Whether these Canons (shall bind). They are of very ill report. Concerning declaration of regal power, trenched upon all Courts for determining prerogative. Taken on them in pulpits to dispute of property. Well when Doctors preach against non-residence. Bad judges of property. Canon against sectaries, provided that not derogate from any former (canon) against them. Doctors were of opinion that (they were) able to take away former canons against Recusants. No proviso, therefore their intention was to dispense with penal laws against Recusants. Oath. That *cannon* charged with three bullets, excommunication, suspension, deprivation.

For the punishment. Let them be laid in their grave by this honourable assembly. Their burial will be more honourable than their birth.

Sir Wm. Strick. They have punished many for being at unlawful conventicles. That they might be called to answer for the abominable proceedings in their conventicle.

Sir Francis Seymour. In their professing to suppress Popery they have brought in crucifixes, images, and themselves worshipped them. King left out of Canons, who certainly is supreme head of Church, notwithstanding what has been said by Dr. Cosins to contrary. Knows not whether Canons or canon-makers more grievous to people. That the Canons may be burnt by hangman, but rather desires reformation than ruin of makers.

Mr. P. That sense of house is that they are un-

Sir John Northcote's Note Book. 63

lawful in respect of the authority or themselves. For manner of taking them away to leave it to house. For makers, to consider them to-morrow, and put to question their illegality.

1. Whether [9] * * *
2. Whether those thus made * *
3. Whether clergy have power to impose oath.
4. Whether benevolence granted be not void in law.

Precedent of an oath imposed by clergy against Lollards, condemned in Parliament, 20 Ric. IInd.

MR. HOLBORNE. Against putting it to question, and will be ready to argue it to-morrow.

[*Debate Adjourned.*]

14th of December.

[SIR W. PENNYMAN.]

Mr. Burdett called to give evidence concerning Captain Yeoward[1] levying money with muskets. By Warrant under Sir William Pennyman's hand.

SIR W. P. Had no such authority from him. The warrant subordinate to an agreement amongst all deputy lieutenants. The Scots had possessed themselves of all bishopric (of Durham). Country prevailed with him to come with his regiment. At Yarm, many irregularities committed, and another law amongst us, and rather put himself upon mercy of the house than the insolency of the Scots.

SIR H. CHOMLEY. That other deputy lieutenants

---

[9] The first two points are given in p. 61.

[1] Captain Ralph Yoward, an officer in Sir William Pennyman's Regiment. (Rushworth.)

had no hand in this warrant, nor privy to raising money for his fortnight's pay. This money levied but at the coming to Parliament, and so no necessity. No necessity for securing the country, if so, the prest soldiers had been fitter than the trained bands. But these trained bands had special relation to Lord Lieutenant, and kept them to act his designs.

SIR WILLIAM PENNYMAN about to reply, but SIR WALTER EARLE says against the order of the house.

MR. PYM. That for matter of fact the party may speak, but for matter of judgment he is to withdraw.

MR. PEARD. That it be referred to Committee for Lord Lieutenants, etc.

SIR WILLIAM P. That Sir Hugh Chomley lately made Deputy Lieutenant. That the order may reach all late Deputy Lieutenants, and that he thought he would not appear a saint.

SIR JOHN HOTHAM. About letters for a levy for money for shiptimber, to which at Sessions returned a denial, and afterwards some of the money levied by Sir William Pennyman's Warrant.

[PETITIONS.]

MR. PYM. Mr. Mallevery's[2] and Mr. Moiser's petition about multiplying issues. Where to appear to receive knighthood, for want of which £400 hath

---

[2] James Mauleverer, of Arncliffe, Yorkshire. The oppressive fees required from those who received the honour of knighthood, and the severe fines imposed upon those who declined it, are well known as among the principal causes of the King's unpopularity. As appears by the text, the profits of this system were often intercepted by the courtiers.

been levied upon him and issues returned for above £2000, and begged by a courtier.

The petition averred.

SIR R. PYE. That this will give a good remonstrance to His Majesty how much more levied than answered to King's purse.

[THE CANONS.]

MR. HOLBORNE.[3] The persons concerned, the clergy in Convocation, and laity in Parliament. As am *servus reipublicæ*, so *filius ecclesiæ*. Question whether these Canons good in law or not. (1.) In respect *constituentis* without confirmation in Parliament, (2) after Parliament. Whether Convocation drawn together became dead body by dissolving Parliament. Another respect—constitution upon the proviso to make none contrary. Whether Convocation can make Canons to bind without Parliament. Not in power to alter prerogative, positive or statute law, for clergy bound to obey magistrate, and can make no canon against it. The canons *quoad mores*, 'tis in power of Convocation to make them with King's consent, by practice, not to speak of power of councils, whose canons regularly hold where they are not at first refused. So in provincial convocations, practice in England from the Conquest to Henry the VIth. Compilation by Linwood,[4] no confirmation of those, scarce of any one canon by Act of Parliament.

---

[3] Adjourned Debate on the Canons. Nalson says that Holborne argued for two hours in defence of them, but he had been unable to obtain any record of his arguments. The speech was evidently an elaborate display of legal learning.

[4] William Lyndwood, Bishop of St. David's, died 1446. He wrote "Provinciale, seu Constitutiones Angliæ."

From Henry VI. to 25th Henry the VIIIth divers convocations. Yet no confirmation in Parliament, yet generally thefe did bind. Parliament 37th Henry the VIIIth Canon to bar Lay Chancellors held till another Parliament took it away. From 25 Henry the VIIIth fubmiffion of clergy not to make canons without King's licenfe, but with profeffion of confidence in that King. So the Church conceived (it) could not but (at) firft be voluntary to have King's confent, *à fortiori* the Parliament's confent not neceffary. From that time to this they never came for confirmation, fo as, if fome law be not produced againft it, this practice is proof of the canons and the power of the Church. *Quoad mores* Convocation, for eftate the Parliament. Conveniency to have corroboration from Parliament, but not neceffity. The King hath fent mandates to Convocation not to trench upon fome cafes. The Parliament fometimes petitioned the King not to confent to their petitions of Clergy, but that could not be concerning their Canons, but for fomewhat elfe. Canon that Clergymen fhould not anfwer a temporal court, againft common law. Standifh's cafe in Kelway. Books that Clergy may make canons to bind Church 30 Henry VIth 13, 20 Edward IVth 45, 4 Henry IVth ca. 3 ftat. The Archbifhop did promife that in a provincial Convocation (he) would make a conftitution, and fhow it the King before next Parliament. Stat. of 25 Henry the VIIIth. They did not yield it then, but did fubmit it. And before that time did it without King's confent. The Writs from King to reftrain them in fome argues that they might in others. (In)

8th King James, the opinion of Judges was afked in the point, and anfwered that they might do it with the limitation of the ftatute. Thefe Canons were not made without fome confideration of the legality. They cannot bind the temporal, but may the Church. In things indifferent they may do fomewhat to bind laity. Many inftances in Linwood.

2. Whether now they have power, Parliament being diffolved, and whether they then are a dead body and incapable of a commiffion. The miftake upon not looking into the feveral writs. Firft for a parliament *ad confentiendum*, but they (had) another writ *ad tractandum et confulendum*. This makes them Convocation, *ad defenfionem ecclesiæ*. This writ no way relative to a Parliament. Find the very writs from and before Henry VIII's time. Of late times they have feldom made proxies to Parliament—16 Henry VII. in Convocation book—20 Henry VII.; 14 Henry VIII. The 21 Henry VIII, the very writs. Convocation after Parliament diffolved remain a body. Twenty precedents of them when no Parliament—18 Ed. 3. Parliament roll. Several writs went out. They were not come before Parliament. King spoke to Archbifhop to punifh them.

Whether, if good power, they have well purfued it. This will trench deeply upon fome of them, but not touch fome of them.

The Canon for Benevolence. The Clergy may bind themfelves. Before Henry VIII. many fuch grants without mention of confirmation in Parliament. No confirmation of the grants of Clergy till 32 Henry VIII.

Objection. Excommunicate and deprive for not payment. 'Tis but concurrence of law, and not their act that they are imprisoned.

Was a benevolence, and not to be forced. True 'twas benevolence before given, but of right afterwards.

Canon for keeping King's inauguration. That against statute that appoints holydays. But this is but to go to prayers, and no holydays. Against 1° of Elizabeth, which appoints book of Common Prayer. This book not made by Convocation. Against 37 Henry VIII, concerning lay Chancellors exercising censures eccles(iastical.) The Canon may stand with it. In 34 Eliz. and 39 of Eliz. Canons that excommunication should not be made by layman.

What to be condemned in the Canons. First, the Oath. And what the power of making an oath. They have power to make an oath in what belongs (to) their jurisdiction. Many oaths made in Linwood. Oath of Simony, 1° King James, a new oath.

18 E. III. an oath made by King and Lords. No act. Oath for judges against divers things, and against corruption. If he broke it, the King to have power of his life and estate. One indicted upon his oath rebellious, and judged to be hanged, and upon the King's asking the Lords it was approved. Dislikes putting doctrine and discipline together. The government of bishops ought to stand. To swear to it little better than perjury. To tie to human laws which may alter with times, hard law. If supreme power alter it, they are freed of their oaths, but if sworn not to give consent, his vote is bound up.

Dislikes first Canon meddling too much with powers of Kings. For property of goods, makes a show as though we were beholding to them. If they meant no more by the oath than has been prest in several places, it may be a slip, and not error of will.

SIR JOHN WRAY. To ask Mr. Holborne where and when he received the communion. (*Answer?*) That he is a due receiver of communion at his parish, but not since the Parliament.

MR. STRANGWAYS.[5] No order made.

MR. ST. JOHN. That there may be convocations out of Parliament, but whether, wanting consent in Parliament, any canons can bind. Canons merely ecclesiastical. Cannot bind clergy by consent. For therein we are bound, for we pay them their wages and tithes, out of which they are bound. If all usurped jurisdiction of Pope given to the King, the clergy shut out of doors, and then no power. Queen Elizabeth declares her restriction of power given by former acts, to have jurisdiction in all causes civil and temporal. 3rd Henry I. at Malmesbury spiritualty and temporalty met. 51 Edward III. 46. 15 Edward III. 26. Consent of Commons to acts of Clergy.[6]

Resolved upon the question. *Voted*, that the clergy convented in any convocation, synod, or otherwise, have no power to make any canons, etc., in doctrine, discipline, or otherwise, to bind the clergy

---

[5] Giles Strangways, member for Bridport, disabled in 1643.

[6] Nalson gives a speech of Sir Benjamin Rudyard, ending thus: "Religious concordance will never be safe nor well at quiet, until these heavy drossy *Cannons* with all their base metal be melted and dissolved. Let us then dismount them and destroy them, which is my humble motion."

or laity without consent in parliament. *Nullo contradicente.*

Mr. K.[7]   Not with the King's consent.

Voted nullo contradicente.

2. Question, that the several canons treated upon by archbishops, etc., in their meeting of 1640, being made without consent in Parliament, are made contrary to laws of the land, and not to bind the clergy or laity or either of them.

Mr. Peard. That a select committee (be appointed) to enquire of the makers and prosecute their crime.

Sir Jo. Culpepper. To have a bill prepared for reviving such canons as shall be thought necessary.

[Elections.]

Mr. Maynard. Report concerning election at Bramber. Sir Edward Bishop's election void for bribery, and made uncapable for this Parliament. The election for Mr. Onslow likewise voted void. Sir Edward Bishop's man Jo. Bramsden for misdemeanour called to the bar, but not here, and sent for as delinquent.

[Petition.]

Ordered that Mr. Malleverye's petition be referred to the committee for drawing the charge against judges.

[Money.]

Mr. Treasurer and Mr. Stroud. For speeding the bill of subsidies, and to the city, and Mr. Harrison to go on in providing the money.

---

[7] Mr. K's addendum is not in Nalson or Rushworth. Mr. K. may have been King or Kirton.

Mr. Harrison. That he has £15,000 ready, and the reſt he will ſpeedily make ready, and reſt upon the bill and goodneſs of the houſe.

[Canons.]

Sir Ed. Hungerford. To puniſh the makers of canons, and tranſmit. *Corpus cum causâ.* That there has been a ſoliçitor amongſt them as well as among the judges.

Mr. Palmer. That the canons not only againſt the law, againſt property. In ſome tending to ſedition, not to conſent to alter, etc. The great commotions 'twixt King and clergy, that they had taken an oath to ſee of Rome, and therefore could not conſent. This clauſe is like the ſetting up another Pope again. In other canon, *in generali juramento ſemper excipitur ſi leges Angliæ permittant.* The ſaving in the oath of homage. Crime charged upon Biſhop of Exeter[8] for receiving homage of his tenants without expreſſing the ſaving homage to King, for which condemned in a fine. Giving the oath to others in clergy, ſchoolmaſters, and all ſcholars.

Mr. Fines. That they contain ſome things deſtructive of fundamental laws of kingdom. Take upon them to define order of kings[9] by divine ordinance. Then democracy and ariſtocracy are

---

[8] The Biſhop of Exeter at this time was Joſeph Hall, "the Engliſh Seneca." Perhaps the ſpeaker may have referred to a former Biſhop.

[9] The firſt Canon declared that "The moſt high and ſacred order of Kings is of Divine right, being the ordinance of God himſelf," &c. Alſo that "Tribute and Cuſtom, and Aid and Subſidy, and all manner of neceſſary ſupport and ſupply be reſpectively due to Kings from their Subjects by the Law of God, Nature, and Nations," &c.

against law of God. All taxes and aids due by law of God and nature.

[MESSAGE FROM LORDS.]

Message by two Chief Justices.

Lords desire conference touching business of Scots, if with convenience.

MR. PIM. That we are entered into matter of great consequence, and that will send answer by messenger of our own.

SIR T. ROWE. To give present meeting.

MR. GOODWYN. For putting it off.

MR. STROUDE. For the weight of the message.

After long debate, to be answered by messenger of own.

[CANONS.]

Question for canons. That these canons and constitutions ecclesiastical are in many of them contrary to the laws and statutes, the King's prerogative, the property and liberty of subjects, and some of them tending to sedition, and of dangerous consequence.

SIR T. WIDDRINGTON. To be added, Against the right of Parliament.

Nullo contradicente.

SIR FRANCIS SEYMOUR. That a committee (be appointed) to prepare it for sending to the Lords, and to consider of the makers.

SIR JOHN HOTHAM. That Lord of Canterbury has been principal active spirit in this business. That every member of house charge him with what he knows.

MR. P. That there was a conspiracy 'twixt Lord Strafford and Lord Canterbury to overthrow the temporal and ecclefiaftical government of kingdom. This prelate greateft incendiary betwixt the two kingdoms.

Sir H. Anderson. Out of the canons that the principal actors have concluded themfelves treafonable.

Mr. Rigby. Words of the book, By advice of our Metropolitan. That the Bifhop's book [1] that Epifcopacy is *jure divino* be referred to Committee.

Mr. Bagshaw. Apology concerning Archbifhop's difpleafure againft him. Produced proclamation and opinion of Judges obtained by Lord of Canterbury for keeping courts in their own name.

Mr. Grimston. That this is charged againft the Judges by the Committee.

Committee appointed to confider who (were) promoters of Canons, and collect the particulars, and draw up a charge againft Lord of Canterbury.

Sir W. Earle. Seventeen years fince, fpeaking of danger of declining to Popery, that if ever it came about, it muft be by the way of Scotland. And laft year moving for readinefs to confer he faid it was an Epifcopal war. Lord of Canterbury.

Mr. Pelham. That Lord Canterbury has monopoly of fines in High Commiffion, where no mitigation but from him, which in other Courts is by a Commiffion. To examine how far (he is guilty) in the fubverfion of laws.

Mr. Weston. That many did not confent to

---

[1] "Epifcopacie by Divine Right. Afferted by Jofeph Hall, Bifhop of Exon." London, 1640. A Committee of thirty-nine was appointed. The names are given by Nalfon. Pym appears to have been chairman.

the Canons. That they may have notice of the refolution of houfe, that they may declare how they were furprifed at Committee. Committee meet at 3 o'clock. That if any have taken or miniftered this oath, (they fhould) be incapable to fit.

Conference with Lords [concerning the Armies.]

To know the refolution of houfe, that they might rely on and deliver to Scots.

To appoint a time to confider of fupply of both armies, that they may anfwer the defire of the Lords for a free conference.

SIR JOHN HOTHAM. To prefs the city to refolve the money.

MR. VASS(ALL). That they expect the paffing of the bill.

MR. P. That Mr. Harrifon's £15,000 may be prefently fent away. And that the Northern parts may now have a greater fhare in proportion to what Yorkfhire had laft.

ALDERMAN PENNINGTON. That he prefumes if the bill were once read the money would be ready.

The Houfe to name committees in the feveral counties for levying the money. The knights and burgeffes to give names to-morrow. *Voted* upon the queftion.

MR. STROUD. To prefs the city to accept fecurity, for that the bill cannot be paffed in little time.

SIR T. ROW. That the refolution of houfe may be prepared to anfwer Lords to-morrow morning concerning the armies and the money. The Scots expect to have £30,000 of this money besides the arrears. That the Scots commissioners will be pressing upon it.

MR. TREASURER. That Alderman P. had informed (him) that they had £20,000 underwritten. That the city would send answer to-morrow morning, and that in the meantime that the paper for the conference be considered.

MR. GRIMSTON. That (a) gentleman of the house would furnish the money. Not name him, but if any scrivener had been sent to they would have done it upon that security.

15 December.

[SIR JOHN ELIOT.]

A committee to take into consideration the commitment of Sir John Elliott and the rest[2] committed 3° *Caroli*, and the reason of dissolving that Parliament. To-morrow 2 o'clock in Court of Wards.

[LORD KEEPER FINCH.]

MR. P. No reading by the clerk, but for a public business.

MR. ROLLS.[3] A letter from Attorney 1 *Caroli*, not suffered to be read.

The substance of it.

Takes notice of the charge, and desires that he may first in person give satisfaction to the house.

MR. P. The like granted to Lord St. Alban's,

---

[2] "The rest" were Sir Peter Hayman, Hollis, Strode, Valentine, Selden, Walter Long, Sir Miles Hobart, Crewe, Bellasis, Sir J. Hotham, Hampden, Pym, and Sir Walter Earle.

[3] John Rolle, member for Truro.

and that, if he will firſt get leave of the upper houſe, that 'tis uſual to be granted.

Mr. Perpoint, one of the committee. That the charge will be ready to deliver to the houſe to-morrow.

Mr. Glin. That there being yet no charge, 'tis too ſoon to order that he ſhall be heard.

Mr. Harrison. That an order be paſſed the like of the laſt, to warrant Sir William Udall to receive his £25,000 beginning of next week, and for him to pay it.

Lord Digby. Moved upon another part of Lord Keeper's letter, of his eſteem of good opinion of this houſe.

Mr. Stroud. That he ſat here when the houſe could not make him ſpeak,[4] who now deſires to be heard. He knows not whether he means before or after the charge.

[The Scots' Articles.]

Mr. P. Report from committee of both houſes.

That Lords' committee had papers from Scots to both houſes. Lord Briſtol, to both houſes from Scots. Firſt, an account of the treaties, and of the articles treated by the commiſſioners.

2. That, after articles read, to preſent declaration of diſtreſs of army.

3. Of ſtate of King's army.

4. Some accuſations preſented by Scots againſt two great perſons.

Articles read by our clerk.[5]

---

[4] Finch, when ſpeaker of a former Parliament, having received orders from the King, had refuſed to put the queſtion on a remonſtrance that had been moved in the Houſe.

[5] The communications from the Scots were, as may be ſuppoſed,

1. That His Majesty would publish the Acts of Parliament. This formally condescended to, for in these they had power for religion and peace.

2. That the castles[6] might be secured. Condescended to.

3. That all may have liberty to swear the Covenant. Agreed that those that live there may so.[7]

4. That incendiaries[8] receive censure (for) that. This much debated. Of two sorts. English to be proceeded (against) here, Scots there.

5. That ships and goods (may be) restored.

6. That damages may be repaired. Not yet concluded till consulted with the kingdom.

7. That declaration (against us as) traitors be re-called.

8. Removing garrisons (from the Borders), and establish a firm peace.

Paper representing necessity of these armies read. That some of our committee had undertaken sending by Parliament two months' pay. Upon this no violence done. The army in great distress, having received but a week('s pay) for two months. Forced to disperse themselves through those (parts) and Cumberland and Westmoreland, to undoing of in-

very long. Sir John Northcote gives the best part of them very concisely.

[6] The Castle of Edinburgh, "and other strengths of the Kingdom of Scotland."

[7] "Condescended to thus far: That such as are of the Scottish Nation dwelling as Inhabitants in England or Ireland shall be subject to the Laws of that Kingdom wherein they live, and so the like to be allowed to our Nation dwelling in Scotland reciprocally, but this not to extend to such as only trade as Merchants and are not Inhabitants."

[8] "Fourthly—That the Common Incendiaries, who have been the Authors of this Combustion in his Majesty's Dominions, may receive their just Censure."

habitants. Except the other £30,000 be speedily sent, are not to be blamed, that their patience is sufficiently known. Lord Bristol (said) that in these expressions they intended not threats.[9] That since coming in had not above twopence a day.

3. Motion for supply (of) King's army. That disorder might come by this necessity. That speedy course for supply, that might be ready to stay disorders. Incendiaries named, C. and Str. (Canterbury and Strafford). Scots commissioners had given remonstrance against them. *Read.*

[THE SCOTS' CHARGE AGAINST LAUD.]

Innovations in religion. Cause of commotion and our present trouble. Alterations pressed against law. New book of Canons. New Liturgy. Of all these prelate of Canterbury (was Author), by fourteen letters subscribed by him to a bishop there; that they should wear whites; for High Commission sitting in Edinburgh; taking down gallery there to make way for altars. Book of canons devised for tyrannical government of clergy; sent by Canterbury, interlining with his own hand. Canons not to come from synods, but from prelates and king's prerogative. That he would put power in their bishops over the consciences, liberty, and property of people. Pressing the Service book. Speaking at *Jointo*[1] of the arch-

---

[9] The Earl of Bristol said that the Scots Commissioners had informed the English Commissioners that, if there were not a present supply of money afforded them, their Army must of necessity plunder; and that this was not spoken by way of threatening, but out of a sense they had of the extreme wants of their army.

[1] After the Pacification at Berwick, he "spared not openly in the hearing of many, often before the King, and privately at the Council Table and the privy *jointo*, to speak of us as Rebels and

rebels and traitors, that the pacification was dishonourable. Oaths devised by him upon their countrymen. Railing against their Assembly. His hand for the restraint of our commissioners. When late Parliament would not contribute to war against them, he after made canons to preach against them, and granted six subsidies. Prayer by him against their nation as traitors. Ready to prove his innovations by Bishop of Edinburgh's and others' papers. That this great firebrand may be removed from His Majesty's presence. Prelates of England, some more, some less, inclinable to Popery.

2. (CHARGE) AGAINST LORD LIEUTENANT READ.
Whose malice set his wits a-working against Church of Scotland.

No less zeal than Canterbury, as appears by advancing Dr. Bramble, his chaplain, to be bishop of Derry, a man forward ("for exalting of Canterburian Popery"). Another chaplain to Dublin (University).

Burning a confession against innovations, pressed by Primate of Ireland, by hand of hangman, though confirmed by former Parliaments.

Countenancing *Lysimachus Nicanor*,[2] and other books against them.

Calling Scots nobility and gentlemen in Ireland to

He made Canons, ordaining that the Clergy should preach four times in the year against the doctrine and proceedings of all Reformed Kirks, &c. "And which is yet worse, and above which Malice itself cannot ascend," he caused a Prayer to be said in all churches during the time of Divine Service, "against our Nation by name of Traitorous Subjects, having cast off all obedience to our Anointed Sovereign, and coming in a rebellious manner to invade England, that shame may cover our faces, as enemies to God and the King."

Traitors," &c.

[2] A pamphlet against the Scottish Reformation.

frame petition, correcting (the petition) himself, containing oath of renunciation of covenant. Such as refused kept close prisoners. Which (Covenant) they had taken forty years before. Many thereupon forced to flee. Some indicted of high treason for refusing it.

By his means Parliament called, and six subsidies granted, that forces should be raised against us as rebels. That would give precedent to Parliament in England. Ships and goods taken in Ireland.

This done, comes into England, and at coming away said he would leave of Scots nor root nor branch.

Stir up King and Parliament here against us, but failing, took course for breaking Parliament, and used all means to be General, to kill and slay. Gave order to officers to give battle. When His Majesty was inclinable (to peace), yet in assembly of Lords (at York) breathed calumnies, that he would whip us out (of England). When cessation was granted, he endeavoured hostility. Governors of garrisons (of Berwick and Carlisle) received order from him. Ports of Ireland stopped. That His Majesty be moved that this incendiary be put to trial.

Last, to present humble desire that might go upon certainty with Scottish Commissioners.

Lord Keeper ended (by saying) that when we had considered upon these, the Lords desire free conference. That Lords desire the papers be returned, and shall be sent back again.

To put two points, (1) for supply, (2) at desire of Scots that Archbishop might be sequestered.

Sir John Northcote's Note Book. 81

Mr. Grimstone.[3] The source of all our infection, the advancer of all that with himself have done (acted). The bringer in of Strafford. Secretary Windebank the broker and pandar to the whore of Babylon. Man(nering), the (Bishop) of Oxford, Bath, Wrenn, these have devoured flock. Guard all projects these ten years. The tobacco licenses. Only man. Scarce complaint brought in, but he interwoven in it. Dangerous that such stand near the King. The course against Earl of Strafford. To resolve to go up and accuse him of high treason.

Mr. Harrison. That this morning he hath sent two gentlemen to get money in gold. That no time given, but immediately charged.

Mr. P. In chair against him. The divers heinous things offered him. That seconded Earl Strafford in dangerous counsel to King. That message go up to accuse him.

Question. That William Laud, Archbishop, shall be forthwith charged to the Lords of high treason.

Voted, nullo contradicente.

The like message for Earl Strafford, accuse him of high treason in name of Commons. That he be sequestered and committed, and in convenient time a charge shall be preferred against him and presented to their lordships.

Mr. Hollis sent with the message.

[Supply of Armies.]

Alderman Pennington. That the city will make ready the money without security.

---

[3] Mr. Grimstone's speech is given by Nalson and Rushworth. Dr. Mainwaring was Bishop of St. David's, Bancroft of Oxford, Pierce

G

Sir John Hotham. For proportioning the money, £30,000 to North, King's army £20,000. To enlarge the number of subsidies. That the army to the 30th of December, £2,000.

Mr. Treasurer. That the last £30,000 pays not by £18,000 to the 8th. Sad condition to leave this army unpaid. This £50,000 will be ready. That Durham (had paid) £25,000. Northumberland paid nothing. That they be considered in the first place, and for enlargement of provision.

Mr. P. That the bill be read to-morrow, and then consider of enlargement. To lay burden upon the authors of it, and not Commonwealth.

Mr. Whistler. That the bill will not be ready to-morrow, though in good readiness.

Sir William Widdrington.[4] Not so much paid in Northumberland by reason of contract between Lords and them before agreement at Ripon. That five troops are now levying the arrears.

Mr. Hamden. For settling the proportioning the money to-morrow.

Resolved upon question, *nullo contradicente*, that £50,000 now to be paid, to be proportioned £20,000 to King's army, £30,000 to North. And to take into consideration for further subsistence of King's army. To send to Lords for free conference.

Moved that Sir Edw. Sans (Edwin Sandys) may have leave to stay from his charge a fortnight.

---

of Bath and Wells, and Wren of Ely, "the least of all these birds, but one of the most unclean."

[4] Sir William Widdrington was member for Northumberland. He was disabled in 1642, created Baron Widdrington in 1643, and killed at the battle of Worcester.

Sir John Hotham. That no such leave be given here, but left to Lord General if he see cause.

[Message from Lords.]

That the Lord Canterbury, according to desire of the House, committed to gentleman usher.

The King's revenue to-morrow.

[Charge against Lord Keeper Finch.]

Mr. St. John.[5] Report that charge against Lord Keeper ready, and charge him with high treason and other misdemeanours. That a charge may be sent him as yesterday. That for the shipping business and articles a conference be desired. 1st Article against him. That traitorously endeavoured to subvert law of kingdom, and to introduce tyrannical government. Many particulars. That though one of them would not make treason, yet all put together would shew his malice sufficiently. Trace his whole course from being Speaker, and in all practised against Law and Liberty. In this house refused something to be read conducing to preservation of King and Kingdom. Concerning his carriage in Forest of Waltham, refused jurors returned by Sheriff, and chose whom he liked, and required them to give presently verdict for King with threats. Promised that judgment should not be entered, but country left at liberty to traverse, which

---

[5] The "Particulars" upon which the Lord Keeper was voted a Traitor, and which were afterwards expanded into an impeachment, were—

i. For refusing to read the Remonstrance against the Lord Treasurer Weston, *4to Caroli*, when the Parliament desired it.

ii. For soliciting, persuading, and threatening the Judges to deliver their opinion for the levying of Ship-money.

iii. For several illegal actions in Forest matters.

iv. For ill offices done in making the King to dissolve the last Parliament, and causing his Declaration thereupon to be put forth.

he refused in Common Pleas, contrary to his oath to maintain laws. Contrived an opinion for warranting ship-writs, and solicited the Judges in it, enjoining secrecy, and to do it presently. After, procured letter from his Majesty to Judges for their opinions. Justices Hutton and Crook refusing, unless he would declare to King that they conformed against their opinions, but he delivered it as their clear opinion. That he laboured B(aron) Denham to retract his opinion (in the case of Hampden). In his circuits did declare what Judges had done, and that (the right of ship money) was so inherent (in the King) as could not be taken (away) by Parliament. Did in Common Pleas subvert order of Court by making orders in his chambers. That did make warrants to set at liberty men in execution, those before judgment to pay five nobles, those after judgment five marks. What concerns Chancery shall be made ready. Being a Councillor, did advise breaking the last Parliament, and set out Declaration.[6]

Of these the Committee received proof to their satisfaction.

That it should be transmitted with the ship-money. That Message be sent to charge him with high treason at bar.

Mr. Finch.[7] To renew yesterday's motion, that he may be admitted to speak for himself before. *Voted.* (written afterwards.)

Mr. P. Being charged with treason, against

---

[6] See afterwards, page 94, note.

[7] John Finch, member for Winchelsea, a kinsman of the Lord Keeper.

course of house (to hear him). (It) was his own rule, that King's counsel was not to be disclosed.

LORD DIGBY. That, being not charged with treason till it be voted, it may be heard.

SIR ED. DEERING. If it may stand with the justice of the house, he is sure it will stand with the honour of the house.

SIR T. MASHAM. That before charge no grand jury hears the party.

SIR FR. SEYMOUR. That may have a short time to come.

MR. NICLAS. The Committee have voted. That we may go to vote too.

SIR H. MILDMAY. The resolution in Lord St. Alban's business. That, if he desired it, he ought to be heard.

SIR W. STRICKLAND. That the motion may be granted.

SERGEANT EVERS (Eure). That the charge of Committee is but an opinion. And that it may be read (heard?). *Inauditi quasi innocentes pereunt.*

MR. GLIN. A person in question. No charge yet against him. If question against him, to what? Nothing against him. Instances of Lord Bacon, and Duke Buck(ingham). Lord Bacon's charge but for injustice, not treason, in which case he may be heard by counsel and witnesses by oath. In felony or treason, not allowed. Duke of Buckingham was charged, and voted, and then desired to be heard.

MR. WALLER. Present at argument in Chequer of ship-money. A general groan ; and upon Judge Crook's going other way, expression of joy. That thereupon Keeper (did) rife in great charge, that he would not fpare the beft man there. If we hear his eloquence that would not hear our groans, much beholden. Though Grand Jury hear not delinquent, yet thofe that commit him did. That not fear his eloquence, and that may be heard. If any of the Grand Jury defire to hear the party charged, 'tis granted,[8] to fatisfy defire of the members.

Mr. Fines. That cannot ftand with order of houfe, being he had no orderly notice of it.

Sir T. Row. That he may take notice by the Committee fent to him and Judges. That he comes not to anfwer heads of charge. Stand with honour of houfe to find men innocent (rather) than guilty. God would go down to fee, &c. That he may be heard. *Inauditus et indefenfus tamquam innocens perire videatur.*

Mr. Stroud. That large Committee have brought opinion, none diffenting. If once fatisfied that 'tis treafon. Whether this the fame with thofe that have been charged without hearing.

Sir R. Hopton. That he may be heard.

Lord Faukland. If we fhould not accufe him of treafon, we accufe ourfelves of charging the others with it. That, there being no charge againft him, he can but make a fpeech in general. That it be put to queftion prefently.

Mr. Capell. Happily he may fubmit himfelf to this houfe. That he defires he may be heard.

Mr. Bellasis. That if, upon intimation from

---

[8] *Quare*, was an accufed perfon ever heard before a Grand Jury?

the gentleman that moved, he come to the door and desire to be heard, he may be admitted.

Sir H. Anderson. That he may go away, and therefore be presently charged.

Mr. Treasurer. That before the report made he desired to be heard, and moved the Lords for leave. The greatest in the Kingdom, being charged from this house, are pressed down with the weight of it. If Lord Strafford or Canterbury had come (the) day before the charge, should have had it. An intimation given by this Lord Keeper to S^t. Alban's of the charge. That he may have Monday morning to come in.

Mr. Win(gate). Birds upon wing fly swiftly. Finches sing sweetly. That it be made sure that we lose him not.[9]

Sir Th. Heale. That he stand body for body (?)

Sir Jo. Hotham. That it may be heard Monday.

Mr. Cooke. To have it resolved, if he be heard, how he shall come into the house.

December 21.

[Monopolies, &c.]

Petition of Weymouth and Melcombe Regis, that they are not prest for Alderman Abell's imposition upon wines, salt, soap. Pressing of soldiers. Coat and conduct money. Sealing of clothes abused.[1]

---

[9] Mr. Wingate was right as to the escape of the Lord Keeper. It was thought that he had friends in the House, who contrived to give him the opportunity.

[1] Sir John Culpeper said, Nov. 9, 1640, "It is a nest of wasps, or swarm of vermin, which have over-crept the land, I mean the Monopoles and Polers of the people.

Sir Jo. Strang (ways.) That goods diftrained be reftored upon fecurity.

Sir Robt. Pye. That it may be examined and fo appear what the fubject lofes, and what the King has gained by it, by particular Committee.

Mr. Warwick.[2] That Lord Treafurer have lately received letters from His Majefty for freeing impofition upon falt.

Mr. Trelawny.[3] That exactions of Cuftomers be referred to Committee. It will appear the King hath been abufed five or fix hundred thoufand pounds. Special Committee of means and all the burgeffes of ports to examine four of King's officers and all under cuftomers of London and other ports.

[Sir Edward Coke.]

Sir T. Row. Council books, will belong to executor of Sir E. Cook, that his Majefty will before Chriftmas day caufe them [to be] delivered to furviving executor Sir Rand. Crewe. That original of Magna Charta is in hands of Sir Jo. Cook.

Mr. Cook. That the books are entailed.

Sir Jo. Cook's fon that he hath fent to his father but yet no anfwer.

Thefe, like the frogs of Egypt, have gotten poffeffion of our dwellings, and leave fcarce a room free from them. They fup in our cup. They dip in our difh. They fit by our fire. We find them in the dye-vat, wafh-bowl, and powdering-tub. They fhare with the butler in his box. They have marked and *fealed* us from head to foot. They will not bate us a pin. We may not buy our own clothes without their brokage."

[2] Philip Warwick, member for Radnor, difabled in 1643, afterwards Secretary to the King.

[3] Robert Trelawny, Royalift member for Plymouth. He was expelled and imprifoned in 1641 for faying that the Houfe had no power to appoint a guard for themfelves without the King's confent. Rufhworth omits his name from his lift of members.

[MR. HOLLIS.]

Sergeant sent for three that arrested three of Mr. Hollis his servants.

[LORD KEEPER FINCH.][4]

Clerk to take notes of Lord Keeper's speech. A chair to sit on, and stool to lay the purse.

SIR SYM. D'EWES. De la Poole[5] Duke of

---

[4] The debate on the ceremonies to be observed in the admission of the Lord Keeper is rather characteristic of the House of Commons, or perhaps of any assembly of Englishmen. Sir S. D'Ewes also tells us that it was disputed whether he should sit or stand, whether he should wear his hat like a member, or stand bare-headed like a petitioner. The question was compromised, or evaded, by a chair being placed, and its being left to his own discretion whether to sit or stand. "The serjeant came in before him, and he brought the purse with the great seal in it himself, and, having made three reverences, he laid the purse on the chair, and stood by it, leaning his left hand on it, and so he made a long and well-composed speech." Before he began to speak, the Speaker said, Your Lordship may sit down if you please. "But he spake standing, and so, having ended his speech, after a reverence made, took up the purse and departed."

Lord Campbell, who classes Finch with Jeffreys as the two worst men who ever disgraced the English ermine, refuses to allow the praise of ability to this famous speech. But such was certainly not the opinion of those who heard it, nor, probably, will it be the opinion of those who read it, either in the full report in Nalson's Collection, which may have been furnished by Finch himself, or in the brief summary in which Sir John Northcote has so well taken the salient points. It is not too much to say that, if no other report existed, a very good speech might be restored from these notes. It must be remembered that the speech was made to a hostile audience, by a man on the very brink of ruin, who might expect at the next moment to be consigned to the Tower, and thence perhaps to the scaffold. It is difficult to conceive any speech better calculated to conciliate the favour of the House, or, if that could not be, at least to test its feeling. That having been ascertained, the Lord Keeper took a boat, dropped down the river, and early next morning was on his way to Holland. He lived to return twenty years afterwards, and to sit in judgment on the regicides.

[5] Sir Simonds D'Ewes "vouching a record" is very characteristic. The case of De la Pole, so often alluded to, is mentioned by Bacon as a precedent, probably to found an argument in his own case. Michael De la Pole, earl of Suffolk, was attainted of high treason in the 11th year of Richard II. (1387.)

90   *Sir John Northcote's Note Book.*

Suffolk came into the houfe without either, and came within the bar.

Sir Ro. Pye. That before he be condemned that honour is to be done [to] the feal.

Sir Gilbt. Gerard.⁶ That when Lord Southam (pton) came they ftood till Mr. Speaker gave order for ftool and that [he] might be covered by direction of houfe.

Mr. Controller. That chair be fet, and left to his difcretion how to demean himfelf.

Sir Jo. Strang. and Mr. Hollis. That no chair (be) placed till he come in and defire to fpeak.

Mr. D. To place chair on left, and that the mace may ftand on right.

[The Lord Keeper's Defence.]

Firft thank for admittance. No defire to preferve felf or fortunes, but their good opinion. Rather go from door to door,⁷ than live without their favour. No intention to juftify words or actions or opinions, but make a clear relation of himfelf and leave to judgment of houfe. Rather been a fuitor that another might have done it. Not with a ftudied fpeech, but to fpeak my heart. If a word flip to give good conftruction, etc. For religion, he hopes none doubts. Lived thirteen years Bencher in Gray's Inn. Doctor Sibs⁸ had beft encouragement from him againft one that would weary him. Fifteen years (of) King's Council. Not advifer of any

---

⁶ Sir Gilbert Gerard, member for Middlefex, fecluded in 1648.

⁷ "And crave *Da obolum Belifario*," &c. Rigby faid, "He would have made us all *Belizaraffes*, to beg for halfpennies."

⁸ Dr. Sibs, "a reverend preacher in my time."

project. Preferred to two places of judicature.[9] Far from thought of one and ambition of other, but King's pleasure. In these hands never touched bribe, eyes never blinded with gift, took heed to friendship and hate which misguides a Judge.[1] I know not particulars of this ill opinion, therefore weakly armed, but in general hope to speak somewhat in allay of ill opinion. Once sat in that chair. Appeal if not served with fidelity and candour, done no ill, but good offices. That last unhappy day, had great share of sorrow for it. Many in House know his expressions of it. After adjournment for two or three days, His Majesty sent for him. That he desired to adjourn once more, but could not discern that he meant to dissolve it. That (the King said) there should be no further speeches, but that after message (he should) come to him. That if voted he should not dare to sit. All these commands delivered by His Majesty before his Council.

For ship business, which in opinion lies heavy on me, shall clearly deliver my carriage in it. Far from justifying, but submit all. Ignorant of first writ, neither authorised nor advised, nor since, for setting forth either.

Made Chief Justice four days before going out of first writ, so as within his time, but not knowledge. His Majesty commanded Lord Richardson,[2] Chief Baron, and self to consider precedents and report to him. His Majesty after that (said) if whole kingdom

---

[9] Chief Justice of Common Pleas, 1634, and Lord Keeper, 1640.
[1] This sentence is not in the speech given by Nalson.
[2] Sir Thomas Richardson, Chief Justice of Common Pleas, 1626-31, of King's Bench, 1631, and afterwards Chief Baron.

concerned, not reasonable to lay burden only upon ports. Upon that, without his knowledge, the King put them the case. Confess was of opinion for it in case of danger. Michaelmas following His Majesty commanded to go to all judges to require their opinions. Not intended by him to be binding opinion to themselves, but for His Majesty's private satisfaction. Did then think that self and judges were bound by oaths to return their opinions. Vow that never used menaces or promises. Left at liberty by His Majesty, and he so left them. The God of Truth will make appear. The discourse of this never so little between judges in business of weight than in this. Not one of judges that subscribed that needed solicitation. None made scruple but Hutton and Crook. The last (scrupled) not at the thing, but (the) introduction, and did subscribe. Justice Hutton never subscribed. When His Majesty would have sent for him again, he moved to leave him to his conscience. A long time after had no speech with any of them till February 26th, (1636), when, by command by His Majesty, judges did assemble in Sergeant's Inn, where much debate, and not deny but did use best arguments could for maintenance of opinion. Then those two did differ in this, whether King were sole judge of danger, not in the rest. Fifteen months' difference from first opinion to this debate. After published in Star Chamber by predecessor. Reason of those two subscriptions was that where most gave votes the rest involved. After came to argument in Chequer,[3] amongst rest he

[3] Hampden's case.

argued. Copies enough of his argument, so as cannot falsify. Only of the necessity, that all the judges were of opinion, in apparent danger. He did deliver that it appeared that danger was so, did deliver that King could not innovate, nor lay any Charge, but by Common Consent. That this judgment did warrant nothing against it, but only danger where whole kingdom concerned. There every man bound. That taking the loss of narrow seas in great danger. He makes protestation he gave opinion never that money to be raised, but that ships be provided according to writ. Humbly submit it to favour and judgment. Far from his thought to introduce new government.

About forest business.[4] That learning far out of way of his study, but commanded to go as attorney upon Mr. Noye's sickness. When came, did King and kingdom service, with extreme danger of himself and fortunes. Concerning perambulation, great difference of opinion. Before did anything, (did) acquaint judges with his objections. They thought them such as fit to be presented. The country upon conference unanimously subscribed. After, commanded to attend service at Essex, and King told him the bounds of forest narrower than ought. He thought to enlarge them no further than Havering. Country refusing conference with him, produced the records for His Majesty's service, but never go about to overthrow charter of forest.

When a judge or two delivered opinion that King

---

[4] Great discontent was caused by the King's pressing his forestal claims, and constantly encroaching on private property. "The royal forests in Essex were so enlarged that they were hyperbolically said to include the whole county." (Hallam.)

might afforest what kind he would, when he came to be judge did declare against it, the King being restrained by the statute but in his own demesnes. In this humbly submit his opinions.

Concerning declaration,[5] 'tis the King's. Bound by duty not to speak without his licence. When may have leave will make it appear that not deserved the least censure.

Humbly thank for patience. If may know what is charged he hopes to give satisfaction. He that was after God's heart was not for wanting infirmities, but that hard heart right to God. Beg that, if not live to serve you, may die in favour and good opinion.

MR. RIGBY. Concerning His Majesty's double capacity, natural and politic, first subject to infirmity, second free from all imperfections. That great crime fallen from Lord Keeper in his narration. That was commanded by King that if being in chair were voted should not sit. That should not lay imputation to the King. That was not authority of that. Expected that would have laid it upon some other, not King. 3rd. Message by secretary for meeting at Sergeant's Inn,—all reflecting on King.

MR. MALLORY. That this favour of his being

---

[5] The King's Declaration to his loving subjects, concerning his reasons for dissolving the Parliament in May 1640, in which he spoke of the "sinister and malicious courses," and the "audacious and insolent way" of the "ill-affected persons of the House of Commons."

The conclusion of the speech is not in Nalson or Rushworth.

The only other speech they give on this occasion is that of Rigby, and their version of it is quite different. Sir S. D'Ewes says, "After his (the Lord Keeper's) departure divers spake; and it was the general sum of all of them that he had rather aggravated than mitigated his crimes by his speech."

heard be no precedent to any other. If any defire it, that may be heard at Committee, not in Houfe.

MR. LANE. Refembled a park. Laws the pale, fubjects deer, King owner. He, the keeper, is charged to pull down pale to make park a foreft. Secondly, to difpofe to deftroy deer by framing fhip writ, which fubverts property and liberty. Third, the greateft crime, to counfel his mafter that pale was broken, and not only to make park a foreft, he went to make this foreft a wildernefs, to move the King that we met here with feditious intentions. That he faid that Scots and French were joining againft us. That was inftrument of taking away the King's weapons, the people's affections. For his words, queftion whether our judgment fhall be guided by words or actions, but muft give vote with Committee, that (he was) culpable and criminal.

ALDERMAN PENNINGTON. That *optimus orator peffimus homo*,[6] and that he was moved little with his eloquence. That may go to vote.

SIR G. PALMES. That he heard nothing from him but rather in aggravation than extenuation of his offence, and defires to vote it.

MR. STROUD. That it be drawn no more in example. He came in great humility. Would God he had been fo when a Judge! As Speaker here, that teftimony would be given with him, that never knew

---

[6] Nalfon reprefents Rigby as faying, "*optimorum putrefactio peffima*," and "Had not this Syren fo fweet a tongue, furely he could never have effected fo much mifchief," here afcribed, no doubt correctly, to Wingate, who previoufly made the fmall joke about finches finging fweetly.

abler man in Chair, but made that obstruction in case of favourite, would not put vote till went to Whitehall. Crime to vouch Majesty that no vote should be put for an adjournment. His silence then cause of all miseries since. Much troubled at what was said of his Majesty commanding concerning Priests and Jesuits. Hoped no more of that kind spoken of his Majesty. [As] to forest, said that part of forest which was not destroyed he left entire. That to his being in Court of Justice nothing said. For voting.

MR. WINGATES. Had not this Syren a sweet tongue, could not have done so much mischief.

MR. BRIDGMAN. Doubt whether to charge him with high treason. The other [charges] were for subverting of Laws and backed with force. Precedents of subverting, without force not high treason. Instance of Cardinal Wolsey for like, and but *premunire*. 10 R. 2. Like of Mich. de la Poole, in Parliament, and not adjudged treason.

MR. WHITELOCKE contrary, yet willing to go the milder way. Whether within Stat. 25 E. 3, those are treasons against King's person, and others left to Parliamentary proceedings, 22 E. 3. Interest of making laws is all we have for our lives, etc. This taken away is as great treason against Commonwealth as any can be against King's person. That when he was in Chair, left it against word of the house, refused to move what was for good of Kingdom. Look upon an individual, it may be thought not treason, but looking upon consequence. Endeavoured to raise own fortunes upon ruin of Commonwealth.

That endeavoured to overthrow Charter (of) foreſt. In Common Pleas ſought to bring it to arbitrary deciſion of cauſes in ſhip buſineſs. Uſed all perſuaſions and threatenings. Subſidies ſtill given by parliament for ſetting out ſhips. He deviſed a way that the King ſhould not need us. Strength of an Army, as Lo. Str. (Lord Strafford) (ſaid) not ſo much as armed with power of judicature, which not ſo eaſily reſiſted as the other might (be). That may go up to charge him with high treaſon.

Mr. Controller. Whether will ſtand with judgment and clemency of houſe. Whether to charge him according to ſtatute or according to judgment of houſe.

Mr. Pim upon difference twixt E. Str. (Earl Strafford) and this. Upon their power to diſſolve Parliament. The Articles preſented by Committee he does agree, though not in Art. 25. 'Twas treaſon before, and left ſo. Takes away legiſlative power of Parliament. Takes away honour of King to be protector of people and goods. The occaſion of troubles in Spain, Scots, and here. Caſes of Wolſey and Ea. De la Poole. Courts cannot go higher than offences require, but may go lower. Liberty of ſubject not ſo aſſaulted in thoſe times as now.

Sir. H. M. (Mildmay).[7] That five or ſix paſt parliaments have been to make up breaches of Commonwealth. Nothing paſſes from King but

---

[7] Sir Henry Mildmay, member for Malden, Eſſex, and therefore intereſted in the "foreſt buſineſs." He was the "maſter of the jewel-houſe," and was accuſed, after the Reſtoration, of having taken ſome of the jewels. He was one of Charles the Firſt's judges, though he did not ſign the ſentence.

upon reference to his Council and Judges. And therefore all depends upon their returns. His concern in Emanuell College,[8] built by his grandfather, that he was principal helper in upholding that College. Dr. Sibs told him that he had been turned out but for his help. Moved to enquire if there were not Judges that embarked in the ship business before him.

Mr. Whist(ler). To be wary that in preserving our liberties we lose not the fairest of them. Not to leave liberty to make treason what will. If not in words of statute, then by parliament. And that must be by bill, and to leave it to the Lords. To declare it treason not safe for them or us.

Mr. Pe(ard). 25 E. was to chalk out the way to Judges, but this treason at Common Law. This person charged 1°, in the Chair, monopolies, and Ship-money. If Speaker will be silent, we are dumb. That blowing up the house without gunpowder.[9] To have an Idle Parliament no Parliament. By saying the King commanded increases the offence. The King would have leaned (to) that Councillor that disadvised. Had been his part to have done

---

[8] Emmanuel College at Cambridge was founded in 1584 by Sir Walter Mildmay, Treasurer to Queen Elizabeth. Its orthodoxy was suspected. One of the articles in the "Considerations for the better settling of the Church Government," presented by Laud to King Charles in 1629, was "That Emanuel and Sydney Colleges in Cambridge, *which are the nurseries of Puritanism,* may from time to time be provided of grave and orthodox men for their governors." Cromwell was of Sidney Sussex College.

[9] Sir S. D'Ewes seems to have understood Peard's speech differently. "Mr. Perd spoke exceeding well to shew that this denying to put the vote *of treason* was to blow up the Parliament without gunpowder." Whereas he appears to have been blaming Finch for not putting the vote for a remonstrance in a former Parliament.

the King right, and upon his confcience he thought he had done the King wrong. More than army to conquer by colour of Law. 2. Foreft. Prefenting prevented fire and meat, but their lands really taken from them. 3. Ship money. Take away all ownerfhip. When judgment was given, thought that not his gown (was his own). We muft thank the King, not Judges, if we had anything. Belknap's cafe, that if Judge gave judgment againft Law was treafon, that was very broken in the bufinefs. One of Judges dying faid, that villain Finch undid me, for he made me to fubfcribe. Four declarations. Not deny that 'twas his Child. If a man arraigned will not deny is worthy to be hanged. Story of foxes.[1]

Mr. Holborne believes the matter of report, but doubts of judgment in Law, fearful in matter of blood, doubtful of confequence, and making treafon by inference. Whether this a fubverfion or rather perverfion of law. One to govern according to will. But when queftion what is the law in foreft and fhip-money, never faid but King muft be governed by law. But great perverfion here. The laws not rightly obferved. If that be *ex errore*, no great crime. Subverfion he thinks clearly treafon. This not treafon in the ftatute. Clear that there are others at Common Law, but thefe courts not try them, but by Parliament. In abfolute monarchy *rex est lex*, but where there is

---

[1] The "Story of foxes" has been unfortunately loft. Allufions to field fports have always been popular with an Englifh audience. In a very fuccefsful fpeech delivered by a ftatefman of the prefent day, a parallel was drawn between the duties of the Leader of the Houfe of Commons and thofe of a mafter of foxhounds.

law, he is bound to govern so, and the dissolution of these treason. Less to give up forts than to destroy bulwark of laws. Empson's [2] case, Henry VIII.'s time, plotted *subvertere leges*, said *proditorie in subversione legis*. Wolsey's maintaining setting up legatine power against our laws. Question upon the Acts in forest and upon the law in ship money. And so perversion, not subversion.

Mr. CREW to point of law. That Tresilian [3] was no swordsman, and that must be wary of proposing to the Lords what is treason but by Bill. It cannot hurt if we declare that subversion of law is treason. We have done the like to Lo. Str. (Strafford) and C. (Archbishop of Canterbury). If Petition of Right be law, judgment in ship money (is) subversion of fundamental laws. Difference of saying he is guilty, and giving a charge in matter of suspicion. Like proceedings many have suffered. Who shall have his vote for pity, and he for justice.

Mr. HIDE. 'Tis treason to kill a judge, much more to slay justice itself.

Voted to be accused of high treason and other misdemeanours.

Voted that message be forthwith sent to Lords to accuse, and to be sequestered and committed. And in convenient time the charge shall be presented to their Lordships.

LORD FAWKLAND sent.

---

[2] Sir Richard Empson and Edmond Dudley, the instruments of Henry VII.'s extortions, executed for high treason in 1510.

[3] The allusion is probably to Chief Justice Tresilian, who was attainted of high treason with De la Pole, under Richard II.

22nd December.

[THE JUDGES.]

Lord Keeper's charge read.

MR. ST. JOHN. That the accusation of Lord Keeper be sent. That (he) being gone, the lords be moved to take caution of judges.

SIR JO. HOTHAM. That the judges charged may be named, and the Lords sent to.

SIR JO. STOWELL. That the same caution be taken of Bishop of Bath as of Ely.

MR. ST. JOHN. Bramston, Chief Baron, Jus. Barkley, Crawley, Trevor, Weston.

MR. P. That messenger go presently after Lord Fawkland to move that they give present caution.

MR. CHADWORTH.[4] That Baron Trevor was solicited by Duke of Buckingham in business of loan 2 Car. to leave out that it should not be drawn into precedent, did oppose rest of judges in many other particulars.

LORD DIGBY. In states no compensation of good actions for ill.[5] That for many motives he yesterday

---

[4] "Mr. Chadworth." William Chadwell sat for St. Michael's. He was disabled in 1643.

[5] This was not the opinion of Lord Macaulay. "Ordinary criminal justice knows nothing of set-off. The greatest desert cannot be pleaded in answer to a charge of the slightest transgression. If a man has sold beer on Sunday morning, it is no defence that he has saved the life of a fellow-creature at the risk of his own. . . . But it is not in this way that we ought to deal with men who, raised far above ordinary restraints, and tried by far more than ordinary temptations, are entitled to a more than ordinary measure of indulgence. . . . Their good and bad actions ought to be fairly weighed; and if on the whole the good preponderate, the sentence ought to be one, not merely of acquittal, but of approbation." *Essay on Lord Clive.*

gave his noe, but now moved that others involved in same crime may not give the slip.

Mr. HOLLIS. That the message against judges be first sent to make them sure.

Mr. WALLER. That they might forthwith be imprisoned to prevent tampering of witnesses this Christmas.

Voted, that whereas there are several informations against the judges, that message be sent they may put in caution by themselves and others forthwith.[6]

[SUPPLY.]

Mr. HARRISON. That he had this morning paid in the last of his money, and so performed what he had undertook.

Bill of subsidies read. Mr. Whistler in the chair.

[PETITIONS.]

Petition against Sir Ro. Bannister, High Sheriff of Warwick, by a constable for refusing to obey his warrant for levying ship money. Strangely abused and committed. Referred to committee for ship money.

A petition against a debauched parson, charging him with lewd language against Parliament. Sent for by a sergeant.

[RECESS.]

Recess at Thursday noon, to meet Tuesday, the House to be called Thursday.

---

[6] A message was sent to the Lords by Mr. Waller, to desire that the Lord Chief Justice Bramston, Lord Chief Baron Davenport, Mr. Justice Berkeley, Mr. Justice Crawley, Baron Trevor, and Baron Weston should put in good security to abide the judgment of Parliament, for informations of Crimes of a high nature against them. The Lords complied with the request, and the Judges accordingly entered into recognizances.

Sir John Northcote's Note Book. 103

[SUPPLY.]

SIR H. VANE. For sending the money speedily to the army, and consider farther supply.

[JUDGES.]

Report by MR. WALLER. That their lordships ordered several judges enter recognizance, 10,000 each, to give like bond with sureties this day seven night.

LORD FAWKLAND. That the Lords resolve instantly to sequester Lord Keeper. That, for commitment, he was fled. That when charge is brought against him, to be to same committee.

MR. PYM. That several committees have complaints against Archbishop and judges. That may be ordered to bring them to the select committee.

23rd December.

[COURTS AT YORK, &c.]

Committee to consider of the courts at York[7] and Ludlow. Taking of four counties from the last. All knights and burgesses of several counties and all the lawyers. Thursday seven night to consider of the foundation and institution of those courts. Court of Wards.

[LOAN.]

ALDERMAN PENNINGTON. That they have 13,500

---

[7] The Court of York, properly the Court of the President and Council of the North, was first established by Henry VIII. after the Northern Rebellion. It was reported on by Hyde in April 1641. The House resolved that its jurisdiction was illegal, and that the Court was unprofitable to His Majesty, and grievous to his subjects. And Mr. Hyde was directed to lay the matter before the Lords, which he did in a long and bitter speech, preserved by Nalson.

ready. To-morrow they have court of aldermen to settle the whole, and those that have subscribed and fail he will bring their names.

MR. STROUD.

[THE STANNARIES.]

MR. OLDSWORTH.[8] Leave to go to Lo. Cant.

To consider court of Stannaries. That the knights and burgesses of west may be appointed of that committee, formerly appointed for committee of Mr. Coriton.

[CHARITY.]

SIR RO. HARLOW.[9] Account of the distribution of the offerings to the preachers and poor of Westminster.

[THE ARMIES.]

MR. THRER. (Treasurer). For reading the letters from Sir Ja. Ashley and Sir Jo. Conyer, and after reading moved concerning martial law, by message from Lord General.

SIR JO. HOTHAM. 3,000 to Bar(wick), 1,000 to Carlisle, 16,000 to army. For (those who were) justly suspected (of recusancy), that oath of allegiance and supremacy be tendered. Ordinance and munition of kingdom liable to danger in Hull and Yorkshire. That for drawing the army near in a body and in posture of defence. That the officers repair to (their) charges. Hath been sent 50,000, as much now going. This pay to the 4th January. There

---

[8] Michael Oldsworth, member for Salisbury.

[9] Sir Robert Harley, member for Herefordshire, secluded in 1648. The money collected at the time of the Members receiving the Sacrament amounted to £78 16s. 2d.

will be 75,000 more due, so as a new supply, or no subsistence for army.

Distribution of the 20,000 voted as before.[1]

For (the) justly suspected, that taking oaths and receiving communion (be enforced).

MR. PIM.[2] Not to make compulsory order here for receiving communion.

Voted for taking the oaths.

Lords Commissioners have thought of a course for returning the monies.

SIR JO. STRANGWAYS. To have our army regulated, that if Scots army break out against will of commanders, that they may be repressed. That the officers of this House may go to their charges. Lord General being sick, that His Majesty be moved to appoint some Commander-in-chief.

MR. STROUD. For reading subsidy bill. That before commanders of the House be sent down, the business for the army be debated in the House, and some of Lords' committee be desired to assist.

MR. PALMER. Upon the request of Sir John Conyers about Martial Law, that it may not pass by colour of approbation of this House. While Courts of Justice open, no Martial Law.

MR. THRER. (Treasurer). That no such thing done, but desire of direction only. No such imputation left on him.

House resolved into Grand Committee to consider of bill of subsidies and to enlarge it.

---

[1] Sir J. Northcote refers to this in a memorandum on the fly-leaf of the Note Book.

[2] Pym would appear to have been enlightened enough to object to the Sacramental Test, which was actually enforced so lately as 1828.

Sir Ben. Radyer (Rudyard). That timely provision be made, or it may cost us more than money, and we not able to sit here and give it. (To) stand hucking here for little money may lose all. If overplus remaining we can soon dispose of it.

Mr. Crew. That if any be against 4 subsidies we may hear his reasons, otherwise go on.

Sir Jo. Culpe(per). To give but so much as to keep army to the time of cessation.

Sir Rob. P. (Pye). For preservation of navy, or else submit ourselves and all we have to King of France. Five or six weeks spent about this business. North country never gave subsidies in Queen Elizabeth's time.

Mr. Capell.[3] Less than 4 subsidies cannot be granted. The expence of three will be out by 4th January. If army should then disband, would require money to send them into country.

Sir H. Vane. A paper that 40,000 of year part to be supplied. 16,000 ordinary expence of Navy, without which ships will be lost. 5,000 for repair of ships set out. Other particulars which will attend committee. 10,000 for next year's supplies. That 60,000 presently supplied for navy, or our walls will be much broken.

Mr. Grimstone. Business of navy of great importance. That four subsidies are the least. The

---

[3] According to Sir S. D'Ewes, the value of two subsidies amounted to about £160,000. This agrees with a letter of Mede's, mentioning that a subsidy was *not above* £80,000. Sir J. Wray is represented as saying that a subsidy in the time of Queen Elizabeth was equal to £12,000. This should no doubt be £120,000.

slow proceedings of the bill, and will require time for levying.

Mr. STROUD. To give three now and another when House is full, that country may see we do it upon necessity and by degrees.

SIR JO. WRAY. That Justice being restored to its splendour, it will be more welcome to give four subsidies than four pence to ship money.

Message by Sergeant Ayleff and Whitfeild. An Act for sale of lands for payment of debts of late E. of Winchelsie.

For equal proportioning subsidies. Beginning of Q. Elizabeth £12,000, now greatest estates not above £50, taken of (off?) by certificates.

Mr. POTTS.[4] For 4 subsidies, and that they be not enhanced, but that the rich be not suffered to go so low.

Mr. PEM (*sic*). That but two subsidies, but those brought to the height of 28th of Q. Elizabeth.

Mr. PRICE.[5] That Northern Counties deserve no relief, for that they made no resistance.

SIR THOS. WIDD(RINGTON). That their arms were taken from them.

Mr. HOLLIS. But for 3 subsidies. The bill being ready, it will easily pass. For two more if there be cause.

SIR FR. SEYMOUR for 4. The Clergy being not named in it, will fall very short.

Mr. P. That the present necessity, not satisfaction

---

[4] Sir John Potts was member for Norfolk. He died soon after this time.

[5] Herbert Price was member for Brecon. He was afterwards disabled.

of country, be looked to. And for 4 subsidies. (We) Have our own treasurer, and many offenders which may bear the future burden.

Question. That 2 subsidies be added to the 2 formerly agreed on, to the use of the former, and to such uses as shall be further declared by house. *Voted nullo contradicente.*

The first payable 10th Feb., second the 10th of May, *so voted.*

Mr. THRER. That sense of house was that Mr. Harrison should receive first 50,000, citizens other 50,000.

Mr. Harrison names for his treasurers Mr. Capell, Sir Ro. Pye, and Sir Thomas Barrington. They all severally undertook it. The city to appoint three more.

Mr. HARRISON. That they may name them, and to have a joint trust.

Exemption heretofore of Cinque Ports and Rumney Marsh.

SIR JO. CULPEPER. The Cinque Ports have divers charters, and were never poorer.

Mr. MAYNARD. The charters are exemptions against King, but not to the use of commonwealth.

SIR P. HAYMAN.[6] That they more charged than others. Subject to press for mariners and pilots, to keep perpetual watch with soldiers, and to furnish 50 ships. Lying upon the sea, are charged with repairing the banks. Never were charged to any payment

---

[6] Sir Peter Hayman, member for Dover, died soon afterwards. The Writ was issued in February following. The local members evidently stood up for the privileges of their constituents.

before or since Conqueft. That till now never had Burgeffes of their country, but recommended. And for refufing, charged by du (Duke?) with billeting. If, now they have half of their country, it fhould pafs, they do them ill fervice.

Mr. St. John. They are to find 57 fhips, 21 men and boys in each, to ferve fifteen days. This fervice not required fince Henry VII.'s time. Have been difcharged from army, but (this) being difcontinued, it would be confidered whether now to be freed.

Sir Jo. Culpeper. That they have never denied. Till then, that they may enjoy their charters.

Sir P. Hayman. That in Portugal voyage, Cales, and all where His Majefty concerned, they have always fet out fome. For army they are as deep charged as any.

Mr. Pim. That they came in as adventurers, and upon return had fhares, and not otherwife charged than other parts.

Report by Mr. Whistler to the houfe, the Speaker (having) returned to the chair, what had been done. Upon his putting the fame queftions, all voted by the houfe *ut supra*.

The alterations of the bill referred to fame committee to make ready againft to-morrow.

[Business of House.]

Mr. Ther. The paper upon Tuefday. The ballaft (*fic*) of King's revenue now to be brought. That the motion for navy be brought firft to that committee.

Sir Edward Savage for contempt of privilege in

administration and fold goods. Mr. Cambell to be sent for, but upon motion of Sir Ro. P. and Mr. Pim stayed, and referred to Committee of privileges to meet this afternoon.

24th December.

[MISCELLANEA.]

Alderman Abell to put in caution. Order to justices to return names of all recusants, and such as pretend to be protected by the lords to return their names, and by whom protected.

MR. MAYNARD reports Mr. Goodwin's[7] election for East Greensteed. *Voted* good.

Wednesday appointed for making reports. Mr. Pim for Irish affairs, Mount Norris, Kildare, Dillon, and Chancellor, be first reported.

MR. HAMDEN. That those that sit in chairs may then present a brief sum of the petitions in their hands conducing to the great causes in hand. *Ordered.*

[THE BISHOPS.]

A draught of articles against Lord of Cant. shall be presented, Wednesday.

That the sub-committee meet Tuesday afternoon.

MR. BAGSHAW. That Bishop Bath and Wells is going. That message be sent to make him sure.

SIR ROB. PYE. That upon enquiries he is satisfied to contrary. He did refuse to give orders *ex institutione* unless take new oath. Enforced payment of new benevolence. If refused he would put arms on them, for that it was *bellum episcopale*. Enjoined penance

---

[7] Robert Goodwyn, member for East Grinstead, Sussex.

Sir John Northcote's Note Book. 111

on churchwardens for catechising, and convented others for preaching in afternoons.

SIR JO. STOWELL.[8] That convented minister and gave oath *ex officio.* Whether not preach twice upon Michaelmas Day to hinder church ales. Did excommunicate Mr. Chambers for not reading book of sports.

SIR HENRY MILDMAY. That he gloried in it that he had put down all lectures. That he had injured divers gentlemen in their patronages.

Message voted for divers heinous crimes tending to the subversion and corruption of religion in that diocese.

SIR HENRY MILDMAY (sent to the Lords).

MR. PEARD (He) is crafty fox, unkennel him.

MR. STROUD. The disorder of carrying messages.

Sergeant sent.

[SUPPLY FOR ARMY.]

SIR W. EARLE attended Lords Commissioners for this house yesterday, concerning receiving and ordering the monies. The Lords answer that four of the committee, Warwick, Mandevil, Paget, Wharton, might receive the money. That they should go for relief of northern counties, to avoid mentioning Scots' army. They desired to know where to receive the money.

ALDERMAN PENNINGTON. That 13,000 in Chamber of London. Moved that might be order for receiving 38,000 out of Chamber of London; 25,000 from C——, 5,000 from Sir W. Udall. *Voted.*

---

[8] Sir John Stowell, or Stawell, member for Somerset, an active Royalist, disabled in 1642.

[MESSAGE.]

Report, That Bishop of Bath was not present, but they had sent for him, and would take caution of him as desired.

[ANNUAL PARLIAMENTS.]

MR. STROUD.⁹ That noised giving 4 subsidies. That somewhat to comfort the people. That Act for yearly holding parliaments. *Read.* That the Tuesday after Easter they assemble without summons, if not a summons by a King's writ before Tuesday after Ash-Wednesday, and sheriffs to send Warrants for choosing, as if writs had been sent. And if Sheriff fail, then the freeholders and Citizens and burgesses to assemble and make choice, and sheriffs to make returns as upon writs. If any proclamation published to contrary, the party to incur penalty of Sta. 16 R. 2. Sheriffs failing their duty to forfeit £500, Citizens 200, and burgesses 200, and freeholders 1000. No parliament to be dissolved within 40 days of meeting without consent of King and both houses.

SIR SIDNEY MOUNT(AGUE).¹ That preamble of bill of subsidies naming Majesty's subjects the Commons is excepted against by Lords, and not used till 1° and 3° Car. That it may breed difference twixt Lords and us.

The bill first read in the house.

---

⁹ This was the Bill which became afterwards the Triennial Act. Cromwell moved the second reading. Clarendon evidently follows Strode's introduction in his mention of it: "It was thought necessary that the people should be refreshed with some behoveful law, at the same time that they found themselves charged with the payment of so many subsidies."

¹ Sir Sidney Montague was member for Huntingdonshire and a Royalist. He was disabled and committed to the Tower, Dec. 1642.

December 28th, 1640.

[Supply.]

Bill of subsidie read.

Mr. Partridge.[2] That the Cinque Ports be exempt.

Referred to Committee, Thursday morning, of whole house.

Sir H. Vane. That speedy course be taken for the Navy.

Sir Robt. Pye. That the general balance of King's revenue be first considered. That it will require two months to prepare it.

That the Lords be sent to for voting the ship-money.

[King's Revenue.]

Sir Ed. Warder called in with a balance of King's revenue made five years since.

First gave thanks that Sir Rob. Pye is joined with him. That he may receive directions from house for drawing new balance, because divers Monopolies likely to be taken off. Revenue £618,990 per annum. Not half answered into Exchequer by reason of defalcations. Recusant's compositions not answered into Exchequer, but into other hands. That in Exchequer always at his Majesty's command. Other monies not so. Assignations duly paid to prejudice of Exchequer. Whole revenue for two years anticipated. That his Majesty may have some supply from the house.

---

[2] Mr. Partridge, I presume, was Sir Edward Parteriche, Bart., member for Sandwich. He was secluded in 1648.

Balance read. Receipts. Great Cuftoms, 150,000. Petty farmes, 60,000. Compo. for houfe, 38,330.

Sir Ro. P. That this war hath coft the King and kingdom two millions.

(A feparate lift.)

Qn. (Queen).	32,594.
Q. Boh. (Bohemia).	19,150.
Cofer.	107,920.
Robes.	5000.
Child(ren).	15,833.
Ward.	26,221.
House.	16,071.
.... (?)	1310.
Jewels.	5810.
Sta. (ftables ?).	41,570.
Caftles.	13,500.
Penfions.	131,000.

Mr. Pim. For prefent confideration of Navy. That cuftomers forbear any payments fave to King's houfe. That the money be affigned for Navy. (Mem. inferted afterwards). *Ordered to make no payments but ut fupra.* That if might have all our defires, if King were not better provided for than we found him.[3] Work not done.

Mr. Thre. (Treafurer). That King's revenue in fuch diftraction that nothing but Parliament can repair it. That fome Patents from the King be called in. That a preparative balance may be brought in in 7 or 8 days. Provifions for Navy to be made at this time of year at much eafier rates.

[3] Pym faid, on one occafion, that they would make the King the richeft King in all Chriftendom.

SIR H. VANE. Method of Navy. Divide expenſe in ordinary and extraordinary. 38,000 for 40 ſhips and ſetting out 4, which was clearly paid till this year 16,000 behind for payment of wages, &c. Hull ſhips for fraught, for King's ſhips paid off, but others daily expected to be provided for. For next, the ordinary will be ſame. That money be forthwith aſſigned, for ſummer guard, ſuitable to ſhips for other princes. Lord Admiral, expence (of) 20 ſhip, 12 or 13,000 preſent pay for victuals. Stores to be ſupplied, ſo as 20,000 will be preſently neceſſary.

[SIR G. RADCLIFFE.]

MR. PIM. From Committee for charge againſt Lord Strafford. Sir Geo. Radcliff ſo interweaved and combined as cannot go without. There being no accuſations againſt him, Lords made ſome ſcruple of examining his articles prepared by Committee againſt him. Upon reading them to ſend to Lords to charge him with treaſon.

Six Articles.

1. That conſpired with Earl Strafford to ſubvert government, and been counſellor in bringing in Iriſh Army to England. Sir Rob. King (brings it) fully home (to him.) King[4] 400,000. 30,000 ſoldiers and ſword by his ſide, if want more not to be pitied. By conference with two others of Ireland, the ſame. Lord Lieutenant (ſaid) abſolute power in the King beſt government. Sir Ro. King replying that would be tyrannical. Sir Geo. Radcliff (ſaid) that government is eaſieſt ſo.

[4] That is, Sir G. Radcliffe ſaid that the King had £400,000, and 30,000 ſoldiers, ſo that he might take whatever he pleaſed.

2. Confederate with him in assuming regal power, and exercised the same over subjects in Ireland. Proofs by extrajudicial proceedings upon paper petitions, fining and imprisoning customers for not conforming.

3. For enabling these designs, taking great sums out of exchequer, 30 or £40,000 at one time employed for tobacco.[5]

4. Abused their power by countenancing papists. Priory built on his own land, and great resort of priests to it. That dissuaded recusants of Ireland from charging him in England.

5. That had stirred up enmity and war twixt Ireland and Scotland. That he spoke in Parliament there that an Army coming from Scotland in Ireland, to incense them.

6. That laboured to subvert rights of Parliament. Mr. Barnwell for standing upon sending parliament men for ancient boroughs, Sir G. R. told him would *session* (billet?) 500 soldiers upon his house.

All during his being councillor there, contrary to his oath and allegiance.

Voted to charge him with high treason.

Voted that these articles should be ground of accusation.

Voted that message forthwith sent to Lords to accuse him, *nullo contradicente*.

MR. STROUD named, but apologised that of late men not so fit have been employed. *Read at bar.*

Message. To know whether it be our desire to have Sir G. Radcliff made sure.

---

[5] "And converting the profits of the same to their own use."

Anſwer by MR. PIMM. That (he) being in cuſtody, they forbore to ſay anything of that till the Articles ſhould be preſented, which will be very ſhortly. Since their Lordſhips have ſent, that they take ſuch courſe for his further reſtraint as ſhall ſeem fit, and that their Lordſhips will be pleaſed to examine ſuch witneſſes as ſhall be produced ſpeedily and ſecretly.

[MISCELLANEA.]

MR. PRYDEAUX.[6] That Dr. Baſtwick's petition be referred to Committee for Burton and Prinne.

Mr. Shepheard ſent for as a delinquent for ſending Mr. Speaker's ſervant to Newgate, and ſaying that if any parliament man break the peace, he would lay him by heels.

[On a ſeparate page.]

Sir Jo. Holland's [7] profeſſion of his integrity in Religion notwithſtanding his *wive's* recuſancy ordered to be entered.

[END OF THE NOTES OF 1640.]

---

[6] Edmund Prideaux, member for Lyme Regis, afterwards Attorney General, and Cuſtos Rotulorum of Devon under the Commonwealth.

[7] Sir John Holland, Bart., member for Caſtle Riſing, Norfolk. This ſhould have been entered under Nov. 24. Sir John H. was one of the firſt who ſpoke upon grievances at the commencement of the Long Parliament.

ENTRIES ON THE FLY LEAVES OF NOTE BOOK.

I.

(*In a clerk's hand, not Sir J. Northcote's.*)

August 16th, 1633.

Keniside. Thomas Johnson hath surrendered to Isabell his daughter, now wife of W^m. Dickson, a tenement there called Whitebanck rented xx^d.

    Saving a moiety thereof to him ye said Tho. Johnson and Katharine his wife and ye longer liver of them.

Dregg. John Kitchin to John his sonn a tenem^t there rented 2^d, and ye said John ye father hath compounded for 2 fines, one upon my late Lord's death, ye other upon this surrender.

Carlton. The same John hath likewise surrendered to Hugh his sonn one tenement there rented xii^d, and hath likewise compounded for 2 fines *ut supra.*

II.

(*In Sir J. Northcote's handwriting.*)

Understood the debate at Committee concerned by his place.[1]

Though of greater value, to quit it, desiring to further general good.

To offer to consideration that the general Liberty

---

[1] A note of the speech of some member, perhaps Sir H. Vane.

Sir John Northcote's Note Book. 119

(be granted) to any that will to put to Sea, without com^on (commission?) or rendering account, I mean of their actions, not of the prizes taken.

Not to retard the intention (?), but provide against the mischief, and submit it to Judgment of house.

III.

Rec.   May 6th, 1640.

		£	s.	d.
Nunm.	Robert Barker . . .	1	0	0
	Rog. fforster . . .	0	10	0
Topc.	Tho. Stevenson . . .	1	0	0
Wros.	Hen. Dixon Lic. . .	0	10	0
Thornton.	Ric. Hill Lic. . . .	0	10	0

IV.

Remem. for Nort.   Lad. 1640.

To take present course for settling of Corbridge.

To Moone for repairing the bridge with timber.

To call upon the rent for Ovingham Mill.   Mem. Wilome fishing.

To settle the tenements in question at Tynmouth.

To enquire concerning Mr. Crage's petition.

To send process for Jo. Wolfe, Tho. Lambert, and Tho. Thorpe of North Sheeles for rescous (rescue?) upon the bailiff.

V.

Rem. for year 1640.

To enquire of the Dutch ship brought in by a Dunkirk at Scarborough, and the corn sold.

Mem. The recovery for Newton upon Darwent delivered Mr. Elmhirst May 6th 1640, to be returned upon all occasions.

VI.

The 20,000 now sent, deducting 4000 for the Garrison will pay but to the beginning of December, so as there is yet no provision to the 4th of January.

To move the Committee concerning executing Martial Law, without which not in the power of officers to prevent disorders in the country.[2]

VII.

	£	s.	d.
Taken with me March 31st, 1640, for Riding Charges	21	0	0
Unde from London to York and at York from the last of March to the 9th of April, ix^l vi^s i^d.	9	6	1

Whereof Mr. Henderson to pay 1. 11. 10.

VIII.

	£	s.	d.
Paid my brother Geo. Potter[3] towards the purchase of the Lands in Idsley, May 22.	50	0	0

---

[2] See Notes, p. 105. This may be a memorandum of what Sir John Northcote himself intended to say in Parliament.

[3] George Potter, here called "my brother," was probably a cousin of Sir John Northcote. His first cousin had married Dr. Barnabas Potter, Bishop of Carlisle, who died in 1642, being the last bishop who died a member of the House of Lords. Perhaps George was a son of his, or he may have been a brother justice. Iddesleigh is a parish in North Devon. The manor still belongs to Sir Stafford Northcote.

Sir John Northcote's Note Book. 121

	£	s.	d.
More paid Mr. Ball's man by my brother's appointment.	114	0	0
More paid Mr. Arthur Chapple upon a bill from my brother, June 16, 1640.	36	0	0
Paid Mr. Keeling by Sir Jo. Melton's appointment, June 5th.	12	0	0
More delivered him for Sir Jo. Melton's ufe, June 14th, 1640.	5	0	0
Lent Mr. Morris Mrs. Gates her fonne upon his bill, June 13th.	2	0	0

(The laſt three entries are croſſed out.)

IX.

	£	s.	d.
To Mr. Selden for drawing his Lordſhip's[4] commiſſions as General, by his Lp's appointment, July 13th, 1640	20	0	0
To his Clerks	0	11	0
More to his clerks			
To Mr. Harris by Mr. Budd's appointment, July 13th	3	0	0
For Maps for his Lordſhip	0	4	0
To Wm. Knight to be repaid to my brother at Michaelmas	1	0	0
Lent Mr. Aſh of Petherton, July 23, 1640	8	0	0
To Mr. Ellis upon his bill of diſburſements in executing Commiſſions from the Admtie, July 21st, 1640, per bill	6	6	8

[4] Probably the Earl of Northumberland, Lord General. It may poſſibly mean the Earl of Bedford, Lord Lieutenant of Devonſhire, under whom Sir John Northcote ſerved at one period of the Civil War.

	£	s.	d.

Difburfed for Sir Jo. Melton, July 28th, 1640, for the fees of his policy. . 7 12 0

More paid Mr. Pryor as fo much laid out for him, per bill 10 0 0

X.

To the Clerk of the Parliament for copies of Scots Articles againft Lord of Cant. and Lord Lieutenant for his Lordfhip, Janu. 12th. 1 0 0

ABSTRACT OF AN ACT OF PARLIAMENT.

On a feparate half-fheet of paper.

This is a fpecimen of an Act of the Commonwealth, long fince expunged from the Statute Book. It may have had some fpecial intereft for Sir John Northcote, as his wife was a Somerfetfhire lady, and Sir John Stowell was member for that county. George Villiers, fecond Duke of Buckingham, was the well-known courtier and minifter of Charles II. Lislebone Long was elected Speaker of Richard Cromwell's Houfe of Commons in 1658, but died a week afterwards. He was member for Wells.

The eftates of Sir John Stowell, G. Duke of Buckingham, etc., declared by the Act, July 15th, 1651, to be forfeited for their feveral treafons againft the Parliament.

Enacted that all the manors, lands, tenements and hereditaments, with the appurtenances which they, the faid Sir John Stowell, G. Duke of Buckingham, etc., or any of them, or any for their ufe, or in truft for any of them, were feized or poffeffed of in poffeffion, reverfion or remainder, on the 20th of May, 1642, or any time fince, and all rights of entry to any the faid manors, etc., which they or any of them had the faid 20th of May or any time fince, be and are hereby vefted, fettled, adjudged and deemed to be in the real and actual poffeffion and feizin of William Skinner, William Robinfon, etc., the furvivors and furvivor of them and their heirs and affigns, and that they and the furvivors, etc., may have the advantage of the faid rights of entry, etc. And that they fhall hold all the premises of the manor of East Greenwich in socage, upon trust nevertheless, That the said W. Skinner, etc., shall hold and enjoy all the premises subject to such uses as by this Act or by Authority of Parliament shall be hereafter directed.

Saving to every person, bodies politic and corporate, their heirs, successors, etc., other than the said Sir John Stowell, G. Duke of Buckingham, etc., or any of them, and all claiming from them since the 20th of the May 1642, and other than the rights of dower of respective wives of any of them, all such estates, interests, rents, incumbrances, charges, rights in law or equity, which any of them had to the said manors, etc., before the said 20th of May;

As also all the estates and interests given, granted, demised, etc., by any Act or Order of Parliament to any who have constantly adhered to this Parliament, if such persons, etc., make their title appear and obtain allowance thereof before Lislebone Long, Ric. Edwards, etc., who are appointed a committee for removing obstructions in the sale of the said lands, and are empowered to receive claims in writing, and to examine and allow them upon proof by oath, and to do all acts which former committees for sale of lands might do before the 1st of December, 1651. Their allowance to be transmitted to the trustees, who are to observe such orders and directions as they shall receive from the said committee.

The said William Skinner, etc., shall stand seized of all the premises vested and settled in them and their heirs, except rectories impropriate, parsonages impropriate, tithes, etc., until the conveyance be made to the purchaser, etc., for satisfying the respective lenders within this Act, and unto such further use as shall be declared by Parliament.

The Trustees to appoint surveyors, etc., who are to return the values of the several premises.

The Trustees to send for particulars of the several lands to the clerk of the commissioners for compounding.

That out of these particulars, they cause abstracts to be made of the said lands in each county.

Provided that they contract not with any other than the immediate tenants for thirty days after his return of the survey.

The several rates they are to sell at.

Instructions for the Trustees, for the Register, the Treasurers, Register Accountant, Surveyor-general, Controller.

Provided that if any double any sum upon forged debentures or false certificates, etc., to forfeit treble the sum of the moiety to the state, the other moiety to the informer.

Provided always, That every person having any estate, right, title or interest, of, in, or to any the lands, tenements, or hereditaments by this Act intended to be put to sale, or that hath any statutory judgment, recognizance, or rent, to which they are liable, and shall make it appear to the committee that such estate, etc., was without fraud had and made before any treason committed, and shall obtain allowance thereof by the committee before the 29th of September, 1651, that then the same shall be good and effectual to such person, etc., to all intents and purposes.

Several savings to particular persons.
Page 1392 mentions 8 per cent. for interest.
Page 1394 allows but 6 per cent.
That is for interest due before the act for reducing it to 6 per cent.

Sir John Northcote's Note Book. 127

MEMORANDA OF THE SESSION OF 1661,

On a separate sheet of paper,
Folded in the form of the Note Book.

Parliament met on May 8, 1661. Sir John Northcote was not a member, but he may have frequented the House from his interest in public affairs. It is possible that he may have been a candidate at the election, and may have claimed the seat by petition, which would account for his presence during the first month or two of the Session. These notes are very different from those of 1640, and of inferior interest. They contain little that might not have been derived from the information of a friend, or from the Journals of the House, but, from the appearance of the manuscript, they would seem to have been taken on the spot. They are not identical with the Journals.

May 18th, 61.

Bill enabling Churchwardens to levy rates for repair of churches, signed by two next justices.

House called over.

Message to Lords for concurrence in burning the Covenant. Vote to deface it in all Churches.

20th.

Report for election of Mr. Evelin and Mr. Morrise at Petersfield.[1]

Petitions of Mr. Chute and some of the Electors read for recommitting it. The bailiff to be taken into custody and brought to the house by the Sergeant to-morrow.

Bill [2] making it treason to attempt anything against

---

[1] *Petersfield.* Hazlemere in the Journals, as in the next page.

[2] This was the Act 13 Charles II. cap. 1.

his Majesty's person or government, and Premunire to preach, print, or speak, against the present government, to say the Long Parliament is yet in being. This to be in force after June 24th.

Mr. SWINFEN offered a Proviso that it should not impeach the Act of Indemnity.

Sergeant Maynard, Mr. Solicitor, and Mr. Swinfen to supply it.

Mr. LEAR for a longer day, and that it might not concern —— (a blot) that all might take notice.

LORD FALKLAND. Report from the Lords that they would send by messenger of their own (concerning the) Covenant.

Conference upon letter from Parliament of Scotland to his Majesty concerning settling some horse and foot for securing the peace of that kingdom. That only natives may be employed. *Ordered* to be debated Monday next.

Message from his Majesty that he is willing to pardon any miscarriage in Sir Jo. Morley, and desires he be admitted into the house.

21*st*.

Bill enabling Mr. Milward to sell land in Derbyshire.

Bill for Mr. Hunt to sell land.

Bailiff of Hazelmere brought to the bar to return Mr. Evelin and Mr. Morris.

Bill for securing his Majesty's person and government. *Voted* to be sent to the Lords.

Lords return their order for burning the Covenant.

Bill for settling Militia. Committed to a grand Committee.

The house to meet 29th to commemorate his Majesty's restoration. Dr. Pierce to preach.

SIR RIC. SPENCER offered a bill for supplying the bill of (indemnity?)

SIR ROB. ATKINS. That provision be made for his Majesty's subsistence, the £120,000 falling much short.

Complaint by a member[3] against an officer of the Lords' house for uncivil usage. *Ordered* the complaint to be sent the Lords.

[*May* 22.]

Bill for settling Mr. Arlebye's[4] estate committed.

All of Bedfordshire to vote.

SIR RALPH ASHTON's scruple concerning receiving sacrament[5] allowed.

ALD. FOWK speaking against the order taken off, and resolved that liberty be granted to none to speak against it.

SIR HENEAG FINCH[6] to the chair.

Concerning bill for Militia.

1 paragr. voted.

2nd after long debate deferred till Monday, and then *de die in diem*.

---

[3] The member was Mr. George Weld.

[4] Mr. "Arlebye." George Orlibear in the Journals.

[5] It had been ordered on May 13 that all members should receive the Communion.

[6] Sir Heneage Finch, Attorney General in 1670, Lord Keeper in 1673, Lord Chancellor, 1675, and Earl of Nottingham, 1681.

May 25th (24th in Journals).

Motion for leave to proceed in fuit againft Mr. Willyams a member, denied.

Bill for confirming an act for fale of Sir Rob. Howard's land.

Bill for mending highways ordered to be read friday.

Bill for incorporating adventure in Lord of Bedford's Level.

And another bill for the 2nd Adventure committed.

Ordered that the King's fupply be firft upon Monday.

2nd parag. of bill of Militia voted.

Act of indemnity to be read Tuefday.

May 27th.

Bill concerning Earl of Worcefter.[7]

Order that Committee of trade bring in a bill for regulating trade in great Corporations.

Petition of Covent Garden.

SERGEANT CHILTON concerning Lords not returning anfwer. Concerning burning covenant, and concerning King's marriage.

Act for High Court of Juftice[8] voted to be burnt.

Act declaring the people of England to be a Commonwealth, to be burnt.

Act for the Engagement to be burnt.

Act for renouncing King to be burnt.

---

[7] *Earl of Worcefter.* "Clothiers of the City of Worcefter" in the Journals.

[8] "That traitorous curfed writing called an Act."

Act for securing the Protector and preserving peace of Nation to be burnt.

Bill enabling Sir Anth. Browne to sell land. *Committed.*

Governor of St. Mawe's[9] to appear.

Letter from Scotland, to be read.

Thanks to be given to Dr. Gunning[1] and Mr. Carpenter, and to print their sermons. Ser. Morrice said Dr. Gunning's was a scandalous sermon.

Militia.

2 parag. voted.

May 28th.

The Six adjacent Counties[2] to the Level to have voices, if not concerned.

Order from the Lords for preventing Riots and tumultuous Petitions.

Bill enabling Sir Ralph Bash to sell Lands, ordered second reading.

Act for confirming Judicial Proceedings, with amendments, to be ingrossed.

Ordered that the Committee bring in a second Bill for those that are omitted.

Lords return the bill for securing his Majesty's person, etc., with saving peerage.[3]

---

[9] The governor of St. Mawe's was Colonel Lewis Tremayne.

[1] Dr. Peter Gunning was consecrated Bishop of Chichester in 1670, and translated to Ely in 1674.

Mr. Carpenter was Chaplain of the House of Commons. Was he the Richard Carpenter who is said to have gone over five times from the Church of England to that of Rome, and *vice versâ* ?

[2] That is, the members for the six adjacent counties.

[3] Proviso that no peer should be tried except by his peers, &c., see p. 134.

May 30th.

Mr. Milward's Bill committed.

Bill for Mr. Howard's invention for tanning without bark, to second reading.

May 31st.

Day of humiliation for great rains.

Bill for Naturaliz,[4] a second reading.

Mr. Harbin's bill to be engrossed.

Bill for Sir Robert Hitcham's (settlements?)

Bill against gathering hands to tumultuous and popular Petitions (13 Charles II. cap. 5).

Bill for highways committed.

June 5th.

Bill for packing butter cast out.

Bill for naturalizing Sabran[5] committed.

Bill for regulating Elections.

Bill concerning Droitwich committed.

Bill enabling Sir Anthony Browne to sell Land, committed.

Mr. Tremayne, Governor of St. Mawe's, to appear to answer misdemeanours.

Letter from Parliament of Scotland for withdrawing garrisons, or that they may be of Natives.

Bill for incorporating Clothiers of Worcester, committed.

---

[4] Bill for naturalizing Francis, son of Lord Brudenell, afterwards Earl of Cardigan, and his sister Anna Maria, Countess of Shrewsbury, the "wanton Shrewsbury" of Pope.

[5] Ranée de Sabran.

Sir John Northcote's Note Book. 133

Bill to enable Sir Ralph Bash to sell, Committed.
Free conference concerning Peerage. Lords adhere.

June 6th.

Nonellye's complaint against Sergeant.

[June 7th.]

Bill to enable Mr. Alg. Peyton to sell.
The like for Mr. Nevill to sell.
Bill sent from the Lords for E. of Dorset's transferring a rent-charge to his hospital, etc., upon Knoll, upon other lands.
Bill for free Present to his Majesty (13 Ch. II. cap. 4).
Quarrel 'twixt Sir Ph. Howard and Sir Rich. Everard. Composed.
Bill disabling Clergymen to bear temporal offices to be repealed. (13 Charles II. cap. 2.)

June 8th.

Bill concerning Wells.
Bill concerning Sir Jo. Hutchinson's seizing monies as belonging to delinquents, but indeed to Orphans.
Bill for Present to his Majesty committed to whole house.
Bill for Militia.
Bill settling salaries upon the Masters of Chancery, and an office to be erected near the Rolls.
Ordered, no private business after 9.

Bill for free Prefent, fecond reading.
Lords concur to amendments concerning Peerage.
Committee voted repeal of the Bill excluding Bifhops.

June 11*th.*

Mr. Harbin's bill for felling, paft.
Mr. Peck's bill ordered to be read.
Bill for repeal of Act difabling Bifhops. *Voted* to be ingroffed.

13*th.*

Report concerning the fens.
Bill for reftoring Mr. Radcliff to his lands in England and Ireland.
Bill for Marquis Winchefter againft Mr. Wallop.
Election for Northampton voted void. The Mayor committed.
Bill for free prefent.
Bill repealing the Act difabling Bifhops to fit in the Lords' houfe paffed and fent to the Lords.
Ordered that the Committee for obferving Receivers of Sacrament report.
Sir Ph. Warwick[6] to bring in Particulars how the £120,000 affigned for his Majefty falls fhort.

[*June* 14*th.*]

Bill for repairing churches committed. All to have voices.

---

[6] Sir Philip Warwick, author of the Memoirs of Charles I. He had fat for Radnor in the Long Parliament.

Act for confirmation of several bills last Parliament, and concerning Act of Indemnity, adjourned.

June 15*th.*

Petition for removing Assizes from Launceston to Bodmin. Laid aside.

Mr. Thomas voted for Cardiff.

Mr. Fitz James for Poole.

Sir Jo. Talbot claims Privilege for a servant of his arrested. The offender sent for.

Report concerning exaction for Ballast. The payment of it to cease till it be heard.

[*June* 18.]

Sir. Ph. Warwick. Estimate of Revenue. Wine Licences £250,000 ;[7] now short.

Norwich. Petition against Excise. Offer xii*d.* per quarter upon Malt.

[*June* 19*th.*]

Militia.

None be charged with horse and foot in one county. None under £100 per annum charged towards horse.

[*June* 20.]

Bill for fees to Masters in Chancery passed.

Grand Committee for Courts of Justice to examine all fees.

[7] Wine Licences, £25,000 in Journals.

Mayor of Northampton at bar. Dismissed with reproof.

Letters from Speaker to several Counties for bringing arr. of Sessn. (arrears of assessments).

Chippenham. Election voted void for want of timely notice and refusing Poll.

Bill for regulating Corporations.

[*June* 21.]

Sir. H. Fredr. Thin's[8] bill for confirming his father's settlement committed.

Mr. Ch. Howard's bill for tanning committed to Committee of trade.

Lime Regis continued Anniversary for raising the King's siege.

---

[8] Sir Henry Frederick Thynne, created a Baronet in 1642, ancestor of the Marquis of Bath. He was probably one of the first English gentlemen who ever bore two Christian names.

THE END.

50A, ALBEMARLE STREET, LONDON,
September, 1877.

MR. MURRAY'S
GENERAL LIST OF WORKS.

ABINGER'S (LORD Chief Baron of the Exchequer) Life. By the Hon. P. CAMPBELL SCARLETT. Portrait. 8vo. 15s.

ALBERT MEMORIAL. A Descriptive and Illustrated Account of the National Monument erected to the PRINCE CONSORT at Kensington. Illustrated by Engravings of its Architecture, Decorations, Sculptured Groups, Statues, Mosaics, Metalwork, &c. With Descriptive Text. By DOYNE C. BELL. With 24 Plates. Folio. 12*l*. 12*s*.

——— HANDBOOK TO, 1s.; or Illustrated Edition, 2s. 6d.

——— (PRINCE) SPEECHES AND ADDRESSES, with an Introduction, giving some outline of his Character. With Portrait. 8vo. 10s. 6d.; or *Popular Edition*, fcap. 8vo. 1s.

ALBERT DÜRER; his Life, with a History of his Art. By DR. THAUSING, Keeper of Archduke Albert's Art Collection at Vienna. Translated from the German. With Portrait and Illustrations. 2 vols. 8vo. [*In the Press.*

ABBOTT'S (REV. J.) Memoirs of a Church of England Missionary in the North American Colonies. Post 8vo. 2s.

ABERCROMBIE (JOHN). Enquiries concerning the Intellectual Powers and the Investigation of Truth. Fcap. 8vo. 3s. 6d.

——— Philosophy of the Moral Feelings. Fcap. 8vo. 2s. 6d.

ACLAND (REV. CHARLES). Popular Account of the Manners and Customs of India. Post 8vo. 2s.

ÆSOP'S FABLES. A New Version. With Historical Preface. By Rev. THOMAS JAMES. With 100 Woodcuts, by TENNIEL and WOLF. Post 8vo. 2s. 6d.

AGRICULTURAL (ROYAL) JOURNAL. (*Published half-yearly*.)

AIDS TO FAITH: a Series of Theological Essays. By various Authors. 8vo. 9s.
Contents:—Miracles; Evidences of Christianity; Prophecy & Mosaic Record of Creation; Ideology and Subscription; The Pentateuch; Inspiration; Death of Christ; Scripture and its Interpretation.

AMBER-WITCH (THE). A most interesting Trial for Witchcraft. Translated by LADY DUFF GORDON. Post 8vo. 2s.

ARMY LIST (THE). *Published Monthly by Authority*.

ARTHUR'S (LITTLE) History of England. By LADY CALLCOTT. *New Edition, continued to* 1872. With 36 Woodcuts. Fcap. 8vo. 1s. 6d.

AUSTIN (JOHN). LECTURES ON GENERAL JURISPRUDENCE; or, the Philosophy of Positive Law. Edited by ROBERT CAMPBELL. 2 Vols. 8vo. 32s.

——— STUDENT'S EDITION, by ROBERT CAMPBELL, compiled from the above work. Post 8vo. 12s.

——— Analysis of. By GORDON CAMPBELL, M.A. Post 8vo. 6s.

ARNOLD (THOS.). Ecclesiastical and Secular Architecture of Scotland: The Abbeys, Churches, Castles, and Mansions. With Illustrations. Medium 8vo. [*In Preparation.*

B

ATKINSON (Dr. R.) Vie de Saint Auban. A Poem in Norman-French. Ascribed to MATTHEW PARIS. With Concordance, Glossary and Notes. Small 4to, 10s. 6d.

ADMIRALTY PUBLICATIONS; Issued by direction of the Lords Commissioners of the Admiralty:—

A MANUAL OF SCIENTIFIC ENQUIRY, for the Use of Travellers. *Fourth Edition.* Edited by ROBERT MAIN, M.A. Woodcuts. Post 8vo. 3s. 6d.

GREENWICH ASTRONOMICAL OBSERVATIONS 1841 to 1846, and 1847 to 1871. Royal 4to. 20s. each.

MAGNETICAL AND METEOROLOGICAL OBSERVATIONS. 1840 to 1847. Royal 4to. 20s. each.

APPENDICES TO OBSERVATIONS.
  1837. Logarithms of Sines and Cosines in Time. 3s.
  1842. Catalogue of 1439 Stars, from Observations made in 1836 to 1841. 4s.
  1845. Longitude of Valentia (Chronometrical). 3s.
  1847. Description of Altazimuth. 3s.
      Twelve Years' Catalogue of Stars, from Observations made in 1836 to 1847. 4s.
      Description of Photographic Apparatus. 2s.
  1851. Maskelyne's Ledger of Stars. 3s.
  1852. I. Description of the Transit Circle. 3s.
  1853. Refraction Tables. 3s.
  1854. Description of the Zenith Tube. 3s.
      Six Years' Catalogue of Stars, from Observations. 1848 to 1853. 4s.
  1862. Seven Years' Catalogue of Stars, from Observations. 1854 to 1860. 10s.
      Plan of Ground Buildings. 3s.
      Longitude of Valentia (Galvanic). 2s.
  1864. Moon's Semid. from Occultations. 2s.
      Planetary Observations, 1831 to 1835. 2s.
  1868. Corrections of Elements of Jupiter and Saturn. 2s.
      Second Seven Years' Catalogue of 2760 Stars for 1861 to 1867. 4s.
      Description of the Great Equatorial. 3s.
  1856. Descriptive Chronograph. 3s.
  1860. Reduction of Deep Thermometer Observations. 2s.
  1871. History and Description of Water Telescope. 3s.

Cape of Good Hope Observations (Star Ledgers). 1856 to 1863. 2s.
—————————————————— 1856. 5s.
—————————————— Astronomical Results. 1857 to 1858. 5s.
Report on Teneriffe Astronomical Experiment. 1856. 5s.
Paramatta Catalogue of 7385 Stars. 1822 to 1826. 4s.

ASTRONOMICAL RESULTS. 1847 to 1871. 4to. 3s. each.

MAGNETICAL AND METEOROLOGICAL RESULTS. 1847 to 1871. 4to. 3s. each.

REDUCTION OF THE OBSERVATIONS OF PLANETS. 1750 to 1830. Royal 4to. 20s each.
——————————————— LUNAR OBSERVATIONS. 1750 to 1830. 2 Vols. Royal 4to. 20s. each.
——————————————— 1831 to 1851. 4to. 10s. each.

BERNOULLI'S SEXCENTENARY TABLE. 1779. 4to. 5s.
BESSEL'S AUXILIARY TABLES FOR HIS METHOD OF CLEARING LUNAR DISTANCES. 8vo. 2s.
ENCKE'S BERLINER JAHRBUCH, for 830. *Berlin*, 1828. 8vo. 9s.
HANSEN'S TABLES DE LA LUNE. 4to. 20s.
LAX'S TABLES FOR FINDING THE LATITUDE AND LONGITUDE. 1821. 8vo. 10s.
LUNAR OBSERVATIONS at GREENWICH. 1783 to 1819. Compared with the Tables. 1821. 4to. 7s. 6d.
MACLEAR ON LACAILLE'S ARC OF MERIDIAN. 2 Vols. 20s. each.

ADMIRALTY PUBLICATIONS—*continued.*
  MAYER'S DISTANCES of the MOON'S CENTRE from the
    PLANETS. 1822, 3*s.*; 1823, 4*s.* 6*d.* 1824 to 1835. 8vo. 4*s.* each.
  ———— TABULÆ MOTUUM SOLIS ET LUNÆ. 1770. 5*s.*
  ———— ASTRONOMICAL OBSERVATIONS MADE AT GOT-
    TINGEN, from 1756 to 1761. 1826. Folio. 7*s.* 6*d.*
  NAUTICAL ALMANACS, from 1767 to 1877, 80*s.* 2*s.* 6*d.* each.
  ———————————— SELECTIONS FROM, up to 1812. 8vo. 5*s.*
    1834-54. 5*s.*
  ———————————— SUPPLEMENTS, 1828 to 1833, 1837 and 1839.
    2*s.* each.
  ———————————— TABLE requisite to be used with the N.A.
    1781. 8vo. 5*s.*
  SABINE'S PENDULUM EXPERIMENTS to DETERMINE THE FIGURE
    OF THE EARTH. 1825. 4to. 40*s.*
  SHEPHERD'S TABLES for CORRECTING LUNAR DISTANCES. 1772.
    Royal 4to. 21*s.*
  ———— TABLES, GENERAL, of the MOON'S DISTANCE
    from the SUN, and 10 STARS. 1787. Folio. 5*s.* 6*d.*
  TAYLOR'S SEXAGESIMAL TABLE. 1780. 4to. 15*s.*
  ———— TABLES OF LOGARITHMS. 4to. 60*s.*
  TIARK'S ASTRONOMICAL OBSERVATIONS for the LONGITUDE
    of MADEIRA. 1822. 4to. 5*s.*
  ———— CHRONOMETRICAL OBSERVATIONS for DIFFERENCES
    of LONGITUDE between DOVER, PORTSMOUTH, and FALMOUTH. 1823.
    4to. 5*s.*
  VENUS and JUPITER: OBSERVATIONS of, compared with the TABLES.
    London, 1822. 4to. 2*s.*
  WALES' AND BAYLY'S ASTRONOMICAL OBSERVATIONS.
    1777. 4to. 21*s.*
  ———— REDUCTION OF ASTRONOMICAL OBSERVATIONS
    MADE IN THE SOUTHERN HEMISPHERE. 1764—1771. 1788. 4to.
    10*s.* 6*d.*

BARBAULD (MRS.). Hymns in Prose for Children. With
  Illustrations. Crown 8vo.

BARCLAY (JOSEPH, LL.D.). The Talmud: being Selected
  Extracts, chiefly illustrating the Teaching of the Bible. With an
  Introduction describing the General Character of the Talmud. 8vo.

BARKLEY (H. C.). Five Years among the Bulgarians and Turks
  between the Danube and the Black Sea. Post 8vo. 10*s.* 6*d.*

————— My Boyhood: a True Story. With Illustrations.
  Post 8vo. A Christmas Book for Schoolboys and others.

BARROW (SIR JOHN). Autobiographical Memoir, from Early
  Life to Advanced Age. Portrait. 8vo. 16*s.*

————— (JOHN) Life, Exploits, and Voyages of Sir Francis
  Drake. Post 8vo. 2*s.*

BARRY (SIR CHARLES). Life and Works. By CANON BARRY.
  With Portrait and Illustrations. Medium 8vo. 15*s.*

BATES' (H. W.) Records of a Naturalist on the River Amazon
  during eleven years of Adventure and Travel. Illustrations. Post 8vo.
  7*s.* 6*d.*

BAX (CAPT. R.N.). Russian Tartary, Eastern Siberia, China, Japan,
  and Formosa. A Narrative of a Cruise in the Eastern Seas. With
  Map and Illustrations. Crown 8vo. 12*s.*

BELCHER (LADY). Account of the Mutineers of the 'Bounty,'
  and their Descendants; with their Settlements in Pitcairn and Norfolk
  Islands. With Illustrations. Post 8vo. 12*s.*

BELL'S (SIR CHAS.) Familiar Letters. Portrait. Post 8vo. 12*s.*

B 2

LIST OF WORKS

BELL (Doyne C.). Notices of the Historic Interments in the Church of St. Peter ad Vincula, in the Tower of London, with an account of the discovery of the remains of Queen Anne Boleyn. With Illustrations. Crown 8vo. 14s.

BELT (Thos.). Naturalist in Nicaragua, including a Residence at the Gold Mines of Chontales; with Journeys in the Savannahs and Forests; and Observations on Animals and Plants. Illustrations. Post 8vo. 12s.

BERTRAM (Jas. G.). Harvest of the Sea: an Account of British Food Fishes, including sketches of Fisheries and Fisher Folk. With 50 Illustrations. 8vo. 9s.

BIBLE COMMENTARY. Explanatory and Critical. With a Revision of the Translation. By BISHOPS and CLERGY of the ANGLICAN CHURCH. Edited by F. C. Cook, M.A., Canon of Exeter. Vols. I. to VI. (The Old Testament). Medium 8vo. 6l. 15s.

| Vol. I. 30s. | Genesis. Exodus. Leviticus. Numbers. Deuteronomy. | Vol. IV. 24s. | Job. Psalms. Proverbs. Ecclesiastes. Song of Solomon. |
| Vols. II. and III. 36s. | Joshua, Judges, Ruth, Samuel, Kings, Chronicles, Ezra, Nehemiah, Esther. | Vol. V. 20s. Vol. VI. 25s. | Isaiah. Jeremiah. Ezekiel. Daniel. Minor Prophets. |

BIGG-WITHER (T. P.). Pioneering in S. Brazil; three years of forest and prairie life in the province of Parana. Map and Illustrations. 8vo. [*In the Press.*

BIRCH (Samuel). History of Ancient Pottery and Porcelain: Egyptian, Assyrian, Greek, Roman, and Etruscan. With Coloured Plates and 200 Illustrations. Medium 8vo. 42s.

BIRD (Isabella). Hawaiian Archipelago; or Six Months among the Palm Groves, Coral Reefs, and Volcanoes of the Sandwich Islands. With Illustrations. Crown 8vo. 7s. 6d.

BISSET (General). Sport and War in South Africa from 1834 to 1867, with a Narrative of the Duke of Edinburgh's Visit. With Map and Illustrations. Crown 8vo. 14s.

BLACKSTONE'S COMMENTARIES; adapted to the Present State of the Law. By R. Malcolm Kerr, LL.D. *Revised Edition,* incorporating all the Recent Changes in the Law. 4 vols. 8vo. 60s.

BLUNT (Rev. J. J.). Undesigned Coincidences in the Writings of the Old and New Testaments, an Argument of their Veracity: containing the Books of Moses, Historical and Prophetical Scriptures, and the Gospels and Acts. Post 8vo. 6s.

────── History of the Church in the First Three Centuries. Post 8vo. 6s.

────── Parish Priest; His Duties, Acquirements and Obligations. Post 8vo. 6s.

────── Lectures on the Right Use of the Early Fathers. 8vo. 9s.

────── University Sermons. Post 8vo. 6s.

────── Plain Sermons. 2 vols. Post 8vo. 12s.

BLOMFIELD'S (Bishop) Memoir, with Selections from his Correspondence. By his Son. Portrait, post 8vo. 12s.

BOSWELL'S (JAMES) Life of Samuel Johnson, LL.D. Including the Tour to the Hebrides. Edited by Mr. CROKER. *Seventh Edition.* Portraits. 1 vol. Medium 8vo. 12s.

BRACE (C. L.) Manual of Ethnology; or the Races of the Old World. Post 8vo. 6s.

BOOK OF COMMON PRAYER. Illustrated with Coloured Borders, Initial Letters, and Woodcuts. 8vo. 18s.

BORROW (GEORGE) Bible in Spain; or the Journeys, Adventures, and Imprisonments of an Englishman in an Attempt to circulate the Scriptures in the Peninsula. Post 8vo. 5s.

———— Gypsies of Spain; their Manners, Customs, Religion, and Language. With Portrait. Post 8vo. 5s.

———— Lavengro; The Scholar—The Gypsy—and the Priest. Post 8vo. 5s.

———— Romany Rye—a Sequel to "Lavengro." Post 8vo. 5s.

———— WILD WALES: its People, Language, and Scenery. Post 8vo. 5s.

———— Romano Lavo-Lil; Word-Book of the Romany, or English Gypsy Language; with Specimens of their Poetry, and an account of certain Gypsyries. Post 8vo. 10s. 6d.

BRAY (MRS.) Life of Thomas Stothard, R.A. With Portrait and 60 Woodcuts. 4to. 21s.

BRITISH ASSOCIATION REPORTS. 8vo.

York and Oxford, 1831-32, 13s. 6d.
Cambridge, 1833, 12s.
Edinburgh, 1834, 15s.
Dublin, 1835, 13s. 6d.
Bristol, 1836, 12s.
Liverpool, 1837, 16s. 6d.
Newcastle, 1838, 15s.
Birmingham, 1839, 13s. 6d.
Glasgow, 1840, 15s.
Plymouth, 1841, 13s. 6d.
Manchester, 1842, 10s. 6d.
Cork, 1843, 12s.
York, 1844, 20s.
Cambridge, 1845, 12s.
Southampton, 1846, 15s.
Oxford, 1847, 18s.
Swansea, 1848, 9s.
Birmingham, 1849, 10s.
Edinburgh, 1850, 15s.
Ipswich, 1851, 16s. 6d.
Belfast, 1852, 15s.
Hull, 1853, 10s. 6d.
Liverpool, 1854, 18s.
Glasgow, 1855, 15s.
Cheltenham, 1856, 18s.
Dublin, 1857, 15s.
Leeds, 1858, 20s.
Aberdeen, 1859, 15s.
Oxford, 1860, 25s.
Manchester, 1861, 15s.
Cambridge, 1862, 20s.
Newcastle, 1863, 25s.
Bath, 1864, 18s.
Birmingham, 1865, 25s.
Nottingham, 1866, 24s.
Dundee, 1867, 26s.
Norwich, 1868, 25s.
Exeter, 1869, 22s.
Liverpool, 1870, 18s.
Edinburgh, 1871, 16s.
Brighton, 1872, 24s.
Bradford, 1873, 25s.
Belfast, 1874. 2)s.
Bristol, 1875, 25s.
Glasgow, 1876, 25s.

BROUGHTON (LORD) Journey through Albania, Turkey in Europe and Asia, to Constantinople. Illustrations. 2 Vols. 8vo. 30s.

———— Visits to Italy. 2 Vols. Post 8vo. 18s.

BRUGSCH (PROFESSOR) History of Egypt, from the earliest period. Derived from Monuments and Inscriptions. *New Edition.* Translated by H. DANBY SEYMOUR. 2 vols. 8vo. [*In Preparation.*

BUCKLEY (ARABELLA B.) Short History of Natural Science, and the Progress of Discovery from the time of the Greeks to the present day, for Schools and young Persons. Illustrations. Post 8vo. 9s.

BURGON (REV. J. W.). Christian Gentleman; or, Memoir of Patrick Fraser Tytler. Post 8vo. 9s.

———— Letters from Rome. Post 8vo. 12s.

BURN (Col.). Dictionary of Naval and Military Technical Terms, English and French—French and English. Crown 8vo. 15s.

BUXTON'S (Charles) Memoirs of Sir Thomas Fowell Buxton, Bart. With Selections from his Correspondence. Portrait. 8vo. 16s. *Popular Edition.* Fcap. 8vo. 5s.

—————— Ideas of the Day. 8vo. 5s.

BURCKHARDT'S (Dr. Jacob) Cicerone; or Art Guide to Painting in Italy. Edited by Rev. Dr. A. Von Zahn, and Translated from the German by Mrs. A. Clough. Post 8vo. 6s.

BYLES' (Sir John) Foundations of Religion in the Mind and Heart of Man. Post 8vo. 6s.

BYRON'S (Lord) Life, Letters, and Journals. By Thomas Moore. *Cabinet Edition.* Plates. 6 Vols. Fcap. 8vo. 18s.; or One Volume, Portraits. Royal 8vo., 7s. 6d.

—————— and Poetical Works. *Popular Edition.* Portraits. 2 vols. Royal 8vo. 15s.

—— Poetical Works. *Library Edition.* Portrait. 6 Vols. 8vo. 45s.

—————— *Cabinet Edition.* Plates. 10 Vols. 12mo. 30s.
—————— *Pocket Edition.* 8 Vols. 24mo. 21s. *In a case.*
—————— *Popular Edition.* Plates. Royal 8vo. 7s. 6d.
—————— *Pearl Edition.* Crown 8vo. 2s. 6d.

—————— Childe Harold. With 80 Engravings. Crown 8vo. 12s.
—————————————————— 16mo. 2s. 6d.
—————————————————— Vignettes. 16mo. 1s.
—————————————————— Portrait. 16mo. 6d.

—————— Tales and Poems. 24mo. 2s. 6d.
—————— Miscellaneous. 2 Vols. 24mo. 5s.
—————— Dramas and Plays. 2 Vols. 24mo. 5s.
—————— Don Juan and Beppo. 2 Vols. 24mo. 5s.
—————— Beauties. Poetry and Prose. Portrait. Fcap. 8vo. 3s. 6d.

BUTTMAN'S Lexilogus; a Critical Examination of the Meaning of numerous Greek Words, chiefly in Homer and Hesiod. By Rev. J. R. Fishlake. 8vo. 12s.

—————— Irregular Greek Verbs. With all the Tenses extant—their Formation, Meaning, and Usage, with Notes, by Rev. J. R. Fishlake. Post 8vo. 6s.

CALLCOTT (Lady). Little Arthur's History of England. *New Edition,* brought down to 1872. With Woodcuts. Fcap. 8vo. 1s. 6d.

CARNARVON (Lord). Portugal, Gallicia, and the Basque Provinces. Post 8vo. 3s. 6d.

CARTWRIGHT (W. C.). The Jesuits: their Constitution and Teaching. An Historical Sketch. 8vo. 9s.

CASTLEREAGH (The) Despatches, from the commencement of the official career of Viscount Castlereagh to the close of his life. 12 Vols. 8vo. 14s. each.

CAMPBELL (Lord). Lord Chancellors and Keepers of the Great Seal of England. From the Earliest Times to the Death of Lord Eldon in 1838. 10 Vols. Crown 8vo. 6s. each.

—————— Chief Justices of England. From the Norman Conquest to the Death of Lord Tenterden. 4 Vols. Crown 8vo. 6s. each.

PUBLISHED BY MR. MURRAY.   7

CAMPBELL (LORD). Lives of Lyndhurst and Brougham. 8vo. 16s.
——————— Shakspeare's Legal Acquirements. 8vo. 5s. 6d.
——————— Lord Bacon. Fcap. 8vo. 2s. 6d.
——————— (SIR GEORGE) India as it may be: an Outline of a proposed Government and Policy. 8vo. 12s.
——————— Handy-Book on the Eastern Question; being a Very Recent View of Turkey. With Map. Post 8vo. 9s.
——————— (THOS.) Essay on English Poetry. With Short Lives of the British Poets. Post 8vo. 3s. 6d.
CAVALCASELLE AND CROWE'S History of Painting in NORTH ITALY, from the 14th to the 16th Century. With Illustrations. 2 Vols. 8vo. 42s.
——————— Early Flemish Painters, their Lives and Works. Illustrations. Post 8vo. 10s. 6d.; or Large Paper, 8vo. 15s.
——————— Life and Times of Titian, with some Account of his Family. With Portrait and Illustrations. 2 vols. 8vo. 42s.
CESNOLA (GEN. L. P. DI). Cyprus; its Ancient Cities, Tombs, and Temples. A Narrative of Researches and Excavations during Ten Years' Residence in that Island. With numerous Illustrations. Medium 8vo. [In Preparation.
CHILD (G. CHAPLIN, M.D.). Benedicite; or, Song of the Three Children; being Illustrations of the Power, Beneficence, and Design manifested by the Creator in his works. Post 8vo. 6s.
CHISHOLM (Mrs.). Perils of the Polar Seas; True Stories of Arctic Discovery and Adventure. Illustrations. Post 8vo. 6s.
CHURTON (ARCHDEACON). Poetical Remains, Translations and Imitations. Portrait. Post 8vo. 7s. 6d.
——————— New Testament. Edited with a Plain Practical Commentary for Families and General Readers. With 100 Panoramic and other Views, from Sketches made on the Spot. 2 vols. 8vo. 21s.
CICERO'S LIFE AND TIMES. His Character as a Statesman, Orator, and Friend, with a Selection from his Correspondence and Orations. By WILLIAM FORSYTH. With Illustrations. 8vo. 10s. 6d.
CLARK (SIR JAMES). Memoir of Dr. John Conolly. Comprising a Sketch of the Treatment of the Insane in Europe and America. With Portrait. Post 8vo. 10s. 6d.
CLIVE'S (LORD) Life. By REV. G. R. GLEIG. Post 8vo. 3s. 6d.
CLODE (C. M.). Military Forces of the Crown; their Administration and Government. 2 Vols. 8vo. 21s. each.
——————— Administration of Justice under Military and Martial Law, as applicable to the Army, Navy, Marine, and Auxiliary Forces. 8vo. 12s.
CHURCH (THE) & THE AGE. Essays on the Principles and Present Position of the Anglican Church. By various Authors. 2 vols. 8vo. 26s.
COLCHESTER (THE) Papers. The Diary and Correspondence of Charles Abbott, Lord Colchester, Speaker of the House of Commons. 1802-1817. Portrait. 3 Vols. 8vo. 42s.
COLERIDGE'S (SAMUEL TAYLOR) Table-Talk. Portrait. 12mo. 3s. 6d.
COLLINGWOOD (CUTHBERT). Rambles of a Naturalist on the Shores and Waters of the China Sea. With Illustrations. 8vo. 16s.
COLONIAL LIBRARY. [See Home and Colonial Library.]

COMPANIONS FOR THE DEVOUT LIFE. Lectures delivered in St. James's Church. 1st Series, 1875. 2nd Series, 1876. New Edition in 1 vol., post 8vo. [*In the Press.*

COOK (Canon). Sermons Preached at Lincoln's Inn. 8vo. 9s.

COOKE (E. W.). Leaves from my Sketch-Book. Being a selection from sketches made during many tours. 25 Plates. Small folio. 31s. 6d.

────── A Second Series of Leaves from my Sketch Book. Consisting chiefly of Views in Egypt and the East. With Descriptive Text. Small folio. [*In the Press.*

COOKERY (MODERN DOMESTIC). Founded on Principles of Economy and Practical Knowledge. By a Lady. Woodcuts. Fcap. 8vo. 5s.

COOPER (T. T.). Travels of a Pioneer of Commerce on an Overland Journey from China towards India. Illustrations. 8vo. 16s.

CORNWALLIS (THE) Papers and Correspondence during the American War,—Administrations in India,—Union with Ireland, and Peace of Amiens. 3 Vols. 8vo. 63s.

COWPER'S (COUNTESS) Diary while Lady of the Bedchamber to Caroline, Princess of Wales, 1714—20. Portrait. 8vo. 10s. 6d.

CRABBE (REV. GEORGE). Life and Poetical Works. With Illustrations. Royal 8vo. 7s.

CRAWFORD & BALCARRES (Earl of). Etruscan Inscriptions. Analyzed, Translated, and Commented upon. 8vo. 12s.

────── Argo; or the Quest of the Golden Fleece. A Metrical Tale, in Ten Books. 8vo. 10s. 6d.

CROKER (J. W.). Progressive Geography for Children. 18mo. 1s. 6d.

────── Stories for Children, Selected from the History of England. Woodcuts. 16mo. 2s. 6d.

────── Boswell's Life of Johnson. Including the Tour to the Hebrides. *Seventh Edition.* Portraits. 8vo. 12s.

────── Early Period of the French Revolution. 8vo. 15s.

────── Historical Essay on the Guillotine. Fcap. 8vo. 1s.

CROWE AND CAVALCASELLE. Lives of the Early Flemish Painters. Woodcuts. Post 8vo, 10s. 6d.; or Large Paper, 8vo, 15s.

────── History of Painting in North Italy, from 14th to 16th Century. Derived from Researches into the Works of Art in that Country. With Illustrations. 2 Vols. 8vo. 42s.

────── Life and Times of Titian, with some Account of his Family, chiefly from new and unpublished records. With Portrait and Illustrations. 2 vols. 8vo. 42s.

CUMMING (R. GORDON). Five Years of a Hunter's Life in the Far Interior of South Africa. Woodcuts. Post 8vo. 6s.

CUNYNGHAME (SIR ARTHUR). Travels in the Eastern Caucasus, on the Caspian and Black Seas, in Daghestan and the Frontiers of Persia and Turkey. With Map and Illustrations. 8vo. 18s.

CURTIUS' (PROFESSOR) Student's Greek Grammar, for the Upper Forms. Edited by DR. WM. SMITH. Post 8vo. 6s.

────── Elucidations of the above Grammar. Translated by EVELYN ABBOT. Post 8vo. 7s. 6d.

────── Smaller Greek Grammar for the Middle and Lower Forms. Abridged from the larger work. 12mo. 3s. 6d.

────── Accidence of the Greek Language. Extracted from the above work. 12mo. 2s. 6d.

────── Principles of Greek Etymology. Translated by A. S. WILKINS, M.A., and E. B. ENGLAND, B.A. 2 vols. 8vo. 15s. each.

CURZON (Hon. Robert). Visits to the Monasteries of the Levant. Illustrations. Post 8vo. 7s. 6d.

CUST (General). Warriors of the 17th Century—The Thirty Years' War. 2 Vols. 16s. Civil Wars of France and England. 2 Vols. 16s. Commanders of Fleets and Armies. 2 Vols. 18s.

—————— Annals of the Wars—18th & 19th Century, 1700—1815. With Maps. 9 Vols. Post 8vo. 5s. each.

DAVIS (Nathan). Ruined Cities of Numidia and Carthaginia. Illustrations. 8vo. 16s.

DAVY (Sir Humphry). Consolations in Travel; or, Last Days of a Philosopher. Woodcuts. Fcap. 8vo 3s. 6d.

—————— Salmonia; or, Days of Fly Fishing. Woodcuts. Fcap. 8vo. 3s. 6d.

DARWIN (Charles). Journal of a Naturalist during a Voyage round the World. Crown 8vo. 9s.

—————— Origin of Species by Means of Natural Selection; or, the Preservation of Favoured Races in the Struggle for Life. Crown 8vo. 7s. 6d.

—————— Variation of Animals and Plants under Domestication. With Illustrations. 2 Vols. Crown 8vo. 18s.

—————— Descent of Man, and Selection in Relation to Sex. With Illustrations. Crown 8vo. 9s.

—————— Expressions of the Emotions in Man and Animals. With Illustrations. Crown 8vo. 12s.

—————— Various Contrivances by which Orchids are Fertilized by Insects. Woodcuts. Crown 8vo. 9s.

—————— Movements and Habits of Climbing Plants. Woodcuts. Crown 8vo. 6s.

—————— Insectivorous Plants. Woodcuts. Crown 8vo. 14s.

—————— Effects of Cross and Self-Fertilization in the Vegetable Kingdom. Crown 8vo. 12s.

—————— Facts and Argument for Darwin. By Fritz Muller. Translated by W. S. Dallas. Woodcuts. Post 8vo. 6s.

—————— Different Forms of Flowers on Plants of the same Species. Crown 8vo. 10s. 6d.

DE COSSON (E. A.). The Cradle of the Blue Nile; a Journey through Abyssinia and Soudan, and a residence at the Court of King John of Ethiopia. Map and Illustrations. 2 vols. Post 8vo. 21s.

DELEPIERRE (Octave). History of Flemish Literature. 8vo. 9s.

DENNIS (George). The Cities and Cemeteries of Etruria. An entirely new Edition, with a new Chapter on Etrurian Bologna. Numerous Illustrations. 2 vols. 8vo. [In the Press.

DENT (Emma). Annals of Winchcombe and Sudeley. With 120 Portraits, Plates and Woodcuts. 4to. 42s.

DERBY (Earl of). Iliad of Homer rendered into English Blank Verse. 10th Edition. With Portrait. 2 Vols. Post 8vo. 10s.

DERRY (Bishop of). Witness of the Psalms to Christ and Christianity. The Bampton Lectures for 1876. 8vo. 10s. 6d.

DEUTSCH (Emanuel). Talmud, Islam, The Targums and other Literary Remains. 8vo. 12s.

DILKE (Sir C. W.). Papers of a Critic. Selected from the Writings of the late Chas. Wentworth Dilke. With a Biographical Sketch. 2 Vols. 8vo. 24s.

DOG-BREAKING, with Odds and Ends for those who love the Dog and Gun. By Gen. Hutchinson. With 40 Illustrations. Crown 8vo. 7s. 6d.

DOMESTIC MODERN COOKERY. Founded on Principles of Economy and Practical Knowledge, and adapted for Private Families. Woodcuts. Fcap. 8vo. 5s.

DOUGLAS'S (Sir Howard) Life and Adventures. Portrait. 8vo. 15s.

——— Theory and Practice of Gunnery. Plates. 8vo. 21s.

——— Construction of Bridges and the Passage of Rivers in Military Operations. Plates. 8vo. 21s.

——— (Wm.) Horse-Shoeing; As it Is, and As it Should be. Illustrations. Post 8vo. 7s. 6d.

DRAKE'S (Sir Francis) Life, Voyages, and Exploits, by Sea and Land. By John Barrow. Post 8vo. 2s.

DRINKWATER (John). History of the Siege of Gibraltar, 1779-1783. With a Description and Account of that Garrison from the Earliest Periods. Post 8vo. 2s.

DUCANGE'S Mediæval Latin-English Dictionary. Translated and Edited by Rev. E. A. Dayman and J. H. Hessels. Small 4to.
[In preparation.

DU CHAILLU (Paul B.). Equatorial Africa, with Accounts of the Gorilla, the Nest-building Ape, Chimpanzee, Crocodile, &c. Illustrations. 8vo. 21s.

——— Journey to Ashango Land; and Further Penetration into Equatorial Africa. Illustrations. 8vo. 21s.

DUFFERIN (Lord). Letters from High Latitudes; a Yacht Voyage to Iceland, Jan Mayen, and Spitzbergen. Woodcuts. Post 8vo. 7s. 6d.

DUNCAN (Major). History of the Royal Artillery. Compiled from the Original Records. With Portraits. 2 Vols. 8vo. 30s.

——— The English in Spain; or, The Story of the Civil War between Christinos and Carlists in 1834 and 1840. Compiled from the Letters, Journals, and Reports of the British Commissioners with Queen Isabella's Armies. With Plates. 8vo.

EASTLAKE (Sir Charles). Contributions to the Literature of the Fine Arts. With Memoir of the Author, and Selections from his Correspondence. By Lady Eastlake. 2 Vols. 8vo. 24s.

EDWARDS' (W. H.) Voyage up the River Amazons, including a Visit to Para. Post 8vo. 2s.

EIGHT MONTHS AT ROME, during the Vatican Council, with a Daily Account of the Proceedings. By Pomponio Leto. Translated from the Original. 8vo. 12s.

ELDON'S (Lord) Public and Private Life, with Selections from his Correspondence and Diaries. By Horace Twiss. Portrait. 2 Vols. Post 8vo. 21s.

ELGIN'S (Lord) Letters and Journals. Edited by Theodore Walrond. With Preface by Dean Stanley. 8vo. 14s.

ELLESMERE (Lord). Two Sieges of Vienna by the Turks. Translated from the German. Post 8vo. 2s.

ELLIS (W.). Madagascar Revisited. Setting forth the Persecutions and Heroic Sufferings of the Native Christians. Illustrations. 8vo. 16s.

——— Memoir. By His Son. With his Character and Work. By Rev. Henry Allon, D.D. Portrait. 8vo. 10s. 6d.

——— (Robinson) Poems and Fragments of Catullus. 16mo. 5s.

ELPHINSTONE (Hon. Mountstuart). History of India—the Hindoo and Mahomedan Periods. Edited by Professor Cowell. Map. 8vo. 18s.

——— (H. W.) Patterns for Turning; Comprising Elliptical and other Figures cut on the Lathe without the use of any Ornamental Chuck. With 70 Illustrations. Small 4to. 15s.

ENGLAND. See Callcott, Croker, Hume, Markham, Smith, and Stanhope.

ESSAYS ON CATHEDRALS. With an Introduction. By Dean Howson. 8vo. 12s.

ELZE (Karl). Life of Lord Byron. With a Critical Essay on his Place in Literature. Translated from the German. With Portrait. 8vo. 16s.

FERGUSSON (James). History of Architecture in all Countries from the Earliest Times. With 1,600 Illustrations. 4 Vols. Medium 8vo.
Vol. I. & II. Ancient and Mediæval. 63s.
Vol. III. Indian and Eastern. 42s.
Vol. IV. Modern. 31s. 6d.

——— Rude Stone Monuments in all Countries; their Age and Uses. With 230 Illustrations. Medium 8vo. 24s.

——— Holy Sepulchre and the Temple at Jerusalem. Woodcuts. 8vo. 7s. 6d.

FLEMING (Professor). Student's Manual of Moral Philosophy. With Quotations and References. Post 8vo. 7s. 6d.

FLOWER GARDEN. By Rev. Thos. James. Fcap. 8vo. 1s.

FORD (Richard). Gatherings from Spain. Post 8vo. 3s. 6d.

FORSYTH (William). Life and Times of Cicero. With Selections from his Correspondence and Orations. Illustrations. 8vo. 10s. 6d.

——— Hortensius; an Historical Essay on the Office and Duties of an Advocate. Illustrations. 8vo. 12s.

——— History of Ancient Manuscripts. Post 8vo. 2s. 6d.

——— Novels and Novelists of the 18th Century, in Illustration of the Manners and Morals of the Age. Post 8vo. 10s. 6d.

——— The Slavonic Provinces South of the Danube; a Sketch of their History and Present State. Map. Post 8vo. 5s.

FORTUNE (Robert). Narrative of Two Visits to the Tea Countries of China, 1843-52. Woodcuts. 2 Vols. Post 8vo. 18s.

FORSTER (John). The Early Life of Jonathan Swift. 1667-1711. With Portrait. 8vo. 15s.

FOSS (Edward). Biographia Juridica, or Biographical Dictionary of the Judges of England, from the Conquest to the Present Time, 1066-1870. Medium 8vo. 21s.

FRANCE (History of). See Markham—Smith—Student's.

FRENCH (The) in Algiers; The Soldier of the Foreign Legion—and the Prisoners of Abd-el-Kadir. Translated by Lady Duff Gordon. Post 8vo. 2s.

FRERE (Sir Bartle). Indian Missions. Small 8vo. 2s. 6d.

——— Eastern Africa as a field for Missionary Labour. With Map. Crown 8vo. 5s.

——— Bengal Famine. How it will be Met and How to Prevent Future Famines in India. With Maps. Crown 8vo. 5s.

GALTON (FRANCIS). Art of Travel; or, Hints on the Shifts and Contrivances available in Wild Countries. Woodcuts. Post 8vo. 7s. 6d.

GEOGRAPHICAL SOCIETY'S JOURNAL. (*Published Yearly.*)

GEORGE (ERNEST). The Mósel; a Series of Twenty Etchings, with Descriptive Letterpress. Imperial 4to. 42s.

—— Loire and South of France; a Series of Twenty Etchings, with Descriptive Text. Folio. 42s.

GERMANY (HISTORY OF). See MARKHAM.

GIBBON (EDWARD). History of the Decline and Fall of the Roman Empire. Edited by MILMAN and GUIZOT. Edited, with Notes, by Dr. WM. SMITH. Maps. 8 Vols. 8vo. 60s.

—— (The Student's Gibbon); Being an Epitome of the above work, incorporating the Researches of Recent Commentators. By Dr. WM. SMITH. Woodcuts. Post 8vo. 7s. 6d.

GIFFARD (EDWARD). Deeds of Naval Daring; or, Anecdotes of the British Navy. Fcap. 8vo. 3s. 6d.

GLADSTONE (W. E.). Financial Statements of 1853, 1860, 63-65. 8vo. 12s.

—— Rome and the Newest Fashions in Religion. Three Tracts. 8vo. 7s. 6d.

GLEIG (G. R.). Campaigns of the British Army at Washington and New Orleans. Post 8vo. 2s.

—— Story of the Battle of Waterloo. Post 8vo. 3s. 6d.

—— Narrative of Sale's Brigade in Affghanistan. Post 8vo. 2s.

—— Life of Lord Clive. Post 8vo. 3s. 6d.

—— Sir Thomas Munro. Post 8vo. 3s. 6d.

GLYNNE (SIR STEPHEN). Notes on the Churches of Kent. With Illustrations. 8vo. [*In Preparation.*

GOLDSMITH'S (OLIVER) Works. Edited with Notes by PETER CUNNINGHAM. Vignettes. 4 Vols. 8vo. 30s.

GORDON (SIR ALEX.). Sketches of German Life, and Scenes from the War of Liberation. Post 8vo. 3s. 6d.

—— (LADY DUFF) Amber-Witch: A Trial for Witchcraft. Post 8vo. 2s.

—— French in Algiers. 1. The Soldier of the Foreign Legion. 2. The Prisoners of Abd-el-Kadir. Post 8vo. 2s.

GRAMMARS. See CURTIUS; HALL; HUTTON; KING EDWARD; ATTHIÆ; MAETZNER; SMITH.

GREECE (HISTORY OF). *See* GROTE—SMITH—Student.

GREY (EARL). Parliamentary Government and Reform; with Suggestions for the Improvement of our Representative System. *Second Edition.* 8vo. 9s.

GUIZOT (M.). Meditations on Christianity. 3 Vols. Post 8vo. 30s.

GROTE (GEORGE). History of Greece. From the Earliest Times to the close of the generation contemporary with the death of Alexander the Great. *Library Edition.* Portrait, Maps, and Plans. 10 Vols. 8vo. 120s. *Cabinet Edition.* Portrait and Plans. 12 Vols. Post 8vo. 6s. each.

—— PLATO, and other Companions of Socrates. 3 Vols. 8vo. 45s.

GROTE (George). ARISTOTLE. 2 Vols. 8vo. 32s.

——— Minor Works. With Critical Remarks on his Intellectual Character, Writings, and Speeches. By ALEX. BAIN, LL.D. Portrait. 8vo. 14s.

——— Fragments on Ethical Subjects. Being a Selection from his Posthumous Papers. With an Introduction. By ALEXANDER BAIN, M.A. 8vo. 7s.

——— Letters on the Politics of Switzerland in 1847. 6s.

——— Personal Life. Compiled from Family Documents, Private Memoranda, and Original Letters to and from Various Friends. By Mrs. GROTE. Portrait. 8vo. 12s.

HALL (T. D.) AND Dr. WM. SMITH'S School Manual of English Grammar. With Copious Exercises. 12mo. 3s. 6d.

——— Primary English Grammar for Elementary Schools. Based on the above work. 16mo. 1s.

——— Child's First Latin Book, including a Systematic Treatment of the New Pronunciation, and a full Praxis of Nouns, Adjectives, and Pronouns. 16mo. 1s. 6d.

HALLAM (HENRY). Constitutional History of England, from the Accession of Henry the Seventh to the Death of George the Second. *Library Edition.* 3 Vols. 8vo. 30s. *Cabinet Edition.* 3 Vols. Post 8vo. 12s.

——— Student's Edition of the above work. Edited by WM. SMITH, D.C.L. Post 8vo. 7s. 6d.

——— History of Europe during the Middle Ages. *Library Edition.* 3 Vols. 8vo. 30s. *Cabinet Edition,* 3 Vols. Post 8vo. 12s.

——— Student's Edition of the above work. Edited by WM. SMITH, D.C.L. Post 8vo. 7s. 6d.

——— Literary History of Europe, during the 15th, 16th and 17th Centuries. *Library Edition.* 3 Vols. 8vo. 36s. *Cabinet Edition.* 4 Vols. Post 8vo. 16s.

——— (ARTHUR) Literary Remains; in Verse and Prose. Portrait. Fcap. 8vo. 3s. 6d.

HAMILTON (GEN. SIR F. W.). History of the Grenadier Guards. From Original Documents in the Rolls' Records, War Office, Regimental Records, &c. With Illustrations. 3 Vols. 8vo. 63s.

HART'S ARMY LIST. (*Published Quarterly and Annually.*)

HAY (SIR J. H. DRUMMOND). Western Barbary, its Wild Tribes and Savage Animals. Post 8vo. 2s.

HEAD (SIR FRANCIS). Royal Engineer. Illustrations. 8vo. 12s.

——— Life of Sir John Burgoyne. Post 8vo. 1s.

——— Rapid Journeys across the Pampas. Post 8vo. 2s.

——— Bubbles from the Brunnen of Nassau. Illustrations. Post 8vo. 7s. 6d.

——— Stokers and Pokers; or, the London and North Western Railway. Post 8vo. 2s.

——— (SIR EDMUND) Shall and Will; or, Future Auxiliary Verbs. Fcap. 8vo. 4s.

HEBER'S (BISHOP) Journals in India. 2 Vols. Post 8vo. 7s.

——— Poetical Works. Portrait. Fcap. 8vo. 3s. 6d.

——— Hymns adapted to the Church Service. 16mo. 1s. 6d.

FOREIGN HANDBOOKS.

HAND-BOOK—TRAVEL-TALK. English, French, German, and Italian. 18mo. 3s. 6d.

——— HOLLAND AND BELGIUM. Map and Plans. Post 8vo. 6s.

——— NORTH GERMANY and THE RHINE,— The Black Forest, the Hartz, Thüringerwald, Saxon Switzerland, Rügen the Giant Mountains, Taunus, Odenwald, Elass, and Lothringen. Map and Plans. Post 8vo. 10s.

——— SOUTH GERMANY,— Wurtemburg, Bavaria, Austria, Styria, Salzburg, the Austrian and Bavarian Alps, Tyrol, Hungary, and the Danube, from Ulm to the Black Sea. Map. Post 8vo. 10s.

——— PAINTING. German, Flemish, and Dutch Schools. Illustrations. 2 Vols. Post 8vo. 24s.

——— LIVES OF EARLY FLEMISH PAINTERS. By CROWE and CAVALCASELLE. Illustrations. Post 8vo. 10s. 6d.

——— SWITZERLAND, Alps of Savoy, and Piedmont. Maps. Post 8vo. 9s.

——— FRANCE, Part I. Normandy, Brittany, the French Alps, the Loire, the Seine, the Garonne, and Pyrenees. Post 8vo. 7s. 6d.

——— Part II. Central France, Auvergne, the Cevennes, Burgundy, the Rhone and Saone, Provence, Nimes, Arles, Marseilles, the French Alps, Alsace, Lorraine, Champagne, &c. Maps. Post 8vo. 7s. 6d.

——— MEDITERRANEAN ISLANDS—Malta, Corsica, Sardinia, and Sicily. Maps. Post 8vo. [In the Press.

——— ALGERIA. Algiers, Constantine, Oran, the Atlas Range. Map. Post 8vo. 9s.

——— PARIS, and its Environs. Map. 16mo. 3s. 6d.
*** MURRAY'S PLAN OF PARIS, mounted on canvas. 3s. 6d.

——— SPAIN, Madrid, The Castiles, The Basque Provinces, Leon, The Asturias, Galicia, Extremadura, Andalusia, Ronda, Granada, Murcia, Valencia, Catalonia, Aragon, Navarre, The Balearic Islands, &c. &c. Maps. 2 Vols. Post 8vo. 24s.

——— PORTUGAL, LISBON, Porto, Cintra, Mafra, &c. Map. Post 8vo. 12s.

——— NORTH ITALY, Turin, Milan, Cremona, the Italian Lakes, Bergamo, Brescia, Verona, Mantua, Vicenza, Padua, Ferrara, Bologna, Ravenna, Rimini, Piacenza, Genoa, the Riviera, Venice, Parma, Modena, and Romagna. Map. Post 8vo. 10s.

——— CENTRAL ITALY, Florence, Lucca, Tuscany, The Marches, Umbria, and late Patrimony of St. Peter's. Map. Post 8vo. 10s.

——— ROME AND ITS ENVIRONS. Map. Post 8vo. 10s.

——— SOUTH ITALY, Two Sicilies, Naples, Pompeii, Herculaneum, and Vesuvius. Map. Post 8vo. 10s.

——— KNAPSACK GUIDE TO ITALY. 16mo.

——— PAINTING. The Italian Schools. Illustrations. 2 Vols. Post 8vo. 30s.

——— LIVES OF ITALIAN PAINTERS, FROM CIMABUE to BASSANO. By MRS. JAMESON. Portraits. Post 8vo. 12s.

——— NORWAY, Christiania, Bergen, Trondhjem. The Fjelds and Fjords. Map. Post 8vo. 9s.

——— SWEDEN, Stockholm, Upsala, Gothenburg, the Shores of the Baltic, &c. Post 8vo. 8s.

——— DENMARK, Sleswig, Holstein, Copenhagen, Jutland, Iceland. Map. Post 8vo. 6s.

PUBLISHED BY MR. MURRAY.   15

HAND-BOOK—RUSSIA, St. Petersburg, Moscow, Poland, and Finland. Maps. Post 8vo. 18s.
———————— GREECE, the Ionian Islands, Continental Greece, Athens, the Peloponnesus, the Islands of the Ægean Sea, Albania, Thessaly, and Macedonia. Maps. Post 8vo. 15s.
———————— TURKEY IN ASIA—Constantinople, the Bosphorus, Dardanelles, Broussa, Plain of Troy. Crete, Cyprus, Smyrna, Ephesus, the Seven Churches, Coasts of the Black Sea, Armenia, Mesopotamia, &c. Maps. Post 8vo. 15s.
———————— EGYPT, including Descriptions of the Course of the Nile through Egypt and Nubia, Alexandria, Cairo, and Thebes, the Suez Canal, the Pyramids, the Peninsula of Sinai, the Oases, the Fyoom, &c. Map. Post 8vo. 15s.
———————— HOLY LAND—Syria, Palestine, Peninsula of Sinai Edom, Syrian Deserts, Petra, Damascus, and Palmyra. Maps. Post 8vo. 20s. *₊* Travelling Map of Palestine. In a case. 12s.
———————— INDIA — Bombay and Madras. Map. 2 Vols. Post 8vo. 12s. each.

ENGLISH HANDBOOKS.
HAND-BOOK—MODERN LONDON. Map. 16mo. 3s. 6d.
———————— ENVIRONS OF LONDON within a circuit of 20 miles. 2 Vols. Crown 8vo. 21s.
———————— EASTERN COUNTIES, Chelmsford, Harwich, Colchester, Maldon, Cambridge, Ely, Newmarket, Bury St. Edmunds, Ipswich, Woodbridge, Felixstowe, Lowestoft, Norwich, Yarmouth, Cromer, &c. Map and Plans. Post 8vo. 12s.
———————— CATHEDRALS of Oxford, Peterborough, Norwich, Ely, and Lincoln. With 90 Illustrations. Crown 8vo. 18s.
———————— KENT, Canterbury, Dover, Ramsgate, Sheerness, Rochester, Chatham, Woolwich. Map. Post 8vo. 7s. 6d.
———————— SUSSEX, Brighton, Chichester, Worthing, Hastings, Lewes, Arundel, &c. Map. Post 8vo. 6s.
———————— SURREY AND HANTS, Kingston, Croydon, Reigate, Guildford, Dorking, Boxhill, Winchester, Southampton, New Forest, Portsmouth, and Isle of Wight. Maps. Post 8vo. 10s.
———————— BERKS, BUCKS, AND OXON, Windsor, Eton, Reading, Aylesbury. Uxbridge, Wycombe, Henley, the City and University of Oxford, Blenheim, and the Descent of the Thames. Map. Post 8vo. 7s. 6d.
———————— WILTS, DORSET, AND SOMERSET, Salisbury, Chippenham, Weymouth, Sherborne, Wells, Bath, Bristol, Taunton, &c. Map. Post 8vo. 10s.
———————— DEVON AND CORNWALL, Exeter, Ilfracombe, Linton, Sidmouth, Dawlish, Teignmouth, Plymouth, Devonport, Torquay, Launceston, Truro, Penzance, Falmouth, the Lizard, Land's End, &c. Maps. Post 8vo. 12s.
———————— CATHEDRALS of Winchester, Salisbury, Exeter, Wells, Chichester, Rochester, Canterbury, and St. Albans. With 130 Illustrations. 2 Vols. Crown 8vo. 36s. St. Albans separately, crown 8vo. 6s.
———————— GLOUCESTER, HEREFORD, and WORCESTER, Cirencester, Cheltenham, Stroud, Tewkesbury, Leominster, Ross, Malvern, Kidderminster, Dudley, Bromsgrove, Evesham. Map. Post 8vo. 9s.
———————— CATHEDRALS of Bristol, Gloucester, Hereford, Worcester, and Lichfield. With 50 Illustrations. Crown 8vo. 16s.

LIST OF WORKS

HAND-BOOK—NORTH WALES, Bangor, Carnarvon, Beaumaris, Snowdon, Llanberis, Dolgelly, Cader Idris, Conway, &c. Map. Post 8vo. 7s.

———— SOUTH WALES, Monmouth, Llandaff, Merthyr, Vale of Neath, Pembroke, Carmarthen, Tenby, Swansea, The Wye, &c. Map. Post 8vo. 7s.

———— CATHEDRALS OF BANGOR, ST. ASAPH, Llandaff, and St. David's. With Illustrations. Post 8vo. 15s.

———— DERBY, NOTTS, LEICESTER, STAFFORD, Matlock, Bakewell, Chatsworth, The Peak, Buxton, Hardwick, Dove Dale, Ashborne, Southwell, Mansfield, Retford, Burton, Belvoir, Melton Mowbray, Wolverhampton, Lichfield, Walsall, Tamworth. Map. Post 8vo. 9s.

———— SHROPSHIRE, CHESHIRE AND LANCASHIRE —Shrewsbury, Ludlow, Bridgnorth, Oswestry, Chester, Crewe, Alderley, Stockport, Birkenhead, Warrington, Bury, Manchester, Liverpool, Burnley, Clitheroe, Bolton, Blackburn, Wigan, Preston, Rochdale, Lancaster, Southport, Blackpool, &c. Map. Post 8vo. 10s.

———— YORKSHIRE, Doncaster, Hull, Selby, Beverley, Scarborough, Whitby, Harrogate, Ripon, Leeds, Wakefield, Bradford, Halifax, Huddersfield, Sheffield. Map and Plans. Post 8vo. 12s.

———— CATHEDRALS of York, Ripon, Durham, Carlisle, Chester, and Manchester. With 60 Illustrations. 2 Vols. Crown 8vo. 21s.

———— DURHAM AND NORTHUMBERLAND, Newcastle, Darlington, Gateshead, Bishop Auckland, Stockton, Hartlepool, Sunderland, Shields, Berwick-on-Tweed, Morpeth, Tynemouth, Coldstream, Alnwick, &c. Map. Post 8vo. 9s.

———— WESTMORLAND AND CUMBERLAND—Lancaster, Furness Abbey, Ambleside, Kendal, Windermere, Coniston, Keswick, Grasmere, Ulswater, Carlisle, Cockermouth, Penrith, Appleby. Map. Post 8vo. 6s.

*** MURRAY'S MAP OF THE LAKE DISTRICT, on canvas. 3s. 6d.

———— ENGLAND AND WALES. Alphabetically arranged and condensed into one volume. Post 8vo. [*In the Press.*

———— SCOTLAND, Edinburgh, Melrose, Kelso, Glasgow, Dumfries, Ayr, Stirling, Arran, The Clyde, Oban, Inverary, Loch Lomond, Loch Katrine and Trossachs, Caledonian Canal, Inverness, Perth, Dundee, Aberdeen, Braemar, Skye, Caithness, Ross, Sutherland, &c. Maps and Plans. Post 8vo. 9s.

———— IRELAND, Dublin, Belfast, Donegal, Galway, Wexford, Cork, Limerick, Waterford, Killarney, Munster, &c. Maps. Post 8vo. 12s.

HERODOTUS. A New English Version. Edited, with Notes and Essays, historical, ethnographical, and geographical, by CANON RAWLINSON, assisted by SIR HENRY RAWLINSON and SIR J. G. WILKINSON. Maps and Woodcuts. 4 Vols. 8vo. 48s.

HERSCHEL'S (CAROLINE) Memoir and Correspondence. By MRS. JOHN HERSCHEL. With Portraits. Crown 8vo. 12s.

HATHERLEY (LORD). Continuity of Scripture, as Declared by the Testimony of our Lord and of the Evangelists and Apostles. 8vo. 6s. *Popular Edition.* Post 8vo. 2s. 6d.

HOLLWAY (J. G.). A Month in Norway. Fcap. 8vo. 2s.

HONEY BEE. By REV. THOMAS JAMES. Fcap. 8vo. 1s.

HOOK'S (DEAN) Church Dictionary. 8vo. 16s.

PUBLISHED BY MR. MURRAY. 17

HOME AND COLONIAL LIBRARY. A Series of Works adapted for all circles and classes of Readers, having been selected for their acknowledged interest, and ability of the Authors. Post 8vo. Published at 2s. and 3s. 6d. each, and arranged under two distinctive heads as follows:—

CLASS A.

HISTORY, BIOGRAPHY, AND HISTORIC TALES.

1. SIEGE OF GIBRALTAR. y JOHN DRINKWATER. 2s.
2. THE AMBER-WITCH. By LADY DUFF GORDON. 2s.
3. CROMWELL AND BUNYAN. By ROBERT SOUTHEY. 2s.
4. LIFE OF SIR FRANCIS DRAKE. By JOHN BARROW. 2s.
5. CAMPAIGNS AT WASHINGTON. By REV. G. R. GLEIG. 2s.
6. THE FRENCH IN ALGIERS. By LADY DUFF GORDON. 2s.
7. THE FALL OF THE JESUITS. 2s.
8. LIVONIAN TALES. 2s.
9. LIFE OF CONDÉ. By LORD MAHON. 3s. 6d.
10. SALE'S BRIGADE. By REV. G. R. GLEIG. 2s.
11. THE SIEGES OF VIENNA. By LORD ELLESMERE. 2s.
12. THE WAYSIDE CROSS. By CAPT. MILMAN. 2s.
13. SKETCHES OF GERMAN LIFE. By SIR A. GORDON. 3s. 6d.
14. THE BATTLE OF WATERLOO. By REV. G. R. GLEIG. 3s. 6d.
15. AUTOBIOGRAPHY OF STEFFENS. 2s.
16. THE BRITISH POETS. By THOMAS CAMPBELL. 3s. 6d.
17. HISTORICAL ESSAYS. By LORD MAHON. 3s. 6d.
18. LIFE OF LORD CLIVE. By REV. G. R. GLEIG. 3s. 6d.
19. NORTH - WESTERN RAILWAY. By SIR F. B. HEAD. 2s.
20. LIFE OF MUNRO. By REV. G. R. GLEIG. 3s. 6d.

CLASS B.

VOYAGES, TRAVELS, AND ADVENTURES.

1. BIBLE IN SPAIN. By GEORGE BORROW. 3s. 6d.
2. GYPSIES OF SPAIN. By GEORGE BORROW. 3s. 6d.
3 & 4. JOURNALS IN INDIA. By BISHOP HEBER. 2 Vols. 7s.
5. TRAVELS IN THE HOLY LAND. By IRBY and MANGLES. 2s.
6. MOROCCO AND THE MOORS. By J. DRUMMOND HAY. 2s.
7. LETTERS FROM THE BALTIC. By a LADY.
8. NEW SOUTH WALES. By MRS. MEREDITH. 2s.
9. THE WEST INDIES. By M. G. LEWIS. 2s.
10. SKETCHES OF PERSIA. By SIR JOHN MALCOLM. 3s. 6d.
11. MEMOIRS OF FATHER RIPA. 2s.
12 & 13. TYPEE AND OMOO. By HERMANN MELVILLE. 2 Vols. 7s.
14. MISSIONARY LIFE IN CANADA. By REV. J. ABBOTT. 2s.
15. LETTERS FROM MADRAS. By a LADY. 2s.
16. HIGHLAND SPORTS. By CHARLES ST. JOHN. 3s. 6d.
17. PAMPAS JOURNEYS. By SIR F. B. HEAD. 2s.
18. GATHERINGS FROM SPAIN. By RICHARD FORD. 3s. 6d.
19. THE RIVER AMAZON. By W. H. EDWARDS. 2s.
20. MANNERS & CUSTOMS OF INDIA. By REV. C. ACLAND. 2s.
21. ADVENTURES IN MEXICO. By G. F. RUXTON. 3s. 6d.
22. PORTUGAL AND GALICIA. By LORD CARNARVON. 3s. 6d.
23. BUSH LIFE IN AUSTRALIA. By REV. H. W. HAYGARTH. 2s.
24. THE LIBYAN DESERT. By BAYLE ST. JOHN. 2s.
25. SIERRA LEONE. By A LADY. 3s. 6d.

. Each work may be had separately.

c

HOOK'S (THEODORE) Life. By J. G. LOCKHART. Fcap. 8vo. 1s.

HOPE (T. C.). ARCHITECTURE OF AHMEDABAD, with Historical Sketch and Architectural Notes. With Maps, Photographs, and Woodcuts. 4to. 5l. 5s.

—————— (A. J. BERESFORD) Worship in the Church of England. 8vo. 9s., or, *Popular Selections from.* 8vo. 2s. 6d.

HORACE; a New Edition of the Text. Edited by DEAN MILMAN. With 100 Woodcuts. Crown 8vo. 7s. 6d.

—————— Life of. By DEAN MILMAN. Illustrations. 8vo. 9s.

HOUGHTON'S (LORD) Monographs, Personal and Social. With Portraits. Crown 8vo. 10s. 6d.

—————————— POETICAL WORKS. *Collected Edition.* With Portrait. 2 Vols. Fcap. 8vo. 12s.

HUME'S (The Student's) History of England, from the Invasion of Julius Cæsar to the Revolution of 1688. Corrected and continued to 1868 Woodcuts. Post 8vo. 7s. 6d.

HUTCHINSON (GEN.) Dog Breaking, with Odds and Ends for those who love the Dog and the Gun. With 40 Illustrations. 6th edition. 7s. 6d.

HUTTON (H. E.). Principia Græca; an Introduction to the Study of Greek. Comprehending Grammar, Delectus, and Exercise-book, with Vocabularies. *Sixth Edition.* 12mo. 3s. 6d.

IRBY AND MANGLES' Travels in Egypt, Nubia, Syria, and the Holy Land. Post 8vo. 2s.

JACOBSON (BISHOP). Fragmentary Illustrations of the History of the Book of Common Prayer; from Manuscript Sources (Bishop SANDERSON and Bishop WREN). 8vo. 5s.

JAMES' (REV. THOMAS) Fables of Æsop. A New Translation, with Historical Preface. With 100 Woodcuts by TENNIEL and WOLF. Post 8vo. 2s. 6d.

JAMESON (MRS.). Lives of the Early Italian Painters— and the Progress of Painting in Italy—Cimabue to Bassano. With 50 Portraits. Post 8vo. 12s.

JENNINGS (LOUIS J.). Field Paths and Green Lanes. Being Country Walks, chiefly in Surrey and Sussex. With Illustrations. Post 8vo. [*In the Press.*

JERVIS (REV. W. H.). Gallican Church, from the Concordat of Bologna, 1516, to the Revolution. With an Introduction. Portraits. 2 Vols. 8vo. 28s.

JESSE (EDWARD). Gleanings in Natural History. Fcp. 8vo. 3s. 6d.

JEX-BLAKE (REV. T. W.). Life in Faith: Sermons Preached at Cheltenham and Rugby. Fcap. 8vo. 3s. 6d.

JOHNS' (REV. B. G.) Blind People; their Works and Ways. With Sketches of the Lives of some famous Blind Men. With Illustrations. Post 8vo. 7s. 6d.

JOHNSON'S (DR. SAMUEL) Life. By James Boswell. Including the Tour to the Hebrides. Edited by MR. CROKER. *New Edition.* Portraits. 4 Vols. 8vo. [*In Preparation.*

—————— Lives of the most eminent English Poets, with Critical Observations on their Works. Edited with Notes, Corrective and Explanatory, by PETER CUNNINGHAM. 3 vols. 8vo. 22s. 6d.

JUNIUS' HANDWRITING Professionally investigated. By Mr. CHABOT, Expert. With Preface and Collateral Evidence, by the Hon. EDWARD TWISLETON. With Facsimiles, Woodcuts, &c. 4to. £3 3s.

KEN'S (BISHOP) Life. By a LAYMAN. Portrait. 2 Vols. 8vo. 18s.
———— Exposition of the Apostles' Creed. 16mo. 1s. 6d.
KERR (ROBERT). GENTLEMAN'S HOUSE; OR, HOW TO PLAN ENGLISH RESIDENCES FROM THE PARSONAGE TO THE PALACE. With Views and Plans. 8vo. 24s.
———— Small Country House. A Brief Practical Discourse on the Planning of a Residence from 2000l. to 5000l. With Supplementary Estimates to 7000l. Post 8vo. 3s.
———— Ancient Lights; a Book for Architects, Surveyors, Lawyers, and Landlords. 8vo. 5s. 6d.
———— (R. MALCOLM) Student's Blackstone. A Systematic Abridgment of the entire Commentaries, adapted to the present state of the law. Post 8vo. 7s. 6d.
KING EDWARD VITH'S Latin Grammar. 12mo. 3s. 6d.
———————————— First Latin Book. 12mo. 2s 6d.
KING GEORGE IIIRD's Correspondence with Lord North, 1769-82. Edited, with Notes and Introduction, by W. BODHAM DONNE. 2 vols. 8vo. 32s.
KING (R. J.). Archæology, Travel and Art; being Sketches and Studies, Historical and Descriptive. 8vo. 12s.
KIRK (J. FOSTER). History of Charles the Bold, Duke of Burgundy. Portrait. 3 Vols. 8vo. 45s.
KIRKES' Handbook of Physiology. Edited by W. MORRANT BAKER, F.R.C.S. 9th Edition. With 400 Illustrations. Post 8vo. 14s.
KUGLER'S Handbook of Painting.—The Italian Schools. Revised and Remodelled from the most recent Researches. By LADY EASTLAKE. With 140 Illustrations. 2 Vols. Crown 8vo. 30s.
———— Handbook of Painting.—The German, Flemish, and Dutch Schools. Revised and in part re-written. By J. A. CROWE. With 60 Illustrations. 2 Vols. Crown 8vo. 24s.
LANE (E. W.). Account of the Manners and Customs of Modern Egyptians. With Illustrations. 2 Vols. Post 8vo. 12s.
LAWRENCE (SIR GEO.). Reminiscences of Forty-three Years' Service in India; including Captivities in Cabul among the Affghans and among the Sikhs, and a Narrative of the Mutiny in Rajputana. Crown 8vo. 10s. 6d.
LAYARD (A. H.). Nineveh and its Remains. Being a Narrative of Researches and Discoveries amidst the Ruins of Assyria. With an Account of the Chaldean Christians of Kurdistan; the Yezedis, or Devil-worshippers; and an Enquiry into the Manners and Arts of the Ancient Assyrians. Plates and Woodcuts. 2 Vols. 8vo. 36s.
*** A POPULAR EDITION of the above work. With Illustrations. Post 8vo. 7s. 6d.
———— Nineveh and Babylon; being the Narrative of Discoveries in the Ruins, with Travels in Armenia, Kurdistan and the Desert, during a Second Expedition to Assyria. With Map and Plates. 8vo. 21s.
*** A POPULAR EDITION of the above work. With Illustrations. Post 8vo. 7s. 6d.
LEATHES' (STANLEY) Practical Hebrew Grammar. With the Hebrew Text of Genesis i.—vi., and Psalms i.—vi. Grammatical Analysis and Vocabulary. Post 8vo. 7s. 6d.
LENNEP (REV. H. J. VAN). Missionary Travels in Asia Minor. With Illustrations of Biblical History and Archæology. With Map and Woodcuts. 2 Vols. Post 8vo. 24s.
———— Modern Customs and Manners of Bible Lands in Illustration of Scripture. With Coloured Maps and 300 Illustrations. 2 Vols. 8vo. 21s.

LESLIE (C. R.). Handbook for Young Painters. With Illustrations. Post 8vo. 7s. 6d.
—— Life and Works of Sir Joshua Reynolds. Portraits and Illustrations. 2 Vols. 8vo. 42s.
LETO (Pomponio). Eight Months at Rome during the Vatican Council. With a daily account of the proceedings. Translated from the original. 8vo. 12s.
LETTERS From the Baltic. By a Lady. Post 8vo. 2s.
—— Madras. By a Lady. Post 8vo. 2s.
—— Sierra Leone. By a Lady. Post 8vo. 3s. 6d.
LEVI (Leone). History of British Commerce; and of the Economic Progress of the Nation, from 1763 to 1870. 8vo. 16s.
LIDDELL (Dean). Student's History of Rome, from the earliest Times to the establishment of the Empire. Woodcuts. Post 8vo. 7s. 6d.
LLOYD (W. Watkiss). History of Sicily to the Athenian War; with Elucidations of the Sicilian Odes of Pindar. With Map. 8vo. 14s.
LISPINGS from LOW LATITUDES; or, the Journal of the Hon. Impulsia Gushington. Edited by Lord Dufferin. With 24 Plates. 4to. 21s.
LITTLE ARTHUR'S History of England. By Lady Callcott. New Edition, continued to 1872. With Woodcuts. Fcap. 8vo. 1s. 6d.
LIVINGSTONE (Dr.). Popular Account of his First Expedition to Africa, 1840-56. Illustrations. Post 8vo. 7s. 6d.
—— Popular Account of his Second Expedition to Africa, 1858-64. Map and Illustrations. Post 8vo. 7s. 6d.
—— Last Journals in Central Africa, from 1865 to his Death. Continued by a Narrative of his last moments and sufferings. By Rev Horace Waller. Maps and Illustrations. 2 Vols. 8vo. 28s.
LIVINGSTONIA. Journal of Adventures in Exploring the Lake Nyassa, and Establishing the above Settlement. By E. D. Young, R.N. Revised by Rev. Horace Waller, F.R.G.S. Maps. Post 8vo.
LIVONIAN TALES. By the Author of "Letters from the Baltic." Post 8vo. 2s.
LOCH (H. B.). Personal Narrative of Events during Lord Elgin's Second Embassy to China. With Illustrations. Post 8vo. 9s.
LOCKHART (J. G.). Ancient Spanish Ballads. Historical and Romantic. Translated, with Notes. With Portrait and Illustrations. Crown 8vo. 5s.
—— Life of Theodore Hook. Fcap. 8vo. 1s.
LOUDON (Mrs.). Gardening for Ladies. With Directions and Calendar of Operations for Every Month. Woodcuts. Fcap. 8vo. 3s. 6d.
LYELL (Sir Charles). Principles of Geology; or, the Modern Changes of the Earth and its Inhabitants considered as illustrative of Geology. With Illustrations. 2 Vols. 8vo. 32s.
—— Student's Elements of Geology. With Table of British Fossils and 600 Illustrations. Post 8vo. 9s.
—— Geological Evidences of the Antiquity of Man, including an Outline of Glacial Post-Tertiary Geology, and Remarks on the Origin of Species. Illustrations. 8vo. 14s.
—— (K. M.). Geographical Handbook of Ferns. With Tables to show their Distribution. Post 8vo. 7s. 6d.
LYTTON'S (Lord) Memoir of Julian Fane. With Portrait. Post 8vo. 5s.
McCLINTOCK (Sir L.). Narrative of the Discovery of the Fate of Sir John Franklin and his Companions in the Arctic Seas. With Illustrations. Post 8vo. 7s. 6d.
MACDOUGALL (Col.). Modern Warfare as Influenced by Modern Artillery. With Plans. Post 8vo. 12s.

MACGREGOR (J.). Rob Roy on the Jordan, Nile, Red Sea, Gennesareth, &c. A Canoe Cruise in Palestine and Egypt and the Waters of Damascus. With Map and 70 Illustrations. Crown 8vo. 7s. 6d.

MAETZNER'S ENGLISH GRAMMAR. A Methodical, Analytical, and Historical Treatise on the Orthography, Prosody, Inflections, and Syntax of the English Tongue. Translated from the German. By CLAIR J. GRECE, LL.D. 3 Vols. 8vo. 36s.

MAHON (LORD), see STANHOPE.

MAINE (SIR H. SUMNER). Ancient Law: its Connection with the Early History of Society, and its Relation to Modern Ideas. 8vo. 12s.

——— Village Communities in the East and West. With additional Essays. 8vo. 12s.

——— Early History of Institutions. 8vo. 12s.

MALCOLM (SIR JOHN). Sketches of Persia. Post 8vo. 3s. 6d.

MANSEL (DEAN). Limits of Religious Thought Examined. Post 8vo. 8s. 6d.

——— Letters, Lectures, and Papers, including the Phrontisterion, or Oxford in the XIXth Century. Edited by H. W. CHANDLER, M.A. 8vo. 12s.

——— Gnostic Heresies of the First and Second Centuries. With a sketch of his life and character. By Lord CARNARVON. Edited by Canon LIGHTFOOT. 8vo 10s. 6d.

MANUAL OF SCIENTIFIC ENQUIRY. For the Use of Travellers. Edited by REV. R. MAIN. Post 8vo. 3s. 6d. (Published by order of the Lords of the Admiralty.)

MARCO POLO. The Book of Ser Marco Polo, the Venetian. Concerning the Kingdoms and Marvels of the East. A new English Version. Illustrated by the light of Oriental Writers and Modern Travels. By COL. HENRY YULE. Maps and Illustrations. 2 Vols. Medium 8vo. 63s.

MARKHAM'S (MRS.) History of England. From the First Invasion by the Romans to 1867. Woodcuts. 12mo. 3s. 6d.

——— History of France. From the Conquest by the Gauls to 1861. Woodcuts. 12mo. 3s. 6d.

——— History of Germany. From the Invasion by Marius to 1867. Woodcuts. 12mo. 3s. 6d.

MARLBOROUGH'S (SARAH, DUCHESS OF) Letters. Now first published from the Original MSS. at Madresfield Court. With an Introduction. 8vo. 10s. 6d.

MARRYAT (JOSEPH). History of Modern and Mediæval Pottery and Porcelain. With a Description of the Manufacture. Plates and Woodcuts. 8vo. 42s. [Post 8vo. 7s. 6d.

MARSH (G. P.). Student's Manual of the English Language.

MASTERS in English Theology. A Series of Lectures delivered at King's Coll., London, 1877. By Canon Barry, D.D., the Dean of St. Paul's; Prof. Plumptre, D.D.; Canon Westcott, D D.; Canon Farrar, D.D.; and Prof. Cheetham, M.A. With an Historical Introduction. Post 8vo. [In Preparation.

MATTHIÆ'S GREEK GRAMMAR. Abridged by BLOMFIELD. Revised by E. S. CROOKE. 12mo. 4s.

MAUREL'S Character, Actions, and Writings of Wellington. Fcap. 8vo. 1s. 6d.

MAYNE (CAPT.). Four Years in British Columbia and Vancouver Island. Illustrations. 8vo. 16s.

MAYO (LORD). Sport in Abyssinia; or, the Mareb and Tackazzee. With Illustrations. Crown 8vo. 12s.

MEADE (HON. HERBERT). Ride through the Disturbed Districts of New Zealand, with a Cruise among the South Sea Islands. With Illustrations. Medium 8vo. 12s.

MELVILLE (HERMANN). Marquesas and South Sea Islands. 2 Vols. Post 8vo. 7s.

MEREDITH'S (MRS. CHARLES) Notes and Sketches of New South Wales. Post 8vo. 2s.

MESSIAH (THE): The Life, Travels, Death, Resurrection, and Ascension of our Blessed Lord. By A Layman. Map. 8vo. 18s.

MICHELANGELO - BUONARROTI, Sculptor, Painter, and Architect. His Life and Works. By C. HEATH WILSON. Illustrations. Royal 8vo. 26s.

MILLINGTON (REV. T. S.). Signs and Wonders in the Land of Ham, or the Ten Plagues of Egypt, with Ancient and Modern Illustrations. Woodcuts. Post 8vo. 7s. 6d.

MILMAN (DEAN). History of the Jews, from the earliest Period down to Modern Times. 3 Vols. Post 8vo. 18s.

——— Early Christianity, from the Birth of Christ to the Abolition of Paganism in the Roman Empire. 3 Vols. Post 8vo. 18s.

——— Latin Christianity, including that of the Popes to the Pontificate of Nicholas V. 9 Vols. Post 8vo. 54s.

——— Annals of St. Paul's Cathedral, from the Romans to the funeral of Wellington. Portrait and Illustrations. 8vo. 18s.

——— Character and Conduct of the Apostles considered as an Evidence of Christianity. 8vo. 10s. 6d.

——— Quinti Horatii Flacci Opera. With 100 Woodcuts. Small 8vo. 7s. 6d.

——— Life of Quintus Horatius Flaccus. With Illustrations. 8vo. 9s.

——— Poetical Works. The Fall of Jerusalem—Martyr of Antioch—Balshazzar—Tamor—Anne Boleyn—Fazio, &c. With Portrait and Illustrations. 3 Vols. Fcap. 8vo. 18s.

——— Fall of Jerusalem. Fcap. 8vo. 1s.

——— (CAPT. E. A.) Wayside Cross. Post 8vo. 2s.

MIVART'S (ST. GEORGE) Lessons from Nature; as manifested in Mind and Matter. 8vo. 15s.

MODERN DOMESTIC COOKERY. Founded on Principles of Economy and Practical Knowledge. *New Edition*. Woodcuts. Fcap. 8vo. 5s.

MONGREDIEN (AUGUSTUS). Trees and Shrubs for English Plantation. A Selection and Description of the most Ornamental which will flourish in the open air in our climate. With Classified Lists. With 30 Illustrations. 8vo. 16s.

MOORE'S (THOMAS) Life and Letters of Lord Byron. *Cabinet Edition*. With Plates. 6 Vols. Fcap. 8vo. 18s.; *Popular Edition*, with Portraits. Royal 8vo. 7s. 6d.

MORESBY (CAPT.), R.N. Discoveries in New Guinea, Polynesia, Torres Straits, &c., during the cruise of H.M.S. Basilisk. Map and Illustrations. 8vo. 15s.

MOTLEY (J. L.). History of the United Netherlands: from the Death of William the Silent to the Twelve Years' Truce, 1609. *Library Edition*. Portraits. 4 Vols. 8vo. 60s. *Cabinet Edition*. 4 Vols. Post 8vo. 6s. each.

——— Life and Death of John of Barneveld, Advocate of Holland. With a View of the Primary Causes and Movements of the Thirty Years' War. *Library Edition*. Illustrations. 2 Vols. 8vo. 28s. *Cabinet Edition*. 2 vols. Post 8vo. 12s.

MOSSMAN (SAMUEL). New Japan; the Land of the Rising Sun; its Annals and Progress during the past Twenty Years, recording the remarkable Progress of the Japanese in Western Civilisation. With Map. 8vo. 15s.

MOUHOT (HENRI). Siam, Cambojia, and Lao; a Narrative of Travels and Discoveries. Illustrations. 2 Vols. 8vo.

MOZLEY'S (CANON) Treatise on Predestination. 8vo. 14s.

——— Primitive Doctrine of Baptismal Regeneration. 8vo. 7s. 6d.

MUIRHEAD'S (JAS.) Vaux-de-Vire of Maistre Jean Le Houx, Advocate of Vire. Translated and Edited. With Portrait and Illustrations. 8vo, 21s.

MUNRO'S (GENERAL) Life and Letters. By REV. G. R. GLEIG. Post 8vo. 3s. 6d.

MURCHISON'S (SIR RODERICK) Siluria; or, a History of the Oldest rocks containing Organic Remains. Map and Plates. 8vo. 18s.

——— Memoirs. With Notices of his Contemporaries, and Rise and Progress of Palæozoic Geology. By ARCHIBALD GEIKIE. Portraits. 2 Vols. 8vo. 30s.

MURRAY'S RAILWAY READING. Containing:—

WELLINGTON. By LORD ELLESMERE. 6d.	MAHON'S JOAN OF ARC. 1s.
NIMROD ON THE CHASE. 1s.	HEAD'S EMIGRANT. 2s. 6d.
MUSIC AND DRESS. 1s.	NIMROD ON THE ROAD. 1s.
MILMAN'S FALL OF JERUSALEM. 1s.	CROKER ON THE GUILLOTINE. 1s.
MAHON'S "FORTY-FIVE." 3s.	HOLLWAY'S NORWAY. 2s.
LIFE OF THEODORE HOOK. 1s.	MAUREL'S WELLINGTON. 1s. 6d.
DEEDS OF NAVAL DARING. 3s. 6d.	CAMPBELL'S LIFE OF BACON. 2s. 6d.
THE HONEY BEE. 1s.	THE FLOWER GARDEN. 1s.
ÆSOP'S FABLES. 2s. 6d.	TAYLOR'S NOTES FROM LIFE. 2s.
NIMROD ON THE TURF. 1s. 6d.	REJECTED ADDRESSES. 1s.
ART OF DINING. 1s. 6d.	PENN'S HINTS ON ANGLING. 1s.

MUSTERS' (CAPT.) Patagonians; a Year's Wanderings over Untrodden Ground from the Straits of Magellan to the Rio Negro. Illustrations. Post 8vo. 7s. 6d.

NAPIER (SIR WM.). English Battles and Sieges of the Peninsular War. Portrait. Post 8vo. 9s.

NAPOLEON AT FONTAINEBLEAU AND ELBA. A Journal of Occurrences and Notes of Conversations. By SIR NEIL CAMPBELL, C.B. With a Memoir. By REV. A. N. C. MACLACHLAN, M.A. Portrait. 8vo. 15s.

NARES (SIR GEORGE), R.N. Official Report to the Admiralty of the recent Arctic Expedition. Map. 8vo. 2s. 6d.

NASMYTH AND CARPENTER. The Moon. Considered as a Planet, a World, and a Satellite. With Illustrations from Drawings made with the aid of Powerful Telescopes, Woodcuts, &c. 4to. 30s.

NAUTICAL ALMANAC (THE). (By Authority.) 2s. 6d.

NAVY LIST. (Monthly and Quarterly.) Post 8vo.

NEW TESTAMENT. With Short Explanatory Commentary. By ARCHDEACON CHURTON, M.A., and ARCHDEACON BASIL JONES, M.A. With 110 authentic Views, &c. 2 Vols. Crown 8vo 21s. bound.

NEWTH (SAMUEL). First Book of Natural Philosophy; an Introduction to the Study of Statics, Dynamics, Hydrostatics, Optics, and Acoustics, with numerous Examples. Small 8vo. 3s. 6d.

——— Elements of Mechanics, including Hydrostatics, with numerous Examples. Small 8vo. 8s. 6d.

——— Mathematical Examinations. A Graduated Series of Elementary Examples in Arithmetic, Algebra, Logarithms, Trigonometry, and Mechanics. Small 8vo. 8s. 6d.

NICHOLS' (J. G.) Pilgrimages to Walsingham and Canterbury. By ERASMUS. Translated, with Notes. With Illustrations. Post 8vo. 6s.

——— (SIR GEORGE) History of the English Poor Laws. 2 Vols. 8vo.

NICOLAS' (SIR HARRIS) Historic Peerage of England. Exhibiting the Origin, Descent, and Present State of every Title of Peerage which has existed in this Country since the Conquest. By WILLIAM COURTHOPE. 8vo. 30s.

LIST OF WORKS

NIMROD, On the Chace—Turf—and Road. With Portrait and Plates. Crown 8vo. 5s. Or with Coloured Plates, 7s. 6d.

NORDHOFF (CHAS.). Communistic Societies of the United States; including Detailed Accounts of the Shakers, The Amana, Oneida, Bethel, Aurora, Icarian and other existing Societies; with Particulars of their Religious Creeds, Industries, and Present Condition. With 40 Illustrations. 8vo. 15s.

NORTHCOTE'S (SIR JOHN) Notebook in the Long Parliament. Containing Proceedings during its First Session, 1640. From the Original MS. in the possession of the Right Hon. Sir Stafford Northcote, Bart., M.P. Transcribed and Edited, with a Memoir. By A. H. A. Hamilton. Crown 8vo. [*In the Press.*

OWEN (LIEUT.-COL.). Principles and Practice of Modern Artillery, including Artillery Material, Gunnery, and Organisation and Use of Artillery in Warfare. With Illustrations. 8vo. 15s.

OXENHAM (REV. W.). English Notes for Latin Elegiacs; designed for early Proficients in the Art of Latin Versification, with Prefatory Rules of Composition in Elegiac Metre. 12mo. 3s. 6d.

PALGRAVE (R. H. I.). Local Taxation of Great Britain and Ireland. 8vo. 6s.

——— NOTES ON BANKING IN GREAT BRITAIN AND IRELAND, SWEDEN, DENMARK, AND HAMBURG, with some Remarks on the amount of Bills in circulation, both Inland and Foreign. 8vo. 6s.

PALLISER (MRS.). Brittany and its Byeways, its Inhabitants, and Antiquities. With Illustrations. Post 8vo. 12s.

——— Mottoes for Monuments, or Epitaphs selected for General Use and Study. With Illustrations. Crown 8vo. 7s. 6d.

PARIS' (DR.) Philosophy in Sport made Science in Earnest; or, the First Principles of Natural Philosophy inculcated by aid of the Toys and Sports of Youth. Woodcuts. Post 8vo. 7s. 6d.

PARKMAN (FRANCIS). Discovery of the Great West; or, The Valleys of the Mississippi and the Lakes of North America. An Historical Narrative. Map. 8vo. 10s. 6d.

PARKYNS' (MANSFIELD) Three Years' Residence in Abyssinia: with Travels in that Country. With Illustrations. Post 8vo. 7s. 6d.

PEEK PRIZE ESSAYS. The Maintenance of the Church of England as an Established Church. By REV. CHARLES HOLE—REV. R. WATSON DIXON—and REV. JULIUS LLOYD. 8vo. 10s. 6d.

PEEL'S (SIR ROBERT) Memoirs. 2 Vols. Post 8vo. 15s.

PENN (RICHARD). Maxims and Hints for an Angler and Chessplayer. Woodcuts. Fcap. 8vo. 1s.

PERCY (JOHN, M.D.). Metallurgy. Vol. I., Part 1. FUEL, Wood, Peat, Coal, Charcoal, Coke, Refractory Materials, Fire-Clays, &c. With Illustrations. 8vo. 30s.

——— Vol. I., Part 2. Copper, Zinc, Brass. With Illustrations. 8vo. [*In the Press.*

——— Vol. II. Iron and Steel. With Illustrations. 8vo. [*In Preparation.*

——— Vol. III. Lead, including part of SILVER. With Illustrations. 8vo. 30s.

——— Vols. IV. and V. Gold, Silver, and Mercury, Platinum, Tin, Nickel, Cobalt, Antimony, Bismuth, Arsenic, and other Metals. With Illustrations. 8vo. [*In Preparation.*

PHILLIPS' (JOHN) Memoirs of William Smith. 8vo. 7s. 6d.

——— (JOHN) Geology of Yorkshire, The Coast, and Limestone District. Plates. 2 Vols. 4to.

——— Rivers, Mountains, and Sea Coast of Yorkshire. With Essays on the Climate, Scenery, and Ancient Inhabitants. Plates. 8vo. 15s.

PHILLIPS' (SAMUEL) Literary Essays from "The Times." With Portrait. 2 Vols. Fcap. 8vo. 7s.

POPE'S (ALEXANDER) Works. With Introductions and Notes, by REV. WHITWELL ELWIN. Vols. I., II., VI., VII., VIII. With Portraits. 8vo. 10s. 6d. each.

PORTER (REV. J. L.). Damascus, Palmyra, and Lebanon. With Travels among the Giant Cities of Bashan and the Hauran. Map and Woodcuts. Post 8vo. 7s. 6d.

PRAYER-BOOK (ILLUSTRATED), with Borders, Initials, Vignettes, &c. Edited, with Notes, by REV. THOS. JAMES. Medium 8vo. 18s. cloth; 31s. 6d. calf; 36s. morocco.

PRINCESS CHARLOTTE OF WALES. A Brief Memoir. With Selections from her Correspondence and other unpublished Papers. By LADY ROSE WEIGALL. With Portrait. 8vo. 8s. 6d.

PUSS IN BOOTS. With 12 Illustrations. By OTTO SPECKTER. 16mo. 1s. 6d. Or coloured, 2s. 6d.

PRIVY COUNCIL JUDGMENTS in Ecclesiastical Cases relating to Doctrine and Discipline. With Historical Introduction, by G. C. BRODRICK and W. H. FREMANTLE. 8vo. 10s. 6d.

QUARTERLY REVIEW (THE). 8vo. 6s.

RAE (EDWARD). Land of the North Wind; or Travels among the Laplanders and Samoyedes, and along the Shores of the White Sea. With Map and Woodcuts. Post 8vo. 10s. 6d.

—— The Country of the Moors. A Journey from Tripoli in Barbary to the City of Kairwan. Crown 8vo. [In the Press.

RAMBLES in the Syrian Deserts. Post 8vo. 10s. 6d.

RANKE (LEOPOLD). History of the Popes of Rome during the 16th and 17th Centuries. Translated from the German by SARAH AUSTIN. 3 Vols. 8vo. 30s.

RASSAM (HORMUZD). Narrative of the British Mission to Abyssinia. With Notices of the Countries Traversed from Massowah to Magdala. Illustrations. 2 Vols. 8vo. 28s.

RAWLINSON'S (CANON) Herodotus. A New English Version. Edited with Notes and Essays. Maps and Woodcut. 4 Vols 8vo. 48s.

—————— Five Great Monarchies of Chaldæa, Assyria, Media, Babylonia, and Persia. With Maps and Illustrations. 3 Vols. 8vo. 42s.

—————— (SIR HENRY) England and Russia in the East; a Series of Papers on the Political and Geographical Condition of Central Asia. Map. 8vo. 12s.

REED (E. J.). Shipbuilding in Iron and Steel; a Practical Treatise, giving full details of Construction, Processes of Manufacture, and Building Arrangements. With 5 Plans and 250 Woodcuts. 8vo.

—— Iron - Clad Ships; their Qualities, Performances, and Cost. With Chapters on Turret Ships, Iron-Clad Rams, &c. With Illustrations. 8vo. 12s.

—— Letters from Russia in 1875. 8vo. 5s.

REJECTED ADDRESSES (THE). By JAMES AND HORACE SMITH. Woodcuts. Post 8vo. 3s. 6d.; or Popular Edition, Fcap. 8vo. 1s.

REYNOLDS' (SIR JOSHUA) Life and Times. By C. R. LESLIE, R.A. and TOM TAYLOR. Portraits. 2 Vols. 8vo.

RICARDO'S (DAVID) Political Works. With a Notice of his Life and Writings. By J. R. M'CULLOCH. 8vo. 16s.

RIPA (FATHER). Thirteen Years' Residence at the Court of Peking. Post 8vo. 2s.

ROBERTSON (CANON). History of the Christian Church, from the Apostolic Age to the Reformation, 1517. Library Edition. 4 Vols. 8vo. Cabinet Edition. 8 Vols. Post 8vo. 6s. each.

ROBINSON (Rev. Dr.). Biblical Researches in Palestine and the Adjacent Regions, 1838—52. Maps. 3 Vols. 8vo. 42s.
——————— Physical Geography of the Holy Land. Post 8vo. 10s. 6d.
——————— (Wm.) Alpine Flowers for English Gardens. With 70 Illustrations. Crown 8vo. 12s.
——————— Wild Gardens; or, our Groves and Shrubberies made beautiful by the Naturalization of Hardy Exotic Plants. With Frontispiece. Small 8vo. 6s.
——————— Sub-Tropical Gardens; or, Beauty of Form in the Flower Garden. With Illustrations. Small 8vo. 7s. 6d.
ROBSON (E. R.). School Architecture. Being Practical Remarks on the Planning, Designing, Building, and Furnishing of School-houses. With 300 Illustrations. Medium 8vo. 18s.
ROME (History of). See Liddell and Smith.
ROWLAND (David). Manual of the English Constitution. Its Rise, Growth, and Present State. Post 8vo. 10s. 6d.
——————— Laws of Nature the Foundation of Morals. Post 8vo. 6s.
RUNDELL'S (Mrs.) Modern Domestic Cookery. Fcap. 8vo. 5s.
RUXTON (George F.). Travels in Mexico; with Adventures among the Wild Tribes and Animals of the Prairies and Rocky Mountains. Post 8vo. 3s. 6d.
SALE'S (Sir Robert) Brigade in Affghanistan. With an Account of the Defence of Jellalabad. By Rev. G. R. Gleig. Post 8vo. 2s.
SCEPTICISM IN GEOLOGY; and the Reasons for It. By Verifier. Crown 8vo. 6s.
SCHLIEMANN (Dr. Henry). Troy and Its Remains. A Narrative of Researches and Discoveries made on the Site of Ilium, and in the Trojan Plain. With Maps, Views, and 500 Illustrations. Medium 8vo. 42s.
——————— Discoveries on the Site of Ancient Mycenæ. With numerous Illustrations, Plans, &c. Medium 8vo. [In Preparation.
SCOTT (Sir G. G.). Secular and Domestic Architecture, Present and Future. 8vo. 9s.
——— (Dean) University Sermons. Post 8vo. 8s. 6d.
SCROPE (G. P.). Geology and Extinct Volcanoes of Central France. Illustrations. Medium 8vo. 30s.
SHADOWS OF A SICK ROOM. With a Preface by Canon Liddon. 16mo. 2s. 6d.
SHAH OF PERSIA'S Diary during his Tour through Europe in 1873. Translated from the Original. By J. W. Redhouse. With Portrait and Coloured Title. Crown 8vo. 12s.
SMILES' (Samuel) British Engineers; from the Earliest Period to the death of the Stephensons. With Illustrations. 5 Vols. Crown 8vo. 7s. 6d. each.
——— George and Robert Stephenson. Illustrations. Medium 8vo. 21s.
——— Boulton and Watt. Illustrations. Medium 8vo. 21s.
——— Life of a Scotch Naturalist (Thomas Edward). With Portrait and Illustrations. Crown 8vo. 10s 6d.
——— Huguenots in England and Ireland. Crown 8vo. 7s. 6d.
——— Self-Help. With Illustrations of Conduct and Perseverance. Post 8vo. 6s. Or in French, 5s.
——— Character. A Sequel to "Self-Help." Post 8vo. 6s.
——— Thrift. A Book of Domestic Counsel. Post 8vo. 6s.
——— Industrial Biography; or, Iron Workers and Tool Makers. Post 8vo. 6s.

PUBLISHED BY MR. MURRAY.   27

SMILES' (SAMUEL) Boy's Voyage round the World. With Illustrations. Post 8vo. 6s.
SMITH'S (DR. WM.) Dictionary of the Bible; its Antiquities, Biography, Geography, and Natural History. Illustrations. 3 Vols. 8vo. 105s.
——— Concise Bible Dictionary. With 300 Illustrations. Medium 8vo. 21s.
——— Smaller Bible Dictionary. With Illustrations. Post 8vo. 7s. 6d.
——— Christian Antiquities. Comprising the History, Institutions, and Antiquities of the Christian Church. With Illustrations. Vol. I. 8vo. 31s. 6d.
——— Biography, Literature, Sects, and Doctrines; from the Times of the Apostles to the Age of Charlemagne. Vol. I. 8vo. 31s. 6d.
——— Atlas of Ancient Geography—Biblical and, Classical. Folio. 6l. 6s.
——— Greek and Roman Antiquities. With 500 Illustrations. Medium 8vo. 28s.
——— Biography and Mythology. With 600 Illustrations. 3 Vols. Medium 8vo. 4l. 4s
——— Geography. 2 Vols. With 500 Illustrations. Medium 8vo. 56s.
——— Classical Dictionary of Mythology, Biography, and Geography. 1 Vol. With 750 Woodcuts. 8vo. 18s.
——— Smaller Classical Dictionary. With 200 Woodcuts. Crown 8vo. 7s. 6d.
——— Smaller Greek and Roman Antiquities. With 200 Woodcuts. Crown 8vo. 7s. 6d.
——— Complete Latin-English Dictionary. With Tables of the Roman Calendar, Measures, Weights, and Money. 8vo. 21s.
——— Smaller Latin-English Dictionary. 12mo. 7s. 6d.
——— Copious and Critical English-Latin Dictionary. 8vo. 21s.
——— Smaller English-Latin Dictionary. 12mo. 7s. 6d.
——— School Manual of English Grammar, with Copious Exercises. Post 8vo. 3s. 6d.
——— Modern Geography, Physical and Political. Post 8vo. 5s.
——— Primary English Grammar. 16mo. 1s.
——— History of Britain. 12mo. 2s. 6d.
——— French Principia. Part I. A First Course, containing a Grammar, Delectus, Exercises, and Vocabularies. 12mo. 3s. 6d.
——— Part II. A Reading Book, containing Fables, Stories, and Anecdotes, Natural History, and Scenes from the History of France. With Grammatical Questions, Notes and copious Etymological Dictionary. 12mo. 4s. 6d.
——— Part III. Prose Composition, containing a Systematic Course of Exercises on the Syntax, with the Principal Rules of Syntax. 12mo. [In the Press.
——— Student's French Grammar. By C. HERON-WALL. With Introduction by M. Littré. Post 8vo. 7s. 6d.
——— Smaller Grammar of the French Language. Abridged from the above. 12mo. 3s. 6d.
——— German Principia, Part I. A First German Course, containing a Grammar, Delectus, Exercise Book, and Vocabularies. 12mo. 3s. 6d.

LIST OF WORKS

SMITH'S (Dr. Wm.) German Principia, Part II. A Reading Book; containing Fables, Stories, and Anecdotes, Natural History, and Scenes from the History of Germany. With Grammatical Questions, Notes, and Dictionary. 12mo. 3s. 6d.

——— Part III. An Introduction to German Prose Composition; containing a Systematic Course of Exercises on the Syntax, with the Principal Rules of Syntax. 12mo.
[*In the Press.*

——— Practical German Grammar. Post 8vo. 3s. 6d.

——— Principia Latina—Part I. First Latin Course, containing a Grammar, Delectus, and Exercise Book, with Vocabularies. 12mo. 3s. 6d.

*** In this Edition the Cases of the Nouns, Adjectives, and Pronouns are arranged both as in the ORDINARY GRAMMARS and as in the PUBLIC SCHOOL PRIMER, together with the corresponding Exercises.

——— Part II. A Reading-book of Mythology, Geography, Roman Antiquities, and History. With Notes and Dictionary. 12mo. 3s. 6d.

——— Part III. A Poetry Book. Hexameters and Pentameters; Eclog. Ovidianæ; Latin Prosody. 12mo. 3s. 6d.

——— Part IV. Prose Composition. Rules of Syntax with Examples, Explanations of Synonyms, and Exercises on the Syntax. 12mo. 3s. 6d.

——— Principia Latina—Part V. Short Tales and Anecdotes for Translation into Latin. 12mo. 3s.

——— Latin-English Vocabulary and First Latin-English Dictionary for Phædrus, Cornelius Nepos, and Cæsar. 12mo. 3s. 6d.

——— Student's Latin Grammar. Post 8vo. 6s.

——— Smaller Latin Grammar. 12mo. 3s. 6d.

——— Tacitus, Germania, Agricola, &c. With English Notes. 12mo. 3s. 6d.

——— Initia Græca, Part I. A First Greek Course, containing a Grammar, Delectus, and Exercise-book. With Vocabularies. 12mo. 3s. 6d.

——— Part II. A Reading Book. Containing Short Tales, Anecdotes, Fables, Mythology, and Grecian History. 12mo. 3s. 6d.

——— Part III. Prose Composition. Containing the Rules of Syntax, with copious Examples and Exercises. 12mo. 3s. 6d.

——— Student's Greek Grammar. By CURTIUS. Post 8vo. 6s.

——— Smaller Greek Grammar. 12mo. 3s. 6d.

——— Greek Accidence. 12mo. 2s. 6d.

——— Plato, Apology of Socrates, &c., with Notes. 12mo. 3s. 6d.

——— Smaller Scripture History. Woodcuts. 16mo. 3s. 6d.

——— Ancient History. Woodcuts. 16mo. 3s. 6d.

——— Geography. Woodcuts. 16mo. 3s. 6d.

——— Rome. Woodcuts. 16mo. 3s. 6d.

——— Greece. Woodcuts. 16mo. 3s. 6d.

——— Classical Mythology. Woodcuts. 16mo. 3s. 6d.

——— History of England. Woodcuts. 16mo. 3s. 6d.

——— English Literature. 16mo. 3s. 6d.

——— Specimens of English Literature. 16mo. 3s. 6d.

SHAW (T. B.). Student's Manual of English Literature. Post 8vo. 7s. 6d.
——— Specimens of English Literature. Selected from the Chief Writers. Post 8vo. 7s. 6d.
——— (ROBERT). Visit to High Tartary, Yarkand, and Kashgar (formerly Chinese Tartary), and Return Journey over the Karakorum Pass. With Map and Illustrations. 8vo. 16s.
SHIRLEY (EVELYN P.). Deer and Deer Parks; or some Account of English Parks, with Notes on the Management of Deer. Illustrations. 4to. 21s.
SIERRA LEONE; Described in Letters to Friends at Home. By A LADY. Post 8vo. 3s. 6d.
SMITH (PHILIP). History of the Ancient World, from the Creation to the Fall of the Roman Empire, A.D. 476. *Fourth Edition.* 3 Vols. 8vo. 31s. 6d.
SIMMONS' (CAPT.) Constitution and Practice of Courts-Martial. *Seventh Edition.* 8vo. 15s.
SPALDING (CAPTAIN). Tale of Frithiof.' Translated from the Swedish of ESIAS TEGNER. Post 8vo. 7s. 6d.
STANLEY (DEAN). Sinai and Palestine, in connexion with their History. Map. 8vo. 14s.
——— Bible in the Holy Land; Extracted from the above Work. Woodcuts. Fcap. 8vo. 2s. 6d.
——— Eastern Church. Plans. 8vo. 12s.
——— Jewish Church. *1st & 2nd Series.* From the Earliest Times to the Captivity. 2 Vols. 8vo. 24s.
——— *Third Series.* From the Captivity to the Destruction of Jerusalem. 8vo. 14s.
——— Epistles of St. Paul to the Corinthians. 8vo. 18s.
——— Life of Dr. Arnold, of Rugby. With selections from his Correspondence. With portrait. 2 vols. Crown 8vo. 12s.
——— Church of Scotland. 8vo. 7s. 6d.
——— Memorials of Canterbury Cathedral. Woodcuts. Post 8vo. 7s. 6d.
——— Westminster Abbey. With Illustrations. 8vo. 15s.
——— Sermons during a Tour in the East. 8vo. 9s.
——— ADDRESSES AND CHARGES OF THE LATE BISHOP STANLEY. With Memoir. 8vo. 10s. 6d.
STEPHEN (REV. W. R.). Life and Times of St. Chrysostom. With Portrait. 8vo. 15s.
ST. JAMES LECTURES. Companions for the Devout Life. 2 Vols. 8vo. 7s. 6d. each.

First Series, 1875.
IMITATION OF CHRIST. CANON FARRAR.
PENSÉES OF BLAISE PASCAL. DEAN CHURCH.
S. FRANÇOIS DE SALES. DEAN GOULBURN.
BAXTER'S SAINTS' REST. ARCHBISHOP TRENCH.
S. AUGUSTINE'S CONFESSIONS. BISHOP ALEXANDER.
JEREMY TAYLOR'S HOLY LIVING AND DYING. REV. DR. HUMPHRY.

Second Series, 1876.
THEOLOGIA GERMANICA. CANON ASHWELL.
FÉNELON'S ŒUVRES SPIRITUELLES. REV. T. T CARTER.
ANDREWES' DEVOTIONS. BISHOP OF ELY.
CHRISTIAN YEAR. CANON BARRY.
PARADISE LOST. REV. E. H. BICKERSTETH.
PILGRIM'S PROGRESS. DEAN HOWSON.
PRAYER BOOK. DEAN BURGON.

ST. JOHN (CHARLES). Wild Sports and Natural History of the Highlands. Post 8vo. 3s. 6d.
——— (BAYLE) Adventures in the Libyan Desert. Post 8vo. 2s.

LIST OF WORKS

STUDENT'S OLD TESTAMENT HISTORY; from the Creation to the Return of the Jews from Captivity. Maps and Woodcuts. Post 8vo. 7s. 6d.

——— **NEW TESTAMENT HISTORY.** With an Introduction connecting the History of the Old and New Testaments. Maps and Woodcuts. Post 8vo. 7s. 6d.

——— **ECCLESIASTICAL HISTORY.** A History of the Christian Church from its Foundation to the Eve of the Protestant Reformation. Post 8vo. 7s. 6d.

——— **MANUAL OF ENGLISH CHURCH HISTORY**, from the Reformation to the Present Time. By Rev. G. G. PERRY, Prebendary of Lincoln and Rector of Waddington. Post 8vo.

——— **ANCIENT HISTORY OF THE EAST**; Egypt, Assyria, Babylonia, Media, Persia, Asia Minor, and Phœnicia. Woodcuts. Post 8vo. 7s. 6d.

——— **GEOGRAPHY.** By REV. W. L. BEVAN. Woodcuts. Post 8vo. 7s. 6d.

——— **HISTORY OF GREECE**; from the Earliest Times to the Roman Conquest. By WM. SMITH, D.C.L. Woodcuts. Crown 8vo. 7s. 6d.
*** Questions on the above Work, 12mo. 2s.

——— **HISTORY OF ROME**; from the Earliest Times to the Establishment of the Empire. By DEAN LIDDELL. Woodcuts. Crown 8vo. 7s. 6d.

——— **GIBBON'S** Decline and Fall of the Roman Empire. Woodcuts. Post 8vo. 7s. 6d.

——— **HALLAM'S HISTORY OF EUROPE** during the Middle Ages. Post 8vo. 7s. 6d.

——— **HALLAM'S HISTORY OF ENGLAND**; from the Accession of Henry VII. to the Death of George II. Post 8vo. 7s. 6d.

——— **HUME'S** History of England from the Invasion of Julius Cæsar to the Revolution in 1688. Continued down to 1868. Woodcuts. Post 8vo. 7s. 6d.
*** Questions on the above Work, 12mo. 2s.

——— **HISTORY OF FRANCE**; from the Earliest Times to the Establishment of the Second Empire, 1852. By REV. H. W. JERVIS. Woodcuts. Post 8vo. 7s. 6d.

——— **ENGLISH LANGUAGE.** By GEO. P. MARSH. Post 8vo. 7s. 6d.

——— **LITERATURE.** By T. B. SHAW, M.A. Post 8vo. 7s. 6d.

——— **SPECIMENS** of English Literature from the Chief Writers. By T. B. SHAW. Post 8vo. 7s. 6d.

——— **MODERN GEOGRAPHY**; Mathematical, Physical, and Descriptive. By REV. W. L. BEVAN. Woodcuts. Post 8vo. 7s. 6d.

——— **MORAL PHILOSOPHY.** By WILLIAM FLEMING, D.D. Post 8vo. 7s. 6d.

——— **BLACKSTONE'S** Commentaries on the Laws of England. By R. MALCOLM KERR, LL.D. Post 8vo. 7s. 6d.

SUMNER'S (BISHOP) Life and Episcopate during 40 Years. By Rev. G. H. SUMNER. Portrait. 8vo. 14s.

STREET (G. E.) Gothic Architecture in Spain. From Personal Observations made during several Journeys. With Illustrations. Royal 8vo. 30s.

——— Italy, chiefly in Brick and Marble. With Notes of Tours in the North of Italy. With 60 Illustrations. Royal 8vo. 26s.

STANHOPE (EARL) England from the Reign of Queen Anne to the Peace of Versailles, 1701-83. *Library Edition.* 8 vols. 8vo. *Cabinet Edition,* 9 vols. Post 8vo. 5s. each.
——————— British India, from its Origin to 1783. 8vo. 3s. 6d.
——————— History of "Forty-Five." Post 8vo. 3s.
——————— Historical and Critical Essays. Post 8vo. 3s. 6d.
——————— French Retreat from Moscow, and other Essays. Post 8vo. 7s. 6d.
——————— Life of Belisarius. Post 8vo. 10s. 6d.
——————— Condé. Post 8vo. 3s. 6d.
——————— William Pitt. Portraits. 4 Vols. 8vo. 24s.
——————— Miscellanies. 2 Vols. Post 8vo. 13s.
——————— Story of Joan of Arc. Fcap. 8vo. 1s.
——————— Addresses on Various Occasions. 16mo. 1s.

STYFFE (KNUT). Strength of Iron and Steel. Plates. 8vo. 12s.

SOMERVILLE (MARY). Personal Recollections from Early Life to Old Age. With her Correspondence. Portrait. Crown 8vo. 12s.
——————— Physical Geography. Portrait. Post 8vo. 9s.
——————— Connexion of the Physical Sciences. Portrait. Post 8vo. 9s.
——————— Molecular and Microscopic Science. Illustrations. 2 Vols. Post 8vo. 21s.

SOUTHEY (ROBERT). Lives of Bunyan and Cromwell. Post 8vo. 2s.

SWAINSON (CANON). Nicene and Apostles' Creeds; Their Literary History; together with some Account of "The Creed of St. Athanasius." 8vo. 16s.

SYBEL (VON) History of Europe during the French Revolution, 1789-1795. 4 Vols. 8vo. 48s.

SYMONDS' (REV. W.) Records of the Rocks; or Notes on the Geology, Natural History, and Antiquities of North and South Wales, Siluria, Devon, and Cornwall. With Illustrations. Crown 8vo. 12s.

THIBAUT (ANTOINE) On Purity in Musical Art. Translated from the German. With a prefatory Memoir by W. H. Gladstone, M.P. Post 8vo. [*In preparation.*

THIELMANN (BARON) Journey through the Caucasus to Tabreez, Kurdistan, down the Tigris and Euphrates to Nineveh and Babylon, and across the Desert to Palmyra. Translated by CHAS. HENEAGE. Illustrations. 2 Vols. Post 8vo. 18s.

THOMS' (W. J.) Longevity of Man; its Facts and its Fiction. Including Observations on the more Remarkable Instances. Post 8vo. 10s. 6d.

THOMSON (ARCHBISHOP). Lincoln's Inn Sermons. 8vo. 10s. 6d.
——————— Life in the Light of God's Word. Post 8vo. 5s.

TITIAN. His Life and Times. With some account of his Family, chiefly from new and unpublished Records. By J. A. CROWE and G. B. CAVALCASELLE. With Portrait and Illustrations. 2 Vols. 8vo. 42s.

TOCQUEVILLE'S State of Society in France before the Revolution, 1789, and on the Causes which led to that Event. Translated by HENRY REEVE. 8vo. 14s.

TOMLINSON (CHARLES); The Sonnet; Its Origin, Structure, and Place in Poetry. With translations from Dante, Petrarch, &c. Post 8vo. 9s.

LIST OF WORKS PUBLISHED BY MR. MURRAY.

TOZER (Rev. H. F.) Highlands of Turkey, with Visits to Mounts Ida, Athos, Olympus, and Pelion. 2 Vols. Crown 8vo. 24s.
———— Lectures on the Geography of Greece. Map. Post 8vo. 9s.

TRISTRAM (Canon) Great Sahara. Illustrations. Crown 8vo. 15s.
———— Land of Moab; Travels and Discoveries on the East Side of the Dead Sea and the Jordan. Illustrations. Crown 8vo. 15s.

TWISLETON (Edward). The Tongue not Essential to Speech, with Illustrations of the Power of Speech in the case of the African Confessors. Post 8vo. 6s.

TWISS' (Horace) Life of Lord Eldon. 2 Vols. Post 8vo. 21s.

TYLOR (E. B.) Early History of Mankind, and Development of Civilization. 8vo. 12s.
———— Primitive Culture; the Development of Mythology, Philosophy, Religion. Art, and Custom. 2 Vols. 8vo. 24s.

VAMBERY (Arminius) Travels from Teheran across the Turkoman Desert on the Eastern Shore of the Caspian. Illustrations. 8vo. 21s.

VAN LENNEP (Henry J.) Travels in Asia Minor. With Illustrations of Biblical Literature, and Archæology. With Woodcuts. 2 Vols. Post 8vo. 24s.
———— Modern Customs and Manners of Bible Lands, in illustration of Scripture. With Maps and 300 Illustrations. 2 Vols. 8vo. 21s.

WELLINGTON'S Despatches during his Campaigns in India, Denmark, Portugal, Spain, the Low Countries, and France. Edited by Colonel Gurwood. 8 Vols. 8vo. 20s. each.
———— Supplementary Despatches, relating to India, Ireland, Denmark, Spanish America, Spain, Portugal, France, Congress of Vienna, Waterloo and Paris. Edited by his Son. 14 Vols. 8vo. 20s. each. *** An Index. 8vo. 20s.
———— Civil and Political Correspondence. Edited by his Son. Vols. I. to V. 8vo. 20s. each.
———— Vol. VI., relating to the Eastern Question of 1829. Russian Intrigues, Turkish Affairs, Treaty of Adrianople, &c. 8vo.
———— Speeches in Parliament. 2 Vols. 8vo. 42s.

WHEELER (G.). Choice of a Dwelling; a Practical Handbook of Useful Information on Building a House. Plans. Post 8vo. 7s. 6d.

WHITE (W. H.). Manual of Naval Architecture, for the use of Officers. Illustrations. 8vo. [In the Press.

WILBERFORCE'S (Bishop) Life of William Wilberforce. Portrait. Crown 8vo. 6s.

WILKINSON (Sir J. G.). Manners and Customs of the Ancient Egyptians, their Private Life, Government, Laws, Arts, Manufactures, Religion, &c. A new edition, with additions by the late Author. Edited by Samuel Birch, LL.D. Illustrations. 3 Vols. 8vo.
———— Popular Account of the Ancient Egyptians. With 500 Woodcuts. 2 Vols. Post 8vo. 12s.

WOOD'S (Captain) Source of the Oxus. With the Geography of the Valley of the Oxus. By Col. Yule. Map. 8vo. 12s.

WORDS OF HUMAN WISDOM. Collected and Arranged by E. S. With a Preface by Canon Liddon. Fcap. 8vo. 3s. 6d

WORDSWORTH'S (Bishop) Athens and Attica. Plates. 8vo. 5s.

YULE'S (Colonel) Book of Marco Polo. Illustrated by the Light of Oriental Writers and Modern Travels. With Maps and 80 Plates. 2 Vols. Medium 8vo. 63s.

BRADBURY AGNEW & CO. PRINTERS, WHITEFRIARS.

www.ingramcontent.com/pod-product-compliance
Lightning Source LLC
Chambersburg PA
CBHW021808230426
43669CB00008B/673